Selected Writings *of*
ELLA HIGGINSON

Edited and with an introduction by
LAURA LAFFRADO

Selected Writings *of*
ELLA HIGGINSON

INVENTING PACIFIC NORTHWEST LITERATURE

Edited and with an introduction by
LAURA LAFFRADO

Whatcom County Historical Society
Bellingham, Washington

Copyright © 2015 Laura Laffrado. All rights reserved.
Manufactured in the United States of America.

Published by the Whatcom County Historical Society
Bellingham, Washington.

Library of Congress Control Number: 2015937755
ISBN 978-0-939576-27-2

Book design and production by Kim Cunningham; typeset in Adobe Caslon Pro. Printed by Gorham Printing in Centralia, Washington.

ON THE COVER
Portrait of Ella Higginson (c. 1885) by Frank G. Abell Studio in Portland, Oregon; from the Ella Higginson Papers, courtesy Center for Pacific Northwest Studies, Western Libraries Heritage Resources, Western Washington University. Background image on cover and title page is White Horse Mountain near Darrington, Washington; photo by Darius Kinsey (1928); courtesy Whatcom Museum, 1978.84.1354.

Contents

Acknowledgments	vii
Introduction	x
Bibliography	xxxix
Works of Ella Rhoads Higginson	xliii
A Note on the Texts	xlv
Chronology of Ella Rhoads Higginson	xlviii

POEMS

"Four-Leaf Clover"	59
"The Snow Pearls"	61
"Yet Am I Not for Pity"	64
"The Lamp in the West"	66
"When the Birds Go North Again"	68
"Sunrise on the Willamette"	70
"Midnight on Brooklyn Bridge"	72
"The College by the Sea"	74
"The Vanishing Race"	76
"To Life"	78

PROSE

"The Mother of 'Pills'"	83
"Patience Appleby's Confessing-Up"	95

PROSE CONT.

"The Takin' In of Old Mis' Lane"	112
"Mrs. Risley's Christmas Dinner"	129
"The Arnspiker Chickens"	134
"A Point of Knuckling-Down"	148
"The Blow-Out at Jenkins's Grocery"	191
"The Stubbornness of Uriah Slater"	197
"M'liss's Child"	213
"The Message of Ann Laura Sweet"	238

MARIELLA, OF OUT-WEST

Chapter XI	269
Chapter XII	274
Chapter XIII	284
Chapter XIV	292

ALASKA, THE GREAT COUNTRY

Chapter I	303
Chapter XXIV	311
Chapter XXV	317
Chapter XXXII	335

Explanatory Notes	343
Whatcom County Historical Society	350

Acknowledgments

I AM VERY HAPPY to acknowledge the generous assistance and support of people and institutions that have helped bring Ella Higginson's work back into print.

First and foremost, Carole Teshima, Kim Cunningham, Lance Lindell, and Gretchen Anderson of the Whatcom County Historical Society devoted their considerable energy and expertise to the publication of this project. This book owes a large part of its existence to their valuable work. Early in this project, Carole Teshima gave me a fountain pen that had been given to Higginson by her sister, Carrie Blake Morgan. It was with a sense of profound fitness (and some needed practice with pen and ink) that I later used that pen to sign the contract for this book.

I received important help from the following individuals: at Western Washington University, Elizabeth Joffrion, Director of Heritage Resources; Tamara Belts, Special Collections Manager, Wilson Library; and Sarah Clark-Langager, Director of the Western Gallery; at the Center for Pacific Northwest Studies, Ruth Steele and Rozalind Koester; at the Whatcom Museum, Jeff Jewell, Archivist/Historian; at the *Bellingham Herald*, Editor Dean Kahn; at C-SPAN BookTV Ashley Hill and Tiffany Rocque; at the Washington State Arts Commission, Janae Huber, Collections Manager; at the Douglas County Museum, Waterville, Washington, Lori Ludeman, Director; and at the Daughters of the Pioneers of Washington State, Edradine Hovde.

From the larger Pacific Northwest community: B. Elaine Bailey; the late Mary Margaret Barker; Martha Benedict;

Belinda Botzong; Joan Clark; Ellen and Don Easterbrook; Leslie Hall; Barbara and Bob Harnden; Gayle Helgoe, formerly of the Bellingham Public Library; Jan Hruthford; Luci Baker Johnson; John and Marcia McWilliams; Helen O'Donnell; Joanne Peterson; Scott Satterfield; Donnie Shea; Barbara SilverSmith; poet/filmmaker Walter Skold; Bellingham historian Gordon Tweit; Todd Warger; and Walter Warren. Russell Carden Higginson's great-great-nephew, Goldthwaite Higginson Dorr III, was gracious and cordial when I phoned him unexpectedly one morning with questions about his great-great-uncle.

My colleagues at Western Washington University provided valuable scholarly assistance, especially Allison Giffen, Bill Lyne, John Purdy, and Bill Smith. Professor Emeritus of English Merrill Lewis generously gave me his notes on Higginson. Mark Sherman put aside his own work to share his technical expertise. Marc Geisler and Bruce Goebel, Chairs of the English Department, strongly supported my research grant applications. Western Washington University generously provided funding for professional leave and research grants that resulted in crucial time for me to focus on this project.

My students have enthusiastically shared my interest in Higginson, especially Jessica Crockett, Anna Lenau, Jessica Lohafer, Caitlin Morris, Tahlia Natachu, and Kayla Shea. My graduate research assistants James Overholtzer and Lindsay Petrie devoted their considerable research skills and many hours of time to this project.

I have benefitted from the work of scholars in the larger academic community who have also conducted extensive research regarding forgotten women writers. In particular, Jennifer Tuttle and Desiree Henderson strongly supported my efforts to recover the importance of Higginson's writings. Monika Elbert's professional advice and help has pro-

Acknowledgments

vided valuable guidance; our friendship often reminds me of the bonds between nineteenth-century US literary women. I continue to learn from the important work of fellow scholars who focus on Pacific Northwest literatures, especially Jana Argersinger, Donna Campbell, and Mary Chapman.

My friends Debbi Hansen, Doug Iannelli, Tara Nebeker, Marcy and Remy O'Rourke, Erik Papritz, and Sharlane Shaffer always welcomed Higginson news.

As always, I am deeply grateful to my family. My sister and brothers are long-term supporters of my work and my mother now knows more about Ella Higginson than she will ever find useful. My nieces and nephews—Jenny, Julie, Anthony, and Andrew—and my young cousins—Brian, Eryn, and Chris—often vividly remind me of those who have gone before and underscore for me the significance of remembrance.

Finally, this project benefitted from the devotion and foresight of Higginson's close friend Catherine Montgomery. Montgomery arranged posthumous publication of a small tribute volume of Higginson's poems. She made sure to preserve Higginson's manuscripts and possessions, donate them to secure places, and honor Higginson's memory even as she was publicly forgotten. Montgomery worked diligently for years to leave a conspicuous paper trail in anticipation of a distant day when someone might stumble upon those papers and so begin the recovery of Higginson's life and works. In token of my admiration for such loyal friendship, this book is dedicated to Catherine Montgomery.

Introduction

"One name will be familiar and reflect credit upon our State long after the names of Senators, Governors, Judges and the history makers of our day shall have sunk into oblivion, for the productions of her intellect will be treasured among all collections of the best literature. That name is Ella Higginson."

(C.H. Hanford letter to Ella Higginson, 14 April 1910)

THOUGH AUTHOR ELLA RHOADS HIGGINSON is little known today, over a century ago she was the most influential Pacific Northwest literary writer in the United States. People across the nation and around the world were first introduced to the Pacific Northwest and the people who lived there when they read Higginson's award-winning poetry, fiction, and nonfiction. Higginson's descriptions of the majestic mountains, vast forests, and scenic waters of the Puget Sound presented the then-remote, unfamiliar Pacific Northwest to eager readers. Her distinctive characterizations of the white women and men who inhabited the region revealed to readers what it was like to live in this particular part of the United States as opposed to other more well-known regions such as New England or the American South. Higginson's celebrated writings were the very first to prominently place the Pacific Northwest on the literary map of the United States.

Higginson's talent was widely recognized during her lifetime. She had a major New York publisher in the prestigious Macmillan Company. She was awarded best short story prizes from well-known magazines such as *Collier's*, *McClure's*,

Peterson's, and *Short Stories*. Many of her poems were set to music and performed internationally by celebrated dramatic singers such as Enrico Caruso. And in 1931, Higginson was chosen to be the first Poet Laureate of Washington State. In her day Higginson and her writing attracted international literary attention to the Pacific Northwest. However, by the time she died in 1940 both she and her work were almost completely forgotten. They remain virtually forgotten today.

It is my hope that this edition of Higginson's stories and poems will accomplish several primary goals. First, I wish to reintroduce Higginson's engaging writings to a new audience of appreciative readers. As one reads Higginson's works, the Pacific Northwest of over a century ago springs to life in precise detail that is rarely found in the other scarce, published writings of the time about the region. Second, I seek to draw attention to the forgotten position of the Pacific Northwest region in American literature from the late nineteenth- and early twentieth centuries. Other regions of the United States are very well-known in earlier American literature while the Pacific Northwest remains overlooked. Finally, I hope to begin to reestablish Higginson's once celebrated literary reputation by restoring both her name and her works to their justly merited places in the history of American literature.

LIFE

"Here comes a woman all the way from Seattle,
breathing the air of the Western mountains and seas."

(Globe Quarterly Review [Philadelphia] 1897)

Ella Rhoads was born in Council Grove, Kansas, probably in 1862, to Charles R. Rhoads and Mary A. Rhoads. She was the youngest of six children, three of whom died before reaching adulthood. When she was two years old, her family moved to Oregon, traveling for eight months by horse-drawn carriage. The family lived in various places in Oregon including the Grand Ronde Valley, Portland, and Milwaukie. By the time Ella was eleven years old, they had settled in Oregon City where Ella was educated in private schools and also independently tutored.

Ella's interests in reading and writing began very early in her life. Her parents possessed what was a substantial library for the time that included books by celebrated American and British authors such as James Fenimore Cooper, Washington Irving, Henry Wadsworth Longfellow, Walter Scott, William Shakespeare, Alfred Lord Tennyson, John Greenleaf Whittier, and others. Ella herself began writing when she was eight years old. Her first publication was the poem, "Dreams of the Past," which appeared locally in *The Oregon City* when she was fourteen. The following year she began work on *The Oregon City Enterprise* newspaper, learning typesetting and editorial writing. She also started publishing short fiction locally and nationally, both anonymously and under various pseudonyms.

In 1885, at age twenty-three, she married Russell Carden Higginson, a druggist and businessman who had moved to Oregon from the Northeast. After her marriage, perhaps feeling authorized by her new status as a wife, Higginson began to publish all her work under her own name. Three years later, the couple moved north to New Whatcom (later Bellingham), Washington, where Higginson lived for the next fifty-two years until her death. Soon after her arrival in Bellingham, Higginson began to earn a national reputation as a literary writer.

In order to attain such a reputation, Higginson conscientiously committed time to her writing. She refused to receive callers because she was busy writing and declined social invitations that would have interfered with her work. However, Higginson nonetheless established and maintained an active social life in Bellingham with a wide and varied range of interests. She played contract bridge with friends and joined newly formed local women's and community groups that eventually helped to found a reading room and a public library. Over the years Higginson also formed several long-standing close friendships with other women, especially Catherine Montgomery, faculty member at the Bellingham State Normal School (later Western Washington University) and a prominent activist for women's rights. Higginson socialized and traveled with these female friends and often referred to them in her correspondence. Though she never bore children, Higginson cultivated affectionate relationships with friends' children and later with area college students. She remained very close to her family, particularly her sister Carrie Blake Morgan, as well as her niece, Ivy Morgan, her sister's daughter.

Among Higginson's many interests was an enduring devotion to her companion animals and a commitment to what we would now recognize as animal rights. A noted animal lover, throughout her life Higginson owned dogs, cats, and horses. She was a dedicated equestrian who rode twice a day for years, exploring the surrounding forests on horseback. The playful names that she assigned to her animals often reflected her literary pursuits. For example, she named one of her horses after a character in British author William Makepeace Thackeray's celebrated novel *Vanity Fair*: "I had a black mare so lovely and so vicious that I named her 'Becky Sharp' " (Higginson letter to Alfred Powers, 22 June 1935). She named one of her dogs "Clover," in reference to her most well-known poem, "Four-Leaf Clover."

Higginson was also an avid admirer of birds, frequently writing in her poems and fiction about bird species found in the Pacific Northwest and their distinctive calls and songs. Her appreciation for songbirds is also seen in her support of the Audubon Society's campaign for milliners to end the cruel practice of slaughtering songbirds in order to acquire plumage then used to decorate women's stylish hats. Additionally, in her book of nonfiction, *Alaska, the Great Country* (1908), Higginson compassionately described the subjection of horses in underground quartz mines, calling attention to the uninterrupted years they spent deep below the earth's surface bereft of fresh air and sunshine. Later in the same book, Higginson depicted the brutality of seal slaughter on St. George Island in the Bering Sea, using blunt language and graphic detail to portray the bloody massacre of helpless animals. In all these cases, Higginson protested the uncompromising domination of animals—for feathers, quartz, pelts, and profit.

Over the years, Higginson regularly traveled within and outside of Washington State. In addition to periodic trips to Oregon to visit her parents, brother, and sister, Higginson journeyed with her husband to the eastern United States to meet his extended family. She and her husband also sailed to Honolulu for two months for his health. In the early twentieth century, Higginson spent four consecutive summers in Alaska, conducting research and gathering information for her book *Alaska, the Great Country*. Higginson's closest friend, Catherine Montgomery, accompanied Higginson to Alaska for two of these trips. As late as October 1936, four years before her death, Higginson traveled again to Oregon with a friend to revisit the scenes of her childhood.

Throughout her adulthood, Higginson's fitness for travel as well as her daily life and literary career were interrupted by frequent episodes of debilitating illness that left her bedridden and unable to write. While these ailments are not explicitly identified in surviving information, Higginson sometimes refers to heart trouble. It is unclear if Higginson was repeatedly unwell with episodes of heart trouble or with unrelated illnesses. As early as 1904, Higginson wrote that her "suffering… was great" and that she had been "very, very ill—not expected to recover" (letter to Lloyd Mifflin, 10 February 1904). Two years later, again unwell, she wrote, "I've had such wretched health this winter" (letter to Lloyd Mifflin, 9 March 1906). Higginson's ill health is a periodic topic in her surviving letters. In 1935, she recounted an episode that had occurred in 1932 when she had been attacked by "ten thousand yellow jackets [from an underground nest that] swarmed up in a solid, golden funnel and stung me almost to death." Severely injured, with "the poison settled in my arms and shoulders," Higginson was unable to hold a pen for almost three years (letter to Alfred Powers, 7 June 1935). In 1937, she reported to a correspondent, "I have a bad heart and visiting and company are positively forbidden" (letter to Etta Schluenz, 14 January 1937).

Even as she described her pain and the ways it limited her daily activities, Higginson displayed fortitude regarding her illnesses. In an undated note to close friends, she wrote, "My love and warmest wishes to the Browns—especially for good health—from one who *hasn't* any health, but who can still laugh and be gay" [emphasis in original] (letter to Brown family). In another letter, having mentioned being again unwell, she added, "Don't be sorry for me. I am as happy and joyous as ever; it is my heart that is playing the deuce; and even that makes me laugh, because I used to think it would be lovely to die of heart trouble!" (letter to Fred Lockley, 30 August 1936).

When she was forty-seven years old, Higginson was widowed after twenty-four years of marriage. After a brief illness, Russell Carden Higginson died at home on 14 May 1909 at age fifty-seven. He left substantial holdings of real estate and stocks, which helped to preserve his wife's continued economic security. Ella Higginson would outlive him by thirty-one years. After his death, she lived alone in Clover Hill, the house that they had built overlooking Bellingham Bay. As time passed, Higginson's sister urged her to return to Oregon to live near her. Higginson considered the move and then later contemplated moving to California to live with her niece, but ultimately chose to remain in Bellingham. For the rest of her life, Higginson divided her time between her house in Bellingham and her ranch in the mountains. Surviving letters document her extensive residence at the ranch. Higginson sometimes spent all winter at the ranch, telling friends that she retreated there for rest and solitude.

Over time, Higginson's house in Bellingham filled with keepsakes of her interesting life, hobbies, and travels. Visitors often commented on the house's unusual contents and furnishings. Higginson avidly collected crystal chandeliers, old Spode china, Meissen vases, Georgian silver, Dutch and French marquetry, antique furniture, and Native American baskets. "I'm crazy about my crystal chandeliers," she wrote to a friend (letter to Etta Schluenz, 14 January 1937). A five-foot long Aleut kayak made of hide with leather bindings and wood interior fittings hung over a bay window. A collection of rosaries bordered the upper walls of one room, while another wall featured a variety of photographs of Higginson at different points in her life. Maps of Alaska entirely papered the walls of her library. In a letter detailing her furnishings, Higginson wrote, "These are the joys of my everyday life" (letter to Etta Schluenz, 14 January 1937). The house became a local attraction, its photograph often featured on postcards. Toward the end of her life Higginson proclaimed in a letter, "I think it [my house] is lovely and I love it better than anything in the world" (letter to Fred Lockley, 30 August 1936).

In 1912, Higginson agreed to serve as political campaign

manager for her friend Frances C. Axtell, who was running for a seat in the Washington State legislature. Axtell was a Republican and cousin of (Democratic) President Grover Cleveland. In her new role as campaign manager, Higginson applied the skills that years earlier had helped to secure her success as a writer. She was organized, disciplined, and mindful of the audience (in this case, voters) that needed to be persuaded. In a revealing newspaper interview, Axtell referred to Higginson as "the boss," humorously remarking on Higginson's competence: "The boss did all the campaigning. I just sat around and watched her work. If you want to go to the legislature just get Mrs. Higginson for a boss; that's all there is to it" (Koert 117). When she was successfully elected, Axtell became Washington's first female member of the State Legislature. Higginson then accompanied Axtell to the Washington State capitol of Olympia for the full legislative session.

Though Higginson never based any of her completed writings on her political experiences, she did begin a draft for an uncompleted play about politics titled *Just Like the Men*. In her notes, Higginson sketched the outlines of a character not unlike herself: "Adelle Carleton, a young, gay and bewitching widow who was Campaign Manager and Political Boss." Higginson described Carleton as "small, dainty, and refined—proves that widows may be merry and honest, too" (Koert 118). An incipient feminism is displayed in Higginson's portrayal of this female character as both conventionally feminine ("small, dainty, and refined") yet unconventionally in command ("Campaign Manager and Political Boss") as well as in Higginson's own commitment to run Axtell's election campaign. These particular aspects of Higginson's life along with many other examples indicate Higginson's dedication to women's autonomy. In short, Higginson was a highly successfully professional woman who cultivated friendships with other similarly independent women, wrote sympathetically about the complications of women's lives, and regularly supported women's community and civic endeavors.

In 1914, Higginson was asked to write a poem in honor of the Bellingham State Normal School (later Western Washington University) which had opened in 1899. Her husband had been one of the original members of the school's Board of Trustees. Higginson's poem, "The Normal [later 'College'] by the Sea," celebrated the school's beautiful natural location. In 1921, a newly completed campus building, Edens Hall, opened with a line from the poem engraved high above the portals of its main entrance: "HERE IS THE HOME OF COLOR AND OF LIGHT." Because Higginson was so well-known, no authorship was assigned to the quotation. It was assumed that the quotation's author would always be immediately recognized. Decades later the inscription remains while its author(ship) is long forgotten.

The entrance of the United States into World War I in 1917 disrupted daily life across the nation including the Pacific Northwest. Higginson suspended her literary writing during the war years. Instead of writing, she devoted much of her time to volunteer work for the newly established American Red Cross chapter in Bellingham. Higginson later recalled that she had worked at the Red Cross office desk three days a week from ten in the morning until five or six o'clock in the evening. Among Higginson's cherished possessions at her death was an American Red Cross medal that she had been awarded.

Throughout her literary career, Higginson had received prizes for her writing from national periodicals such as *McClure's* and *Collier's*. She was awarded her last major literary honor in 1931 when the Washington State Federation of Women's Clubs chose her as Poet Laureate of Washington State. The letter informing Higginson of this honor explained that she had been chosen by the organization "because you inspire in our hearts a love and devotion that we would wish all the world to know." In response, Higginson expressed her gratitude but demurred, first writing, "I cannot but feel that you should have chosen a younger woman—one better fitted physically to do something for you in the future," and then added that "on account of ill health" she could not promise to attend the meeting at which the honor would be bestowed. But, she concluded, "if after considering that, you still want me, I will gratefully accept the honor" (letter to Etta Schluenz, 11 April 1931). As it happened, Higginson was able to attend the meeting and her appointment was reported and celebrated in newspapers across the state and the nation. For the rest of her life, articles and interviews identified Higginson as Poet Laureate of Washington State. Nearly eighty years later in 2007, the Washington State Legislature would pass a bill that established the official position of State Poet Laureate. Before that time, however, the post of Poet Laureate was not regulated by the State Legislature. Thus while Higginson is not the first Poet Laureate appointed as an act of the State Legislature, she is indeed the first widely recognized Poet Laureate of Washington State.

 Toward the end of her life, Higginson was contacted by Oregon literary historian Alfred J. ("Dean") Powers who wrote to her hoping to gather information for his comprehensive study, *History of Oregon Literature* (1935). Powers's initial request led to an extensive correspondence with Higginson. Though Powers's letters to Higginson have not been recovered, Powers preserved the detailed letters that Higginson wrote in response to his queries about her life, her writings, and other writers she had known. In these letters, Higginson dedicated herself to helping Powers with his project of preserving Oregon literature, an endeavor she admired and viewed as important. Much of what we know about Higginson's life is contained in these letters.

The twenty letters that survive from this correspondence were written from May 1935 to December 1938 and comprise over one hundred pages of Higginson's writing along with clippings of literary reviews; photos of Higginson, her house, and her dogs; and poems by Higginson that she copied for Powers in her own hand. In these letters, Higginson reflected on her childhood in Oregon and provided substantial information about her family and her literary career. Very early in this correspondence, she recognized that she was, uncharacteristically, revealing a great deal: "And now, insatiable man, what shall I say to you! I have told you a thousand times more about my 'inmost me' than I have told all others together—yet here you come… crying for 'more'" (22 June 1935). Higginson also seemed aware that this might be her final opportunity to recount her life as she wished it to be viewed. In the same letter she emphasized, "I have lived a full, rich, *joyous* everyday life" [emphasis in original].

Higginson died at her home at age seventy-eight on 27 December 1940, having been ill most of the year. Her sizable assets were valued at about $60,000. Higginson expected her estate to be managed after death by her niece, Ivy Morgan, her heir and only close surviving relative. But then Morgan herself died unexpectedly on 3 March 1941, a little more than two months after Higginson's death. Higginson's will had stipulated that her estate was to be bequeathed to Morgan and that after Morgan's death whatever remained of the estate would then be inherited by Russell Carden Higginson's family. However, Morgan's untimely death led to Morgan's father's relatives challenging that distribution, arguing that they should inherit Higginson's estate from Morgan. A two-year legal battle resulted that was ultimately decided in favor of Russell Carden Higginson's relatives.

Introduction

Ella Higginson is buried in Bayview Cemetery, Bellingham, Washington, beneath a self-designed granite marker. The monument, which is in the shape of a bench, features a large granite cross. The armrests of the bench are decorated with four-leaf clovers, in reference to "Four-Leaf Clover," Higginson's most well-known poem. Lower tiers of the monument are engraved with both the title of Higginson's sonnet sequence, "Yet Am I Not For Pity," and the last line of that poem, "Trembling, I have come face to face with God." Beneath these lines appears "Ella Higginson, Poet-Writer." As she designed her memorial marker, Higginson knew all too well that most of her works were long out of print and that her reputation had largely faded. Despite those realities or perhaps because of them, Higginson prominently and publicly identified herself on the monument as a poet and a writer.

LITERARY CAREER

Over the course of her lifetime, Higginson primarily wrote poetry and short fiction, as well as essays, newspaper columns, nonfiction, novels, and screenplays. In addition to the books published by Macmillan, she also had several books published by small Pacific Northwest presses. Her major works are *From the Land of the Snow Pearls and Other Stories* (1897; originally published as *The Flower That Grew in the Sand and Other Stories* [1896]); *A Forest Orchid and Other Stories* (1897); *When the Birds Go North Again* (poems, 1898); *Four-Leaf Clover* (poems, 1901); her only completed novel, *Mariella, of Out-West* (1902); *The Voice of April-Land and Other Poems* (1903); *Alaska, the Great Country* (travel, 1908); and *The Vanishing Race and Other Poems* (1911).

Higginson was the author of over one hundred short stories which regularly appeared in leading periodicals of the day such as *The Atlantic, Collier's, Harper's Bazaar, Lippincott's,* and *McClure's Magazine.* Many of her stories were later reprinted widely in other magazines and newspapers across the nation. Higginson's stories were published alongside writings by prominent American and British authors such as A. Conan Doyle, Thomas Hardy, Sarah Orne Jewett, Harriet Prescott Spofford, Robert Louis Stevenson, Mark Twain, and Walt Whitman. Most of the stories collected in her three books of short stories were first published in periodicals.

Higginson's short fiction frequently explores the lives of Pacific Northwest white women. Reflecting Pacific Northwest demographics of the time, the white women in these stories occupy a region that is peopled by more white men than white women. Given this, for these women marriage is a likely possibility, even a ready choice. However, though Higginson's stories recognize the economic stability sometimes provided for women by marriage, marital life in these texts is nonetheless rarely bearable. As I will discuss in a later section of this introductory essay, Higginson's employment of Pacific Northwest regional conditions of remoteness, a largely male population, and a predisposition toward white women's enfranchisement enabled her to depict a less settled region inhabited by white women who are, like their region, often less settled and more self-determined.

Like her stories, Higginson's poems appeared regularly in leading periodicals with works by other renowned authors. Higginson was the author of over three hundred poems. Approximately fifty of Higginson's poems were set to music during her lifetime by well-known composers such as Leila Brownell, Charles Willeby, Horatio Parker, and Whitney Coombs. Such poems included "Four-Leaf Clover," "Cradle Song of the Fisherman's Wife," "Hey, Alder, Hang Thy Tassels Out," "The Lamp in the West," and others. The songs were then performed internationally and recorded by notable dramatic singers such as Enrico Caruso, Emma Calvé, John McCormack, and Ada Crossley.

In her poetry, Higginson often takes as her focus natural elements of the Pacific Northwest region. Birds, bodies of water, flowers, mountains, plants, and trees that are native to the area appear as regular subjects in Higginson's poems. The seasons, the weather, and the night sky of the region are also frequently found in her poems. Many of Higginson's poems celebrate specific locations in Washington and, though less often, in both Oregon and Alaska. A reading of the contents in Higginson's books of poetry yields titles such as "The Grand Ronde Valley," "The Little Church at Sitka," "Moonrise in the Rockies," "The Opal-Sea," "Orcas Isle," "Semiahmoo Spit," and "Sunrise on the Willamette." Additionally, Higginson's poems also often center on subjects such as prayer, love, and grief.

Higginson's poems display her sophisticated mastery of form and her awareness of form's possibilities to convey nuanced, layered meaning. She regularly worked with forms such as the sonnet and sonnet sequences, as well as variations on the common ballad form or hymn form. Her poems indicate a very close attention to both rhyme and metrical schemes. However, Higginson's poems also make clear that she did not rigidly adhere to standard poetic forms. She often altered customary meter, rhyme, and stanza length in order to convey her meaning more precisely. Her poetry reveals an acute awareness of the power of variation and prosodic rupture. Unlike some popular women poets of the late nineteenth century, Higginson's attention to poetic form is never mechanical. Though fairly regular, her meter is musical. That characteristic musicality as well as her innovative play with prosodic structures are hallmarks of Higginson's striking poetic expertise.

Though Higginson had been writing and publishing from

Introduction

an early age, her national reputation as a writer began in 1890 with publication of the immediately popular poem "Four-Leaf Clover." The poem was first published in Portland, Oregon's *West Shore* magazine. It was subsequently reprinted in a variety of periodicals and appeared regularly on postcards, greeting cards, and calendars. Additionally, "Four-Leaf Clover" was set to music and the sheet music for the song was also widely available. "Four-Leaf Clover" remains the one poem by Higginson that continues to be easily located today.

Higginson's literary ambition is seen in the ways that she strategically employed the popularity of "Four-Leaf Clover" to increase her regional and national reputation. Higginson immediately and avidly adopted the four-leaf clover as both her personal and literary emblem. In addition to naming her dog Clover, her house Clover Hill, and including the clover motif on her self-designed grave marker, Higginson also wore four-leaf clover jewelry and nominated the wild clover as the official state flower. Further, no fewer than five of Higginson's books featured the four-leaf clover on their spines; a four-leaf clover was imprinted on her bookplates; and for years Higginson wrote a literary column titled "Clover Leaves." Additionally, in 1902 Higginson's husband and his real estate partners named a newly completed Bellingham office building the Clover Building, in honor of the poem and in hope for good fortune. In these ways and others, Higginson regularly publicized her authorship of "Four-Leaf Clover" and promoted her status as a nationally recognized literary author.

Higginson's literary reputation increased as she accrued national honors. In 1893, she was awarded the best short story prize from New York's *McClure's* for "The Mother of 'Pills.' " The following year Higginson again won first prize, also from *McClure's*, for the story "The Takin' In of Old Mis' Lane." *McClure's* printed 80,000 copies of the issue in anticipation of high demand. Her correspondence with editor S. S. McClure reflects her work's appeal for reading audiences. McClure wrote to Higginson that the issue in which "Mis' Lane" appeared "is selling splendidly. Although we printed 80,000 we may not have many left" (11 December 1894).

Higginson was well-established as both a poet and a short story writer when she began work on what would become her only completed novel, *Mariella, of Out-West* (1902). A fascinating drama of family struggle, romance, and cultural change set in the early Pacific Northwest, *Mariella* is one of the earliest published novels written by a woman born west of the Mississippi. Reviews of *Mariella* repeatedly compared the book to novels by well-known authors such as Jane Austen, Leo Tolstoy, and Émile Zola, among others. A review in the *San Francisco Bulletin* read, "Her characters are as strong, as individual, as any created by Dickens or Thackeray." The *Buffalo Express* wrote, "The author's style and breadth and power are American, and ... 'Mariella' is a fine American novel." Originally published in 1902, *Mariella* was so successful that new editions were issued again in 1902 and then in 1903, 1905, and 1924.

A few years after publication of *Mariella*, Higginson turned her attention to book-length nonfiction and began to write about Alaska. In preparation, she spent four consecutive summers traveling in Alaska and also thoroughly researched the intersection of Russian and Alaskan history. She later wrote about her disciplined work schedule for the book: "When I was writing *Alaska, the Great Country* I was at my desk at eight o'clock in the morning and worked till five o'clock in the afternoon; then from eight at night till one or two in the morning, for a full year" (Powers 433). An extensive bibliographic appendix at the end of *Alaska* lists the many works that Higginson consulted as she wrote. The resulting book is a highly readable combination of history and travel narrative, mixed with descriptions of Higginson's encounters with people living in Alaska.

It is important to note that *Alaska* is Higginson's only work to feature explicit discussion of the disastrous effects of white settlement on Native American groups. In her fiction set in Western Washington, Higginson generally incorporated passing references to Salish Native groups into her writing. For example, in these works Higginson often described Lummi and Nooksack Native practices and occasionally used Chinook Jargon. However, when Higginson discussed the Alaskan Native groups that she had encountered, she wrote much more extensively. This noteworthy awareness of Native American groups in Alaska may have emerged because Higginson was writing book-length nonfiction and travel narrative. This new literary task required comprehensive research and detailed observation in order to accurately describe a region unfamiliar to her readers. In *Alaska* then, Higginson writes in detail regarding the history and customs of the Kwakiutl, Thlinkits, and Tinneh groups, among others. Further, in *Alaska* Higginson, in a striking shift from her fiction, significantly expands her sustained attention to women's lives to include an interested awareness in the conditions and lives of Alaskan women of various Native groups.

The book's concentration on Alaska, then considered a remote area associated with tales of Gold Rush wealth and wildness, attracted much interest. The *Chicago Tribune* wrote, "One cannot read Mrs. Higginson's *Alaska* without wanting to pack his bag and start off immediately for the North." The *Boston Herald* warned, "Despite the fact that Mrs. Higginson disclaims having found the secret of putting the spell of Alaska into words, the reader who does not wish to become a convert to her faith should beware of this book. It is a fascinating volume." *Alaska's* popularity resulted in its being reprinted regularly. In 1914, Higginson's publisher, the Macmillan Company, asked her to extensively update the book for reissue. For months Higginson turned down numerous social engagements in order to devote herself to the task. The updated edition with new material was published in 1919. Higginson was very pleased with the edition, writing to Charles T. Conover, "I am proud of my *lovely* new edition of *Alaska, the Great Country*" [emphasis in original].

Throughout her life, Higginson's distance from Northeast publishing centers and lack of nearby literary writers deprived her of the immediacy of a close professional community that would have been available to her had she lived, for example, in Boston. As an alternative, Higginson created a long-distance literary community for herself through varied correspondence with authors, editors, and publishers. She sought advice about her work from well-known writers such as Bret Harte, Sarah Orne Jewett, Lloyd Mifflin, Joaquin Miller, and Louise Chandler Moulton. To cite a few examples, influential Boston writer and critic Moulton advised Higginson how to progress with the plot of *Mariella* when Higginson was unsure how to proceed. Miller praised Higginson's poetry and sent her galley proofs of his own poems, seeking her critique. Higginson also conducted a lengthy and detailed correspondence with Pennsylvania painter/poet Mifflin in which they critiqued each other's writings. After Mifflin had praised her fiction, Higginson responded gratefully, "If you only knew what it is to have always lived where one has none to ask for advice or criticism" (29 November n.d.).

Also among Higginson's surviving letters is a cordial, infrequent correspondence with Jewett, whose work she greatly admired ("The tenderness, poetry and delicate humor of Miss Jewett's stories are unequaled" [Koert 21]). In a 26 December note, Jewett responded to Higginson's having mailed her a copy of "Four-Leaf Clover" and a small piece of fir branch (in reference to Jewett's book *Country of the Pointed Firs* [1896]). In reply, Jewett wrote that she had asked her publisher to send Higginson a copy of her latest book, enclosed a blossom from her yard, and praised "Four-Leaf Clover," exclaiming, "It is *exquisite*! I like it best of all!" [emphasis in original]. In a 17 January postcard printed with a picture of her South Berwick, Maine home, Jewett wrote, "I want to return your kind Christmas card with late enough New Year wishes—but I have been ill. How I wish that I could open your door and that you could come to mine!" In another letter, now lost, Jewett wrote, "There is a different quality in your verse which must come from your unworn surroundings" (qtd. in Washington State Federation 81).

Higginson also maintained long-term, cordial letter-writing relationships with her publishers and editors including George Platt Brett, Sr., head of Macmillan Publishing, well-known for his promotion of regional literature; Herbert P. Williams, editor at Macmillan; and S.S. McClure. In surviving letters, these men appeal to Higginson to send them more of her writing. For example, McClure advises Higginson: "I think it would be a good plan if we could follow up your prize story with other stories from your pen and make your name well-known to readers of *McClure's Magazine*. Three stories, for instance, produces ten times the effect of one story." At the end of the same letter McClure reiterates, "I wish you would send me some more short stories. With good illustrations and advertising I could add greatly to your reputation as a short story writer, especially in the East" (5 March 1894). In these ways and others, Higginson navigated the constraints of her remote location, creating and sustaining a valuable literary network.

Introduction

In addition to such correspondence, Higginson was shrewdly attentive to the business aspects of her literary career. For example, she was a member of the Authors League of America (later the Authors Guild, when the association reorganized in 1921), the professional society of published authors founded in 1912 to advise writers regarding copyright, contracts, and other matters. Her letters also chart keen alertness to contracts, payments, permissions, and royalties. Higginson resolutely protected her interests in such literary matters. She rejected publication offers she considered low-paying and often insisted on (and received) higher prices for her work. A late nineteenth-century letter from Philadelphia's *Ladies Home Journal* is a case in point. Written in response to a letter in which Higginson had apparently criticized their payment scale as low, the tone of editor William George Jordan is contrite: "We regret that the prices paid for your manuscripts by the *Journal* have not proved so large as those you receive from other sources. This is not an incurable disease. We will be very glad to meet you in this matter, and to pay you whatever you feel you could receive for your stories elsewhere" (24 August 1897).

Throughout her life, Higginson read widely and wrote of her admiration for other authors. She often praised literary works by authors such as Hamlin Garland, Jewett, Jack London, and Owen Wister who, like her, located their writings in specific regions of the nation. Higginson also referred to well-known writers of the past and present such as Emily Brontë, Emily Dickinson, Ralph Waldo Emerson, Nathaniel Hawthorne, William Dean Howells, George Meredith, Edgar Allan Poe, Sappho, Alfred Lord Tennyson, Edith Wharton, Walt Whitman, and others. Such references reflect Higginson's informed knowledge concerning both literary matters and well-regarded books and authors despite her distance from urban literary and publishing centers.

Introduction

Higginson was fortunate that the earlier years of her literary career intersected with an enormous growth in United States periodicals. Schneirov notes that "magazine circulation tripled between 1890 and 1905 while the total circulation of newspapers only rose from 36 million to 57 million during the same period. By 1900 the total circulation of monthly magazines was 65 million or about three magazines for every four people" (5). In the "booming [regional literary] marketplace" of the second half of the nineteenth century, "women who lived far distant from the thriving centers of eastern civilization" benefitted from new publishing opportunities (Inness and Royer 4). Zagarell links regionalism's popularity to "new publishing opportunities" that by the late 1870s had emerged from "developments in the production of print material," "professionalization of editorial work and authorship," "expanding networks of distribution, and the emergence of proto-modern marketing techniques." For Higginson and others, these conditions "created unprecedented opportunities for writers with few or no literary connections" (xii). Higginson and other non-Eastern writers such as Mary Hunter Austin found new prospects in what Hoppenstand describes as "San Francisco's dramatic rise to commercial and cultural prominence on the West Coast during the mid-nineteenth century," accompanied by "the equally dramatic proliferation of the city's literary journals" (221). This regional growth introduced new periodicals which published Higginson's work and created readership for her work in California and beyond.

In addition to writing fiction, nonfiction, plays, and poetry, Higginson also regularly wrote for newspapers and worked as an editor on the staff of various periodicals throughout her life. These included Portland, Oregon's literary magazine *West Shore;* Seattle's *Sunday Times* newspaper; Seattle magazines *The Pacific* and *The Westerner;* and Portland, Oregon's *Pacific*

Monthly, which with a circulation of 87,000 "was considered the largest illustrated magazine in the nation" (Powers 426; Koert 106). Higginson's column "Clover Leaves" appeared regularly in the *Seattle Times* for three years beginning in 1900. In these editorial positions, Higginson often wrote essays, reviewed newly published books, and promoted writings by other Pacific Northwest and West Coast authors.

In her correspondence with Alfred Powers toward the end of her life, Higginson responded forthrightly to one of Powers's questions about her literary career: "You ask—'particularly what caused you to become a writer?' Nothing but the consuming desire to write. It is the only thing I ever really wanted to do" (11 May 1935). That consuming desire is unmistakably evident in the decades of writing that resulted in Higginson's impressive list of publications, her prestigious awards and honors, and her extensive work in editing positions. Throughout her life, Higginson unstintingly devoted her time, energy, and remarkable talent to her literary career. As she clearly perceived in the last years of her life, writing had been her one indisputable, irresistible passion.

Region

"I love the twin states of the Northwest next to God and my country; and if either should cease to claim me as one of her writers my heart would be broken."

(Higginson letter to Alfred Powers, 11 May 1935)

A quality that particularly distinguished Higginson's writing during her lifetime was her locating her work in the Pacific Northwest. The majority of Higginson's writings are set in the states of Oregon and Washington, with infrequent forays into Alaska, British Columbia, and Idaho. During this time, the Pacific Northwest region was, as detailed below, thinly populated, remote, and largely male, a place in which white women were more readily granted enfranchisement and about which Eastern readers manifested keen curiosity. This region became the fundamental public marker of Higginson's literary identity as well as one of her principal literary devices. In her fiction in particular, Higginson employed region "to foreground a critique of the location of women" (Fetterley and Pryse 38). Higginson's fictive women are habitually marked as Pacific Northwesterners in their independence, determination, and passion. Such characterizations appear in stories published in a wide range of periodicals across the decades of Higginson's literary career. These texts demonstrate the meanings of region beyond geographic setting and also exhibit how regional discourses about the early Pacific Northwest function.

The demographic environment in which Higginson lived and set the majority of her writing differed significantly from other United States regions. Most fundamentally, the Pacific Northwest was markedly underpopulated compared, for example, to the United States Northeast, an area strongly associated with literary regionalism. For instance, the 1900 US Census lists the population of the New England states as 5,592,017; and as 8,166,341 in 1930. Conversely, the 1900 United States Census lists the combined populations of Washington and Oregon as 931,639; and as 2,517,182 in 1930. For a mix of imperialist reasons, the Pacific Northwest experienced contact and colonization later and more gradually than many regions of what became the United States, including California. For example, George Vancouver began exploration of the region in 1792. Schwantes writes, "When Oregon achieved territorial status in the late 1840s, two generations had passed since the opening battles of the Revolutionary War, thirty states had entered the Union, eleven men had served as president of the United States, Harvard College was already two hundred years old, and the population of New York City was… [almost] seven hundred thousand" (15). In these ways, the Pacific Northwest was "geographically remote from the East Coast and chronologically distant from the mainstream of American history" (Schwantes 16). Later colonization combined with the perception and reality of the Pacific Northwest as remote and difficult to reach helped determine lower regional population. As this data demonstrates, Higginson's regional literary setting was far less populated than settings employed by most regionalist writers of the time. Correspondingly, very few published literary authors lived in the Pacific Northwest during the late nineteenth and early twentieth centuries.

The ratio between female and male populations also differed considerably across the country. For example, the 1860 United States Census, the first to attempt to formally count the population of Washington territory, listed the population as nearly 75% male. Because the census undercounted Coast Salish peoples and left uncounted African Americans, this percentage was composed largely of white men. Further, in 1900 New England states had 98 men for every 100 women; while the Pacific Northwest had 128 men for every 100 women. The sparsely populated region in which Higginson lived and wrote transformed during her life. Between 1860 and 1870 the population of Washington territory almost doubled. By 1880, total population had tripled, with the great majority of residents coming from other regions and nations (HistoryLink.org). Washington itself became a state in 1889. Indeed, according to Census records, men continued to outnumber women in Washington State until about 1970.

Prevailing assumptions regarding women's agency and self-determination also evolved during this period. While full extensive female suffrage in the United States was finally achieved in 1920 with the nineteenth amendment to the United States Constitution, Western states and territories achieved more extensive female suffrage much earlier than those in the East. With certain restrictions, female suffrage was approved in Idaho in 1896; Washington in 1910; and Oregon in 1912. However, it is important to note that various oppressive citizenship laws continue to deny many non-white women the right to vote. As early as 1854, Washington had proposed that women be granted voting rights, a measure defeated by a single vote. Bennion summarizes conjectures regarding the success of women's suffrage in the West, ranging from the less settled aspect of the West compared to the East, the role of "frontier spirit promot[ing] a sense of equality as women and men worked together," and the hope that suffrage would bring publicity and so more settlers to the West (56).

The Northeast, then, had a larger population than the Pacific Northwest, with a greater percentage of women than men, more authors, literary publications with higher circulations, and more readers. However, Easterners displayed avid interest in western regions, perhaps particularly so because many men had left the postbellum Northeast in search of work in the West. This attention is reflected in the widespread circulation of western periodicals, "letters from eastern readers" in these periodicals, and the "western news in eastern papers [some of which] came from western periodicals" (Bennion vii).

Higginson's employment of the Pacific Northwest region and her incorporation of its qualities are reflected in virtually all reviews of her work. For example, the *New Orleans Picayune* described her as "writ[ing] of the far West with the sympathy of one who loves it" (qtd. in Horner 55-56). The *Kansas City Star's* review of her short story collection *From the Land of the Snow Pearls* noted, "[Here] is revealed the wildness and witchery of that northwestern corner where, watched by immemorial pines, Puget Sound lies sparkling in the clean air, and the horizon sweeps down to the great blue ocean" (24 October 1897). Thomas Wentworth Higginson (distant cousin of Ella Higginson's husband) maintained, "In dealing with the remoter region of the Northwest we find but one novelist who has made her mark. Her name is Ella Higginson" (qtd. in Washington State Federation 80). A 15 November 1903 review of Higginson's novel *Mariella, of Out-West* in Ohio's *Toledo Blade* proclaimed that Higginson's "characters are of the west, the vast, wildly beautiful sweep of land beyond the Rockies where impulse rules and emotions are volcanic"; while a review of the short story collection *A Forest Orchid and Other Stories* in Philadelphia's *Godey's Magazine* argued, "The large scenery of the Puget Sound region enlarges the emotions of Miss Higginson's characters." A May 1899 review of Higginson's book of poetry, *The Snow Pearls*, in San Francisco's *Overland Monthly* referenced her short stories, describing Higginson as "writ[ing] from the heart, of the plain, everyday folk she meets," noting "her sympathetic comprehension of the trials and joys, the hardships and the romances of humble, hard-working people who constitute her characters" (436). Higginson's employment of empathy generated readers' inaugural recognitions of Pacific Northwest white women and led to readers' sympathetic contemplation of the often impoverished conditions and more marginal status of these women.

Reviewers across the United States highly praised Higginson's writing. For example, the *New York Independent* stated, "Some of the incidents are sketched so vividly and so truthfully that persons and things come out of the page as if life itself were there" (qtd. in *Native Sons of Oregon* 241-2). In a review of *Mariella*, the *San Francisco Examiner* wrote, "Jack London of Oakland and Ella Higginson of Seattle are putting forth more and better works of fiction than any other writers on the Coast" (14 December 1902). Philadelphia's *Godey's Magazine* began its review of the short story collection *From the Land of the Snow Pearls*, "Here is a book of genuine power" (October 1897). The *Chicago Tribune* praised her writing as having "a breadth of treatment and knowledge of human verities that equals much of the best work of France" and proclaimed, "Ella Higginson has the hallmark of genius" (n.d.). And New York's *Outlook* classified Higginson as "one of the best American short-story writers"(Horner 56). Reviewers and readers across the United States regularly judged Higginson's writing—its regionalism, artistry, and sympathetic character development—to be a valuable, appealing part of popular regionalist United States literature.

Particularly in her fiction, Higginson charts the social and material conditions of white women in the Pacific Northwest. Higginson's writing reflects the demographics of the Pacific Northwest in her representations of white women who expect to perform physical labor in a beautiful landscape surrounded by men. Higginson's setting her writing in the Pacific Northwest was a fundamental public marker of her literary identity. As a review of *Mariella* in the *Chicago Dial* plainly stated, Higginson "represents the far Northwest—the Puget Sound country—in our imaginative literature, and may almost be said to have annexed this region to the literary map" (1 April 1903).

Later Obscurity

In the last decades of her life most of Higginson's books went out of print and her prominence dramatically diminished. Revealing her awareness that her reputation had declined, Higginson wrote on a folder of saved correspondence: "Letters from famous folks; and from publishers, proving that I didn't need to seek publishers—*they* sought *me*" [emphasis in original]

(Note). The 1930 United States Census records Higginson's occupation as "author," while the 1940 United States Census identifies her as "retired." Considered together, both descriptions, presumably Higginson's responses to the census taker, reflect her recognition of her fading literary reputation.

Higginson papers were to be managed after her death by her niece, Ivy Morgan, her one close surviving relative. However, with Morgan's unexpected death soon following Higginson's own death, only distant relatives remained, none close enough geographically or emotionally to preserve or promote Higginson's work and reputation. And so Higginson's works and reputation, already discounted by the time she died, remained forgotten along with the works and the reputations of many other once well-known women writers.

A mix of reasons informs this long neglect. In broad terms, during the first half of the twentieth century, many if not most once-popular United States women writers experienced a similar eclipse of earlier literary success. Very few women were literary scholars in these decades and so it was white male scholars who shaped the contours of the literary work that was studied, published, and admired. It is important to note that these men performed valuable scholarly work. For example, their efforts led to renewed attention to neglected nineteenth-century United States male authors such as Herman Melville. But their common biases about women, authorship, and literary writing resulted in the works of many once well-known women authors remaining almost wholly ignored.

With the dawn of the feminist movement of the 1970s and the subsequent endeavors of feminist literary critics, new scholarly attention was focused on locating forgotten women's writing. During this important time, the texts and the literary reputations of many women writers such as New England's Mary E. Wilkins Freeman and Sarah Orne Jewett, the

American Southwest's and California's Mary Hunter Austin, and Appalachia's Mary Noailles Murfree were restored to prominence. However, Higginson and her work still remained entirely overlooked. Higginson's regional location, far from northeast literary establishments and from the literary locations of other writers, was a factor in this neglect. For instance, her papers were collected in Pacific Northwest archives, still remote from the papers of writers with whom she had been classed in her lifetime. This separation made it less likely that her works would be stumbled upon, rediscovered, and retrieved with theirs.

However, with the turn into the twenty-first century, literary scholars began to search for overlooked writings from areas of the United States that were less represented in well-known American literature. It is this welcome new focus that has finally led to attention being directed to the works and reputation of Ella Higginson. Scholarly articles on Higginson's work have begun to be published, interviews about Higginson and her work have been conducted, and Higginson's writings are starting to be taught. After far too long, the literary recovery has begun of the work and the reputation of the Pacific Northwest region's foundational writer, Ella Higginson.

Bibliography

Bennion, Sherilyn Cox. *Equal to the Occasion: Women Editors of the Nineteenth-Century West*. Reno and Las Vegas: U Nevada P, 1990. Print.

Chicago Tribune. N.d. N. pag. Ella Higginson Papers. Center for Pacific Northwest Studies, Bellingham, Washington. Print.

Coyney, Josephine L(aura). "Interview With the Greatest Western Writer, Ella Higginson in Her Home." N.d. N. pag. Ella Higginson Papers. Center for Pacific Northwest Studies, Bellingham, Washington. Print.

Fetterley, Judith and Marjorie Pryse. *Writing Out of Place: Regionalism, Women, and American Literary Culture*. Urbana and Chicago: U of Illinois P, 2003. Print.

Globe Quarterly Review Philadelphia, 1897. Thorne, William Henry. "A New Literary Genius." Rev. of *The Flower that Grew in the Sand and Other Stories* by Ella Higginson. Internet Archive Digital Library of Free Books, http://www.archive.org/stream/theglobe07philuoft/theglobe07philuoft_djvu.txt. Web. 1 Sept. 2014.

Hanford, C. H. Letter to Ella Higginson. 14 April 1910. MS. Ella Higginson Papers. Center for Pacific Northwest Studies, Bellingham, Washington.

Higginson, Ella. Letter to Brown family. N.d. MS. Whatcom Museum, Bellingham, Washington.

---. Letter to Charles T. Conover. 2 December n.d. MS. University of Washington Libraries Special Collections, Seattle, Washington.

---. Letter to Fred Lockley. 30 August 1936. MS. Brown University Library, Providence, Rhode Island.

---. Letter to Lloyd Mifflin. 29 November n.d. MS. Franklin and Marshall College, Lancaster, Pennsylvania.

---. Letter to Lloyd Mifflin. 10 February 1904. MS. Franklin and Marshall College, Lancaster, Pennsylvania.

---. Letter to Lloyd Mifflin. 9 March 1906. MS. Franklin and Marshall College, Lancaster, Pennsylvania.

---. Letter to Alfred Powers. 11 May 1935. MS. Oregon Historical Society Research Library, Portland, Oregon.

---. Letter to Alfred Powers. 7 June 1935. MS. Oregon Historical Society Research Library, Portland, Oregon.

---. Letter to Alfred Powers. 22 June 1935. MS. Oregon Historical Society Research Library, Portland, Oregon.

---. Letter to Etta Schluenz. 11 April 1931. MS. Douglas County Historical Society, Waterville, Washington.

---. Letter to Etta Schluenz. 14 January 1937. MS. Douglas County Historical Society, Waterville, Washington.

---. Note. Ella Higginson Papers. Center for Pacific Northwest Studies, Bellingham, Washington.

HistoryLink.org. *The Free Online Encyclopedia of Washington State History*. Timeline Essays. 1 Sept. 2014. Web.

Hoppenstand, Gary. "Ambrose Bierce and the Transformation of the Gothic Tale in the Nineteenth-century American Periodical." *Periodical Literature in Nineteenth-Century America*. Ed. Kenneth M. Price and Susan Belasco Smith. Charlottesville: University Press of Virginia, 1995. 220-238. Print.

Horner, John B. *Oregon Literature*. Portland, Oregon: JK Gill Company, 1902. Web. 1 Sept. 2014.

Inness, Sherrie A. and Diana Royer, eds. *Breaking Boundaries: New Perspectives on Women's Regional Writing.* Iowa City: U of Iowa P, 1997. Print.

---. Introduction. *Breaking Boundaries: New Perspectives on Women's Regional Writing.* Ed. Sherrie A. Inness and Diana Royer. Iowa City: U of Iowa P, 1997. 1-16. Print.

Jewett, Sarah Orne. Letter to Higginson. 26 December n.d. MS. Ella Higginson Papers. Center for Pacific Northwest Studies, Bellingham, Washington.

---. Letter to Higginson. 17 January n.d. MS. Ella Higginson Papers. Center for Pacific Northwest Studies, Bellingham, Washington.

Jordan, William George. Letter to Higginson. 24 August 1897. MS. Ella Higginson Papers. Center for Pacific Northwest Studies, Bellingham, Washington.

Koert, Dorothy. *The Lyric Singer: A Biography of Ella Higginson.* Bellingham, Washington: Center for Pacific Northwest Studies and Fourth Corner Registry. 1985. Print.

S. S. McClure. Letter to Higginson. 5 March 1894. MS. Ella Higginson Papers. Center for Pacific Northwest Studies, Bellingham, Washington.

---. Letter to Higginson. 11 December 1894. MS. Ella Higginson Papers. Center for Pacific Northwest Studies, Bellingham, Washington.

Native Sons of Oregon. *Oregon Native Son and Historical Magazine.* Native Son Publishing, 1899. Print.

Powers, Alfred. *History of Oregon Literature.* Portland: Metropolitan Press, 1935. Print.

Rev. of *Alaska*, by Ella Higginson. *Boston Herald.* N.d. N. pag. Print.

Rev. of *Alaska*, by Ella Higginson. *Chicago Tribune* N.d. N. pag. Print.

Rev. of *A Forest Orchid and Other Stories*, by Ella Higginson. *Godey's Magazine* March 1898: n. pag. Print.

Rev. of *From the Land of the Snow Pearls*, by Ella Higginson. *Godey's Magazine* Oct. 1897. Print.

Rev. of *From the Land of the Snow Pearls*, by Ella Higginson. *Kansas City Star* 24 October 1897. Print.

Rev. of *Mariella, of Out-West*, by Ella Higginson. *The Buffalo Express* 22 Nov. 1902: n. pag. Print.

Rev. of *Mariella, of Out-West*, by Ella Higginson. *Chicago Dial* 1 April 1903: n. pag. Print.

Rev. of *Mariella, of Out-West*, by Ella Higginson. *San Francisco Bulletin*. N.d. N. pag. Print.

Rev. of *Mariella, of Out-West*, by Ella Higginson. *San Francisco Examiner* 14 December 1902: N. pag. Print.

Rev. of *Mariella, of Out-West*, by Ella Higginson. *Toledo Blade* 15 November 1903: N. pag. Print.

Rev. of *The Snow Pearls*, by Ella Higginson. *Overland Monthly* May 1899: N. pag. Print.

Schneirov, Matthew. *The Dream of a New Social Order: Popular Magazines in America 1893-1914*. New York: Columbia UP, 1994. Print.

Schwantes, Carlos Arnaldo. *The Pacific Northwest: An Interpretive History*. Lincoln: University of Nebraska Press, 1996. Print.

Washington State Federation of Women's Clubs, ed. *Ella Higginson: A Tribute*. Bellingham, Washington: Union Printing Company Press, 1941. Print.

Zagarell, Sandra A. Introduction. *A New England Nun and Other Stories* by Mary E. Wilkins Freeman. Ed. Sandra A. Zagarell. NY: Penguin, 2000. ix-xxiv. Print.

Works of Ella Rhoads Higginson

HIGGINSON WAS THE AUTHOR of over 300 poems and over 100 short stories that were published in regional and national periodicals. Higginson was also the author of many essays that appeared regularly in newspapers and literary magazines. Ella Higginson's papers are archived at the Center for Pacific Northwest Studies in Bellingham, Washington. The collection includes short stories, poems, plays, a novel, correspondence, clippings, photographs, and ephemera. Many materials in the collection are handwritten and typed drafts.

VOLUMES OF POETRY

A Bunch of Western Clover (Bellingham, Washington: Edson & Irish, 1894).

When the Birds Go North Again (New York: Macmillan, 1898).

The Snow Pearls: A Poem by Ella Higginson (Seattle: Lowman and Hanford, 1897).

Four-Leaf Clover (Bellingham, Washington: Edson & Irish, 1901).

The Voice of April-Land and Other Poems (New York: Macmillan, 1903).

The Vanishing Race and Other Poems (Bellingham, Washington: C.M. Sherman, 1911).

Volumes of Short Fiction

The Flower That Grew in the Sand and Other Stories (Seattle: The Calvert Company, 1896).

From the Land of the Snow-Pearls: Tales From Puget Sound (New York: Macmillan, 1897).

A Forest Orchid and Other Stories (New York: Macmillan, 1897).

Novel

Mariella, of Out-West (New York: Macmillan, 1902).

Nonfiction

Alaska, the Great Country (New York: Macmillan 1908).

A Note on the Texts

THE VERSIONS OF HIGGINSON'S WORKS collected here are taken from the books and periodicals listed below. Since many of Higginson's collected stories and poems were initially published in periodicals, the periodical citations are also given when possible.

The excerpts included here from both *Mariella, of Out-West* and *Alaska, the Great Country* are reprinted from the first editions of these books.

Whenever possible, the works in this edition are presented as they originally appeared. I have made very few silent emendations. I have corrected obvious printer errors and have also standardized font sizes and styles. I have maintained Higginson's use of dialect in her fiction except in rare instances when the usage would create confusion for readers. I also have retained anachronistic spellings and punctuation when possible.

The Flower That Grew in the Sand and Other Stories (Seattle: The Calvert Company, 1896): "The Mother of 'Pills' " (*Short Stories: A Magazine of Select Fiction*, February 1894); "Patience Appleby's Confessing-Up" (*Peterson's Magazine*, October 1894); "The Takin' In of Old Mis' Lane" (*McClure's Magazine*, December 1894); "Mrs. Risley's Christmas Dinner" (*Lippincott's*, January 1895); "A Point of Knuckling-Down" (*McClure's Magazine*, December 1895).

A Forest Orchid and Other Stories (New York: Macmillan, 1897): "The Arnspiker Chickens" (*The Outlook*, July 1895).

From the Land of the Snow-Pearls: Tales From Puget Sound (New York: Macmillan, 1897): "The Blow-Out at Jenkins's Grocery" (*The Black Cat*, December 1896).

"The Stubbornness of Uriah Slater" (*Harper's Bazaar*, 1899).

Prize Stories From Collier's, v. 2 (New York: Collier's, 1916): "M'liss's Child" (*Collier's Magazine*, 4 November 1905).

Prize Stories From Collier's, v. 3 (New York: Collier's, 1916): "The Message of Ann Laura Sweet" (*Collier's Magazine*, 26 December 1914).

Mariella, of Out-West (New York: Macmillan, 1902).

Alaska, the Great Country (New York: Macmillan, 1908).

The Snow Pearls (Seattle: Lowman and Hanford, 1897): "The Snow Pearls."

When The Birds Go North Again (New York: Macmillan, 1898): "Four-Leaf Clover" (*The West Shore Magazine*, 1890); "The Lamp in the West"; "Yet Am I Not For Pity" (*McClure's Magazine*, December 1897); "When the Birds Go North Again"; "Sunrise on the Willamette."

The Voice of April-Land and Other Poems (New York: Macmillan, 1903): "Midnight on Brooklyn Bridge."

A Note on the Texts

Supplement to the Bulletin of the State Normal School Bellingham, XV.3 (Olympia, Washington: 1904): "The College By the Sea" (originally titled "The Normal By the Sea").

The Vanishing Race (Bellingham, Washington: C.M. Sherman, 1911): "The Vanishing Race"; "To Life."

Chronology of Ella Rhoads Higginson

1862? Ella Rhoads is born on January 28 in Council Grove, Kansas, to Charles Reeve Rhoads (1821-1881) and Mary A. Rhoads (1826-1898). She is the youngest of six children, three of whom died before reaching adulthood.

1863? The family—her father, mother, older sister Carrie (1850-1926), older brother Mahlon (1853-1906), and Ella—travels by horse-drawn carriage throughout the eight-month journey from Kansas to Oregon.

1863-1873 The family first settles in Eastern Oregon's Grand Ronde Valley. In 1868, they move to Portland, then to a farm near Milwaukie, then to Oregon City. Ella is privately tutored and also attends public school.

1875 When Ella is fourteen years old, her first published poem "Dreams of the Past" appears in *The Oregon City* newspaper.

1876 Ella begins what will become regular editorial work with a job at the newspaper office of *The Oregon City Enterprise*, where she learns typesetting and editorial writing. She starts publishing short fiction anonymously and under various pseudonyms (such as "Ann Lester," "Ethelind Ray," and "Enid").

1878-1914 Ella Higginson publishes over 100 short stories and over 300 poems in major periodicals of the day.

1881 Her father Charles Reeve Rhoads dies. He is buried in Mountain View Cemetery in Oregon City, Oregon.

1885 At age 23, she marries Russell Carden Higginson (1852-1909), age 33, a druggist, who had moved to Oregon from New Jersey. He is a distant cousin of New England writer and abolitionist Thomas Wentworth Higginson. During their marriage she will travel to the Northeastern United States to visit his family. She begins publishing her writing under her own name.

1888 Ella and Russell Higginson move to New Whatcom (later Bellingham), Washington.

1889 On November 11, Washington territory becomes the 42nd state of the United States.

1890 Ella Higginson serves as editor of the "Fact and Fancy for Women" department for Portland, Oregon's *West Shore*, a literary magazine. Her first article appears March 8. Its controversial topic is divorce. Higginson's argument that early marriage is more of a problem for women than divorce garners Higginson national notice.

1890 What will become Higginson's most well-known and most frequently reprinted poem, "Four-Leaf Clover," is published in Portland, Oregon's *West Shore*.

1890 The Higginson house in Bellingham is built at Pine and High Street across from what is now Western Washington University's Edens Hall. Higginson names the house "Clover Hill."

1891 She becomes associate editor of Seattle's *The Pacific* magazine.

1893 Higginson's story "The Mother of 'Pills' " wins *Short Stories* magazine's award for best story.

1894 *A Bunch of Western Clover*, a book of poetry, is published.

1894 Higginson wins *McClure's* magazine short fiction contest, with a prize of $500, for "The Takin' In of Old Mis' Lane." *McClure's* prints 80,000 copies of the issue in anticipation of high demand.

1896 *The Flower That Grew In the Sand and Other Stories* is published.

1897 *The Snow-Pearls*, a poem by Higginson with illustrations by Maud Miner Biglow, is published.

1897 Macmillan republishes *The Flower That Grew In the Sand and Other Stories*. Macmillan replaces one story, adds another, and titles the collection *From the Land of the Snow Pearls: Tales From Puget Sound*.

1897 *A Forest Orchid and Other Stories* is published.

1898 *When the Birds Go North Again*, a book of poetry, is published. New England author Sarah Orne Jewett writes Higginson, praising her work.

1898 Higginson's mother, Mary A. Rhoads, dies. She is buried next to her husband in Mountain View Cemetery in Oregon City, Oregon.

1899 New Whatcom State Normal School (later Western Washington University) opens in September.

1900-1903? Higginson writes a regular column, "Clover Leaves," in the *Seattle Daily Times* newspaper.

1901 *Four-Leaf Clover*, a book of poetry, is published.

1902 Higginson's only completed novel *Mariella, of Out-West* is published. Reviewers compare the book to novels by Jane Austen, Leo Tolstoy, and Émile Zola. New editions are published again in 1902, then in 1903, 1905, and 1924.

1903 *The Voice of April-Land and Other Poems* is published.

1905 Higginson serves as associate editor for the Seattle magazine, *The Westerner*.

1906 Higginson writes regular book reviews for Portland, Oregon's *Pacific Monthly*.

1906-1909 Sometime during this period, Higginson travels to Honolulu with her husband for his health.

1906-1909 Higginson spends four consecutive summers traveling in Alaska, conducting research for her book on Alaska.

1908 *Alaska, the Great Country*, an account of her travel in Alaska as well as a history of Alaska, is published.

1909 On May 14, Russell Higginson, age 57, dies after a short illness. Ella Higginson is 47 years old.

1910 Washington State grants the right to vote to women who can read and speak English. (Various oppressive citizenship laws continue to deny many non-white women the right to vote.)

1911 *The Vanishing Race and Other Poems* is published.

1912 Higginson begins to serve as campaign manager for State Republican candidate Frances C. Axtell, cousin of US President Grover Cleveland. Axtell becomes the first female member of the Washington State Legislature.

1912 *Alaska* is republished as part of the *Macmillan Travel Series*.

1914 Higginson's story "The Message of Ann Laura Sweet" is named *Collier's* magazine prize story and awarded a prize of $500 by a panel consisting of former US President Theodore Roosevelt and investigative journalists Mark Sullivan and Ida Tarbell.

1914 Higginson extensively updates *Alaska* for reissue.

1915-1918 Higginson volunteers for the Red Cross, suspending her writing during World War I.

1919 New edition of *Alaska* with new material is published.

1921 Edens Hall opens on the Western Washington University campus. Above the portals of its main entrance is engraved, "HERE IS THE HOME OF COLOR AND OF LIGHT" a line from Higginson's poem, "The College by the Sea."

1922 On December 12, Higginson's brother-in-law, John B. Morgan, dies, age 82.

1926 Higginson's sister, Caroline "Carrie" Blake (Rhoads) Morgan, dies, age 76.

1930 On October 17, Higginson renews the copyright of *Mariella, of Out-West*.

1931 Higginson is named Poet Laureate of Washington State by the Washington Federation of Women's Clubs.

1940 On December 27, Higginson dies at home at age 78, having been ill most of the year. She leaves an estate of about $60,000. She is buried in Bayview Cemetery, Bellingham, Washington beneath a self-designed granite monument adorned with four-leaf clovers, a reference to her most well-known poem. The inscription on her gravestone quotes the title and the final line of her sonnet sequence, "Yet Am I Not for Pity": "YET AM I NOT FOR PITY—TREMBLING I HAVE COME FACE TO FACE WITH GOD." Beneath the quotation is engraved, "ELLA HIGGINSON, POET-WRITER."

1951 Higginson's friend, Catherine Montgomery, a founding faculty member of what will become Western Washington University, donates three acres of forest land on the Mount Rainier Chinook Pass Highway to the State parks system in honor of Higginson. The tract of land is named Ella Higginson Grove.

1961 Higginson Hall on the campus of Western Washington University is dedicated in honor of Ella and Russell Carden Higginson in recognition of their early support of the university.

SELECTED WRITINGS *of*
ELLA HIGGINSON

Poems

"Four-Leaf Clover"
• 1890 •

I know a place where the sun is like gold,
    And cherry blossoms burst with snow,
And down underneath is the loveliest nook
    Where the four-leaf clovers grow.

One leaf is for hope, and one is for faith,
    And one is for love, you know,
And God put another in for luck—
    If you search, you will find where they grow.

But you must have hope, and you must have faith,
    You must love and be strong—and so—
If you work, if you wait, you will find the place
    Where the four-leaf clovers grow.

"Four-Leaf Clover," Higginson's most well-known work, was published in 1890 in Portland, Oregon's *West Shore* magazine. It also appeared in Higginson's books *When The Birds Go North Again* (1898) and *Four-Leaf Clover* (1901), and was widely reprinted in her lifetime. Higginson regularly received letters from people seeking permission to reprint "Four-Leaf Clover" on calendars, greeting cards, postcards, and other items. "Four-Leaf Clover" was set to music and performed internationally by renowned dramatic singers of the day. In the twenty-first century, "Four-Leaf

Clover" continues to be popular. It appears as a common verse for St. Patrick's Day cards, on many websites, and as a frequently reprinted poem sometimes inaccurately attributed to Emily Dickinson.

Higginson responded to the poem's popularity by adopting the clover as her identifying symbol. She named her house "Clover Hill," her dog "Clover," and wore four-leaf clover jewelry. In 1892, she campaigned unsuccessfully for wild clover to be the Washington State flower. In 1899, her husband—druggist and real estate investor Russell Carden Higginson—named a building in downtown Bellingham, Washington, the Clover Building, in reference to the poem. In 1900, Higginson began writing a regular column called "Clover Leaves" in the *Seattle Times* newspaper. Images of clovers adorn Higginson's self-designed gravestone and "Four-Leaf Clover" was sung at her funeral.

Later in life, Higginson corrected the common interpretation that the poem was about luck. She explained that instead it was a poem about industrious effort: "We should never lack for 'good luck' which is another name for work" (Washington State Federation of Women's Clubs 11). Having devoted her energies to becoming a prolific, professional writer in the years since she had written the poem, Higginson presented success as earned. In Higginson's poem, the person who finds a four-leaf clover does so as the result of sustained, committed labor and not as the result of random chance.

"The Snow Pearls"
• 1897 •

I love the pale green emerald,
    The ruby's drop of flame,
The rare and precious sardonyx
    Of deeply envied fame;
I love the opal's restless fire
    With green lights interwove,
And e'en the royal amethyst,—
    But most of all I love
The string of snow-pearls set around
    This great blue sapphire, Puget Sound.

The modest garnet, finely cut,
    Gleams like some rich old wine;
I hold the diamond's crimson flash
    As something half divine;
The turquoise—chill December's gem—
    Blue as the blue above,
Is precious unto every heart—
    But more than these I love
The string of snow-pearls linked around
    This cool, blue sapphire, Puget Sound.

When up Mount Baker's noble dome
    Struggles the morning sun,
And waves of crimson and of gold
    Across the pale sky run;

When every fir-tree flashes out
   Like a tall gilded spire,
Sweet as a hope rooted in Heaven,
   Springs a soft, sudden fire
Upon the snow-pearls strung around
   This deep blue sapphire, Puget Sound.

Take, then, all jewels of the earth
   Which only gold can buy—
Not one is worth that glistening chain
   Linked in God's pale green sky!
Let him who will, roam East or West,
   On prairie or on sea,
Searching for empty gems—but oh!
   Let us contented be
With these pure snow-pearls clasped around
   Our own blue sapphire, Puget Sound.

"The Snow Pearls" is a poem that was published as an illustrated book in 1897.

In the book version of this poem, striking pen-and-ink lithographic illustrations of Mount Baker and the Puget Sound region by Pacific Northwest artist Maud Miner Biglow were integrated with the poem. Each stanza was printed on a single page that was then followed by two pages of illustrations.

In "The Snow Pearls," Higginson writes within the poetic tradition of Romantic depictions of nature. Like British poet William Wordsworth and others, Higginson in this poem both closely describes the speaker's physical environment and expresses the religious fervor experienced in response to the sublime natural splendor with which the speaker is surrounded. "The Snow Pearls"

"The Snow Pearls"

delivers the speaker's inspired reaction to the magnificent nature of the Puget Sound region.

"Yet Am I Not for Pity"
• 1897 •

For me there are no cities, no proud halls,
    No storied paintings—nor the chiseled snow
    Of statues; never have I seen the glow
Of sunset die upon the deathless walls
Of the pure Parthenon; no soft light falls
    For me in dim cathedrals, where the low,
    Still seas of supplication ebb and flow;
No dream of Rome my longing soul enthralls.
But oh, to gaze in a long tranced delight
    On Venice rising from the purple sea!
    Oh, but to feel one golden evening pale
On that famed island from whose lonely height
    Dark Sappho sank in burning ecstasy!
    But once—but once—to hear the nightingale!

Yet am I not for pity. This blue sea
    Burns with the opal's deep and splendid fires
    At sunset; these tall firs are classic spires
Of chaste design and marvelous symmetry
That lift to burnished skies. Let pity be
    For him who never felt the mighty lyres
    Of Nature shake him thro' with great desires.
These pearl-topped mountains shining silently—
They are God's sphinxes and God's pyramids;
    These dim-aisled forests His cathedrals, where
    The pale nun Silence tiptoes, velvet shod,

And Prayer kneels with tireless, parted lips;
And thro' the incense of this holy air
Trembling—I have come face to face with God.

THE SONNET SEQUENCE "Yet Am I Not For Pity" appeared in *McClure's Magazine* in December 1897. It was reprinted in Higginson's collection *When The Birds Go North Again* (1898) and in periodicals such as *The Nation* (1898) and *The Christian Register* (June 1899). Higginson chose to have the poem's title and its final line inscribed on her self-designed gravestone. "Yet Am I Not For Pity" is still reprinted often today, though many times without attributing the poem to Higginson.

This sonnet sequence dramatizes the often vexed position of the white settler in the United States West. The speaker initially mourns the knowledge that to dwell in such a remote region is to forfeit the precious opportunity to experience the distant worlds of exquisite European art. Though still recognizing how much is lost by residing in the Pacific Northwest, the speaker then describes what is gained by living in this wild location. In this poem, the white settler in the West is, regrettably, far from European art but as a result of that very distance lives a privileged life surrounded by the divine art of nature.

"The Lamp in the West"
· 1898 ·

Venus has lit her silver lamp
    Low in the purple West,
Breathing a soft and mellow light
    Upon the sea's full breast;
It is the hour when velvet winds
    Tremble the alder's crest.

Far out, far out, the restless bar
    Starts from a troubled sleep,
Where roaring thro' the narrow straits
    The meeting waters leap.
But still that shining pathway leads
    Across the lonely deep.

When I sail out the narrow straits,
    Where unknown dangers be,
And cross the troubled, moaning bar,
    To the mysterious sea—
Dear God, wilt Thou not set a lamp
    Low in the West for me?

"THE LAMP IN THE WEST" was published in 1898 in Higginson's book *When The Birds Go North Again*. It was frequently set to music during Higginson's lifetime, notably by American composer Horatio Parker (1863-1919). It became one of Parker's most popular commercial songs. "The Lamp in the West" continues to be reprinted often.

In "The Lamp in the West," nature is used as a site for religious consideration of the subjects of dying and the passage to an afterlife. Rather than address these challenging topics explicitly, the speaker instead depicts a dangerous path in nature that is made passable only by the light of the bright planet Venus. Describing that hazardous natural path and the crucial light that successfully guides one through it allows the speaker the courage to then envision the moment of dying and the hope of religious salvation.

"When the Birds Go North Again"
• 1898 •

Oh, every year hath its winter,
    And every year hath its rain—
But a day is always coming
    When the birds go North again.

When new leaves swell in the forest,
    And grass springs green on the plain,
And the alder's veins turn crimson—
    And the birds go North again.

Oh, every heart hath its sorrow,
    And every heart hath its pain—
But a day is always coming
    When the birds go North again.

'Tis the sweetest thing to remember,
    If courage be on the wane,
When the cold dark days are over—
    Why, the birds go North again.

"WHEN THE BIRDS GO NORTH AGAIN" was published in 1898 in Higginson's book *When The Birds Go North Again*. It was set to music by American composer Richard Henry Warren (1859-1933). It continues to be reprinted often.

"When the Birds Go North Again" aligns the cycles of nature with the cycles of human experience. In the poem, the speaker reassures readers that consolation from the challenges of human life may be found by recognizing that humans are not separate from nature and its patterns, but instead are a crucial element of the wide physical world of birds, seasons, and all forms of life.

"Sunrise on the Willamette"
• 1898 •

The sun sinks downward thro' the silver mist
    That looms across the valley, fold on fold,
And sliding thro' the fields that dawn has kissed,
    Willamette sweeps, each dimple set with gold.

Sweeps onward ever, curving as it goes,
    Past many a hill and many a flowered lea,
Until it pauses where Columbia flows,
    Deep-tongued, deep-chested, to the waiting sea.

O lovely vales thro' which Willamette slips!
    O vine-clad hills that hear its soft voice call!
My heart turns ever to those sweet, cool lips!
    That, passing, press each rock or grassy wall.

Thro' pasture lands, where mild-eyed cattle feed,
    Thro' marshy flats, where velvet tulés grow,
Past many a rose-tree, many a singing reed,
    I hear those wet lips calling, calling low.

The sun sinks downward thro' the trembling haze,
    The mist flings glistening needles high and higher,
And thro' the clouds—O fair beyond all praise!—
    Mount Hood leaps, chastened, from a sea of fire.

"Sunrise on the Willamette" was published in 1898 in Higginson's book *When the Birds Go North Again*. It has been reprinted often, particularly in reference to the literature of Oregon.

Though Higginson lived her entire adult life in Washington, she held an enduring love for Oregon, where she spent her childhood. Through detailed description of the Willamette River this poem exalts the magnificence of Pacific Northwest nature and promotes the opportunities available to whites who settle in the West. The speaker's depiction of the river at sunrise and its progress towards the sea invokes the hopeful beginning (represented by the sunrise) of white settlement in the West and what was seen as its unstoppable progress toward greater things (represented by the vast sea).

"Midnight on Brooklyn Bridge"
• 1903 •

Ah, me! I know how large and cool and white
  The moon lies on the brow of Sehome Hill,
And how the firs stand shadowy and still,
  Etched on that luminous background this soft night;
How the nighthawk sinks from his starry height,
  And breathes his one note, mournfully and shrill,
And crickets clamor in the marsh until
  The dusk grows vocal with their deep delight.

City, a lifetime spent in thee were not
  Worth one night in my western solitude!
They pulse is feverish, thy blood is hot,
  Thine arteries throb with passion heavily;
But oh, how sweet I hear, in interlude,
  The beating, moon-lured tides of Puget Sea.

"MIDNIGHT ON BROOKLYN BRIDGE" is a sonnet published in Higginson's *The Voice of April-Land* in 1903. The poem was most likely written during Higginson's visit to her husband's family in the Northeastern United States.

  In this poem, the speaker argues for the Pacific Northwest as a more authentic American region than the Northeast. Using New York's Brooklyn as an urban contrast, the speaker portrays the Northwest as the America of the nation's imagination: natural, beautiful, and offering a democracy of wide open spaces that the speaker imagines are available to all.

"The College by the Sea"
• 1904 •

Below, the sea!—blue as a sapphire—set
    Within a sparkling, emerald mountain chain
Where fir and hemlock needle sift like rain
    Thro' the voluptuous air. The soft winds fret
The waves, and beat them wantonly to foam.
    The golden distances across the sea
Are shot with rose and purple. Languorously
    The silver seabirds in wide circles roam.
The sun moves slowly down the flaming west
    And flings its rays across to set aglow
The islands rocking on the cool waves' crest
    And the great glistening domes of snow on snow.
And thro' the mist the Olympics flash and float
    Like opals linked around a beating throat.

Inspired by God were they that chose this place
    Wherein to build these walls of softest rose;
Whose every slender pane at sunset glows
    Like burnished gold, and fires with mystic grace
The wooded loveliness of Sehome Hill.
    Here is the home of color and of light
Perfume of balm-tree; singing birds delight.
    Splendor of mist and rainbow—and the still,
Slow, flight of butterflies. Sweet, liquid-clear,
    The lark flings to dawn his lyric notes.
And what inspired psalmist have we here?

What song pure, enthralling sweetness floats
From yonder elm-tree in the midnight hush?
'Tis the entrancing love-song of the hermit-thrush.

"The College By the Sea" (originally titled "The Normal By the Sea") was published in 1904 in the *Supplement to the Bulletin of the State Normal School Bellingham,* vol. XV, no. 3.

The poem's subject is the beautiful Pacific Northwest setting of the Bellingham State Normal School (now Western Washington University). Higginson was asked to write the poem by Dr. George Williston Nash, second President of the Bellingham State Normal School. A line from the poem—"HERE IS THE HOME OF COLOR AND OF LIGHT"—is engraved over Edens Hall (built in 1921), one of the earliest buildings on the Western Washington University campus.

Rather than describe the educational mission, students, or other particulars of the college referenced in the poem's title, the speaker instead depicts the college's stunning natural setting. Focusing on the sea, mountains, firs, hemlock, and birds, the speaker implicitly associates the natural world with formal education. In this poem, the physical world that surrounds the college becomes the college itself, a world of learning embedded in nature that is available to all students.

"The Vanishing Race"
• 1911 •

Into the shadow, whose illumined crest
   Speaks of the world behind them where the sun
Still shines for us whose day is not yet done,
   Those last dark ones go drifting. East or West,
Or North or South—it matters not; their quest
   Is toward the shadow whence it was begun;
Hope in it, Ah, my brothers! there is none;
   And yet—they only seek a place to rest.

So mutely, uncomplainingly, they go!
   How shall it be with us when they are gone,
When they are but a mem'ry and a name?
   May not those mournful eyes to phantoms grow—
When wronged and lonely, they have drifted on
   Into the voiceless shadow whence they came?

THE SONNET "The Vanishing Race" was published in Higginson's book *The Vanishing Race* in 1911. The poem was written in response to a 1904 photograph of the same name by well-known, prolific Seattle-based photographer and ethnographer Edward S. Curtis (1868-1952). The photograph features a line of Navaho Indians on horseback riding slowly away from the camera.

   This poem accurately reflects the meanings that are suggested by Curtis's photograph. Both the photograph and the poem sympathetically endorse the then-dominant myth of American Indians as a vanished race, destroyed by colonization, disease, and assimilation.

"To Life"
• 1911 •

Take not endeavor from me. To the last
   Give me the quick blood and the eager heart;
The ecstasy of striving; and the smart
   Of failure's needles pricking fine and fast
To goad me to achievement. Unaghast,
   Let me endure to tread, alone, apart—
Led by the soft, compelling hand of Art—
   The paths by which lone, toiling ones have passed.

Yea, let me joy and suffer, live and love;
   Soar boundless heights on Aspiration's wing,
Or speak with God in wide and desolate plains.
   Let me know all! The quiet of the dove;
The sage's wisdom; and the exquisite sting
   Of liquid fire-drops burning in my veins.

THE SONNET "To Life" was published in Higginson's book *The Vanishing Race* in 1911.

   The poem is an intense entreaty from the aging artist. The speaker petitions fiercely to retain the whole, nuanced range of artistic struggle—resolve, effort, solitude, passionate response to success and failure—and so to be fully alive to absolute artistic endeavor until the last breath.

   Among all of Higginson's poems, "To Life" perhaps most

completely locates the artist in nature. Here the world of art is the world of nature. In this poem, artistic effort becomes life itself. For the poem's speaker, to create art is to live and to lose that ability to create is to die.

Prose

"The Mother of 'Pills'"
• 1894 •

"Pills! Oh, Pills! You Pillsy!"

The girl turned from the door of the drug-store, and looked back under bent brows at her mother, who was wiping graduated glasses with a stained towel, at the end of the prescription counter.

"I wish you wouldn't call me that," she said; her tone was impatient but not disrespectful.

Her mother laughed. She was a big, good-natured looking woman, with light-blue eyes and sandy eyebrows and hair. She wore a black dress that had a cheap, white cord-ruche at the neck. There were spots down the front of her dress where acids had been spilled and had taken out the color.

"How particular we are gettin'," she said, turning the measuring glass round and round on the towel which had been wadded into it. "You didn't use to mind if I called you 'Pills,' just for fun."

"Well, I mind now."

The girl took a clean towel from a cupboard and began to polish the show-cases, breathing upon them now and then. She was a good-looking girl. She had strong, handsome features, and heavy brown hair, which she wore in a long braid down her back. A deep red rose was tucked in the girdle of her cotton gown and its head lolled to and fro as she worked. Her hands were not prettily shaped, but sensitive, and the ends of the fingers were square.

"Well, Mariella, then," said Mrs. Mansfield, still looking amused; "I was goin' to ask you if you knew the Indians had all come in on their way home from hop pickin'."

Mariella straightened up and looked at her mother.

"Have they, honest, ma?"

"Yes, they have; they're all camped down on the beach."

"Oh, I wonder where!"

"Why, the Nooksacks are clear down at the coal-bunkers, an' the Lummis close to Timberline's Row; an' the Alaskas are all on the other side of the viaduct."

"Are they goin' to have the canoe race?"

"Yes, I guess so. I guess it'll be about sundown to-night. There, you forgot to dust that milk-shake. An' you ain't touched that shelf o' patent medicines!"

She set down the last graduate and hung the damp towel on a nail. Then she came out into the main part of the store and sat down comfortably behind the counter.

Long before Mariella was born her father had opened a drug-store in the tiny town of Sehome, on Puget Sound. There was a coal mine under the town. A tunnel led down into it, and the men working among the black diamonds, with their families, made up the town. But there was some trouble, and the mine was abandoned and flooded with salt water. The men went away, and for many years Sehome was little more than a name. A mail boat wheezed up from Seattle once a week; and two or three storekeepers—Mr. Mansfield among them—clung to the ragged edge of hope and waited for the boom. Before it came, Mr. Mansfield was bumped over the terrible road to the graveyard and laid down among the stones and ferns. Then Mrs. Mansfield "run" the store. The question "Can you fill perscriptions?" was often put to her fearfully by timid customers, but she was equal to the occasion.

"Well, I guess I can," she would say, squaring about and looking her questioner unwaveringly in the eye. "I guess I'd ought to. I've been in the store with my husband, that's dead, for twenty years. I'm not a regular, but I'm a practical—an' that's better than a regular any day."

"It's not so much what you know in a drugstore as what you *look* like you know," she sometimes confided to admiring friends.

It is true Mrs. Mansfield was often perplexed over the peculiar curdled appearance of some mixture—being as untaught in the mysterious ways of emulsions as a babe—but such trifles were dismissed with a philosophical sigh, and the prescriptions were handed over the counter with a complaisance that commanded confidence. The doctor hinted, with extreme delicacy, at times, that his emulsions did not turn out as smooth as he had expected; or that it would be agreeable to find some of his aqueous mixtures tinged with cochineal; or that it was possible to make pills in such a way that they would not—so to speak—melt in the patient's mouth before he could swallow them. But Mrs. Mansfield invariably laughed at him in a kind of motherly way, and reminded him that he ought to be glad to have even a "practical" in a place like Sehome. And really this was so true that it was unanswerable.

So Mrs. Mansfield held the fort; and as her medicines, although abominable to swallow, never killed any one, she was looked upon with awe and respect by the villagers and the men in the neighboring logging-camps.

Mariella was brought up in the drug-store. She had the benefit of her mother's experience, and, besides that, she had studied the "dispensatory"—a word, by the way, which Mrs. Mansfield began with a capital letter because of the many pitfalls from which it had rescued her.

"Mariella is such a good girl," her mother frequently declared; "she got a real good education over at the Whatcom schools, an' she's such a help in the drug-store. She does make a beautiful pill."

Indeed, the girl's pill-making accomplishment was so appreciated by Mrs. Mansfield that she had nick-named her "Pills"—a name that had been the cause of much mirth between them.

Mariella was now sixteen, and the long-deferred "boom" was upon them. Mrs. Mansfield and her daughter contemplated it from the store door daily with increasing admiration. The wild clover no longer velveted the middle of the street. New buildings, with red, green or blue fronts and nondescript backs, leaped up on every corner and in between corners. The hammers and saws made music sweeter than any brass band to Sehome ears. Day and night the forests blazed backward from the town. When there were no customers in the store Mariella stood in the door, twisting the rope of the awning around her wrist, and watched the flames leaping from limb to limb up the tall, straight fir-trees. When Sehome hill was burning at night, it was a magnificent spectacle; like hundreds of torches dipped into a very hell of fire and lifted to heaven by invisible hands—while in the East the noble, white dome of Mount Baker burst out of the darkness against the lurid sky. The old steamer *Idaho* came down from Seattle three times a week now. When she landed, Mrs. Mansfield and Mariella, and such customers as chanced to be in the store, hurried breathlessly back to the little sitting-room, which overlooked the bay, to count the passengers. The old colony wharf, running a mile out across the tide-lands to deep water, would be "fairly alive with 'em," Mrs. Mansfield declared daily, in an ecstasy of anticipation of the good times their coming foretold. She counted never less than a hundred and fifty; and so many walked three and four abreast that it was not possible to count all.

Really, that summer everything seemed to be going Mrs. Mansfield's way. Mariella was a comfort to her mother and an attraction to the store; business was excellent; her property was worth five times more than it had ever been before; and, besides—when her thoughts reached this point Mrs. Mansfield smiled consciously and blushed—there was Mr. Grover! Mr. Grover kept the dry-goods store next door. He had come at the very beginning of the boom. He was slim and dark and forty. Mrs. Mansfield was forty and large and fair. Both were "well off." Mr. Grover was lonely and "dropped into" Mrs. Mansfield's little sitting-room every night. She invited him to supper frequently, and he told her that her fried chicken and "cream" potatoes were better than anything he had eaten since his mother died. Of late his intentions were not to be misunderstood, and Mrs. Mansfield was already putting by a cozy sum for a wedding outfit. Only that morning she had looked at herself in the glass more attentively than usual while combing her hair. Some thought made her blush and smile.

"You ought to be ashamed!" she said, shaking her head at herself in the glass as at a gay, young thing. "To be thinkin' about gettin' married! With a big girl like Pills too. One good thing: He really seems to think as much of Pills as you do yourself, Mrs. Mansfield. That's what makes me so—happy, I guess. I believe it's the first time I ever was real happy before." She sighed unconsciously as she glanced back over her years of married life. "An' I don't know what makes me so awful happy now. But sometimes when I get up of a mornin' I just feel as if I could go out on the hill an' sing—foolish as any of them larks holler'n' for joy."

"Mariella," she said, watching the duster in the girl's hands, "what made you flare up so when I called you 'Pills?' You never done that before, an' I don't see what ails you all of a sudden."

"I didn't mean to flare up," said Mariella. She opened the cigar-case and arranged the boxes carefully. Then she closed it with a snap and looked at her mother. "But I wish you'd stop it, ma. Mr. Grover said—"

"Well, what 'id he say?"

"He said it wasn't a nice name to call a girl by." Mariella's face reddened, but she was stooping behind the counter.

Mrs. Mansfield drummed on the show-case with broad fingers and looked thoughtful.

"Well," she said with significance, after a pause, "if he don't like it, I won't do it. We've had lots o' fun over it, Pills, ain't we—I mean Mariella—but I guess he has a right to say what you'll be called, Pi—my dear."

"Oh, ma," said Mariella. Her face was like a poppy.

"Well, I guess you won't object, will you? I've been wond'rin' how you felt about it."

"Oh, ma," faltered the girl; "do you think, honest, he—he—"

"Yes, I do," replied her mother, laughing comfortably and blushing faintly. "I'm sure of it. An' I'm happier 'n I ever was in my life over it. I don't think I could give you a better stepfather, or one that would think more of you."

Mariella stood up slowly behind the counter and looked—stared—across the room at her mother, in a dazed, uncomprehending way. The color ebbed slowly out of her face. She did not speak, but she felt the muscles about her mouth jerking. She pressed her lips more tightly together.

"I hope you don't think I oughtn't to marry again," said her mother, returning her look without understanding it in the least. "Your pa's been dead ten years"—this in an injured tone. "There ain't many women—Oh, good mornin', Mr. Lester? Mariella, 'll you wait on Mr. Lester?" Well—beaming good naturedly on her customer—"how's real estate this mornin'? Any new sales afoot?"

"*Are* there?" repeated that gentleman, leaning on the show-case and lighting his cigar, innocent of intentional discourtesy. "Well, I should *smile*—and smile broadly too, Mrs. Mansfield. There's a Minneapolis chap here that's buyin' right an' left; just *slashin'* things! He's bought a lot o' water-front property, too; an' let me tell *you*, right now, that Jim Hill's behind him; an' Jim Hill's the biggest railroad man in the U. S. to-day, an' the Great Northern's behind *him!*"

"Well, I hope so." Mrs. Mansfield drew a long breath of delight. Mr. Lester smiled, shrugged his shoulders, spread out his hands, and sauntered out with the air of a man who has the ear of railroad kings.

"Are you goin' to the canoe races to-night, Mariella?" began her mother, in a conciliatory tone.

"I don't know. Might as well, I guess."

The girl was wiping the shelf bottles now; her face was pale, but her back was to her mother.

"Well, we will have an early supper, so you can get off. Mercy, child! Did you break one o' them glass labels? How often 'v' I told you not to press on 'em so hard? What one is it? The tincture cantharides! Well, tie a string around it, so we'll know what it is. There ain't no label on the aconite bottle, nor the Jamaica ginger either—an' them settin' side by side, too. I hate guessin' at things in a drug-store—'specially when one's a poison. Have you scoured up them spatulas?"

"Yes'm."

"Well, I'll go in an' do up the dishes, an' leave you to 'tend store. Don't forget to make Mr. Benson's pills. "

But Mr. Benson's pills were not made right away. When her mother was gone, Mariella got down from the step-ladder and leaned one elbow on the show-case and rested her chin in her hand. Her throat swelled in and out fitfully, and the blue veins showed, large and full, on her temples. For a long time she stood thus, twisting the towel in her hand and looking at the fires on the hill without seeing them. Some of their dry burning seemed to get into her own eyes.

Mr. Grover, passing, glanced in.

"Mariella," he said, putting one foot across the threshold, "are you goin' to the canoe races?"

The girl had darted erect instantly, and put on a look of coquettish indifference.

"Yes, I am." Her eyes flashed at him over her shoulder from the corners of their lids as she started back to the prescription-case, "I'm goin' with Charlie Walton!"

When Mariella had gone to the races that night, and customers were few and far between, Mr. Grover walked with a determined air through Mrs. Mansfield's store and, pushing aside the crimson canton-flannel portieres, entered her cheerful sitting-room. On the floor was a Brussels carpet, large-flowered and vivid. A sewing-machine stood in one corner and Mariella's organ in another. The two narrow windows overlooking the sound were gay with blooming geraniums and white curtains tied with red ribbons. There was a trunk deceptively stuffed and cretonned into the semblance of a settee; and there was a wicker-chair that was full of rasping, aggravating noises when you rocked in it. It had red ribbon twisted through its back and arms. Mrs. Mansfield was sitting in it now, reading a novel, and the chair was complaining unceasingly.

Mr. Grover sat down on the trunk.

"Mrs. Mansfield," he said, looking squarely at her, "I've got somethin' to ask of you, an' I'm goin' to do it while Mariella's away."

"That so?" said Mrs. Mansfield.

The color in her cheek deepened almost to a purple. She put one hand up to her face, and with the other nervously wrinkled the corners of the leaves of her novel. She lowered her lids resolutely to hide the sudden joy in her eyes.

"I guess you know what I've been comin' here so much for. I couldn't help thinkin', too, that you liked the idea an' was sort of encouragin' me."

Mrs. Mansfield threw one hand out toward him in a gesture at once deprecating, coquettish and helpful.

"Oh, you!" she exclaimed, laughing and coloring more deeply. There was decided encouragement in her honest blue eyes under their sandy lashes.

"Well, didn't you, now?" Mr. Grover leaned toward her.

She hesitated, fingering the leaves of her book. She turned her head to one side; the leaves swished softly as they swept past her broad thumb; the corners of her mouth curled in a tremulous smile; the fingers of her other hand moved in an unconscious caress across her warm cheek; she remembered afterward that the band across the bay on the long pier, where the races were, was playing "Annie Laurie," and that the odor of wild musk, growing outside her window in a box, was borne in, sweet and heavy, by the sea winds. It was the one perfect moment of Mrs. Mansfield's life—in which there had been no moments that even approached perfection; in which there had been no hint of poetry—only dullest, everyday prose. She had married because she had been taught that women should marry; and Mr. Mansfield had been a good husband. She always said that; and she did not even know that she always sighed after saying it. Her regard for Mr. Grover was the poetry—the wine—of her hard, frontier life. Never before that summer had she stood and listened to the message of the meadow-lark with a feeling of exaltation that brought tears to her eyes; or gone out to gather wild pink clover with the dew on it; or turned her broad foot aside to spare a worm. Not that Mr. Grover ever did any of these things; but that love had lifted the woman's soul and given her the new gift of seeing the beauty of common things. No one had guessed that there was a change in her heart, not even Mariella.

It was well that Mrs. Mansfield prolonged that perfect moment. When she did lift her eyes there was a kind of appealing tenderness in them.

"I guess I did," she said.

"Well, then,"—Mr. Grover drew a breath of relief—"you might's well say I can have her. I want it all understood before she gets home. I want to stop her runnin' with that Walton. Once or twice I've been afraid you'd just as leave she'd marry him as me. I don't like to see girls gallivant with two or three fellows."

Mrs. Mansfield sat motionless, looking at him. Her eyes did not falter; the smile did not wholly vanish from her face. Only the blood throbbed slowly away, leaving it paler than Mariella's had been that morning. She understood her mistake almost before his first sentence. While he was speaking her thoughts were busy. She felt the blood coming back when she remembered what she had said to Mariella. If *only* she had not spoken!

"Well," she said, calmly, "have you said anything to Mariella?"

"Yes, I have; lots o' times. An' I know she likes me; but she's some flirtish, and that's what I want to put a stop to. So, with your permission, I'll have a talk with her to-night."

"I'd like to talk to her first myself." Mrs. Mansfield looked almost stern. "But I guess it'll be all right, Mr. Grover. If you'd just as soon wait till to-morrow, I'd like to be alone and make up my mind what to say to her."

Mr. Grover got up and shook hands with her awkwardly.

"I'll make her a good husband," he said, earnestly.

"I don't doubt that," replied Mrs. Mansfield.

Then he went out and the crimson curtain fell behind him.

...

When Mariella came home her mother was sitting, rocking, by the window. The lamp was lighted.

"The Mother of 'Pills'"

"Pills," she said, "I want you to stop goin' with that fello'."

The girl looked at her in silence. Then she took off her turban and stuck the long black pins back into it.

"I thought you liked him," she said, slowly.

"I do, but Mr. Grover wants you—an' I like him better."

"Wants *me!*" Mariella drew up her shoulders proudly.

"Yes, you," replied Mrs. Mansfield, laughing. The humor of the situation was beginning to appeal to her. "He says he'd told you. You must of laughed after I told you he wanted me."

"Oh, ma, does he want me, honest?"

"Yes, he does." She was still laughing.

"An' don't you mind, ma?"

"Not a mite," said the widow, cheerfully. "I'd rather he'd marry you than me; only, I thought he was too nice a man to be lost to the fam'ly."

"Oh, ma!"

"Well, get to bed now. He's comin' in the mornin' to see you."

She took up the lamp and stood holding it irresolutely.

"Pills," she said, looking embarrassed, "You won't ever tell him that I—that I—"

"Never, ma!" exclaimed the girl, earnestly; "as long as I live."

"All right, then. Look out! You're droppin' tallo' from your candle! Don't hold it so crooked, child! I wouldn't like him to laugh about it. Good-night."

As she passed through the kitchen she called out: "Oh, Pills! Mr. Jordan brought in a mess of trout. We'll have 'em fried for breakfast."

The girl came running after her mother, and threw her arms around her.

"Oh, ma, are you sure you don't care a bit?"

"Not a bit," said Mrs. Mansfield, kissing her heartily. "I just thought he ought to be in the family. I'm glad it's turned out this way. Now, you go to bed, an' don't forget to roll up your bangs."

She went into her room and shut the door.

"The Mother of 'Pills,' " Ella Higginson's first story to win a national award, was chosen as the Best Original Story by *Short Stories: A Magazine of Select Fiction*. It was published in February 1894 and reprinted in Higginson's collections *The Flower That Grew in the Sand and Other Stories* (1896) and *From The Land of the Snow-Pearls: Tales From Puget Sound* (1897).

In "The Mother of 'Pills,' " Higginson dramatizes the shifting understandings between a mother and her daughter in the tiny town of Sehome on Puget Sound in the late-nineteenth-century United States. The subject of the mother/daughter relationship in struggling Pacific Northwest towns is one that Higginson will often return to in her fiction over the course of her career. The setting of the "The Mother of 'Pills' " is a drugstore that is owned and operated by the main character, the widowed Mrs. Mansfield. Higginson's detailed description of the store and the various medicines prepared there reflect the knowledge that she had acquired while working in drugstores owned by her husband (Russell Carden Higginson, a druggist) in Oregon and then in Washington.

"Patience Appleby's Confessing-Up"
• 1894 •

"It must be goin' to rain! My arm aches me so I can hardly hold my knitting needles."

"Hunh!" said Mrs. Wincoop. She twisted her thread around her fingers two or three times to make a knot; then she held her needle up to the light and threaded it, closing one eye entirely and the other partially, and pursing her mouth until her chin was flattened and full of tiny wrinkles. She lowered her head and looking at Mrs. Willis over her spectacles with a kind of good-natured scorn, said—"Is that a sign o' rain?"

"It never fails." Mrs. Willis rocked back and forth comfortably. "Like as not it begins to ache me a whole week before it rains."

"I never hear tell o' such a thing in all my days," said Mrs. Wincoop, with unmistakable signs of firmness, as she bent over the canton flannel night-shirt she was making for Mr. Wincoop.

"Well, mebbe you never. Mebbe you never had the rheumatiz. I've had it twenty year. I can't get red of it, anyways. I've tried the Century liniment—the one that has the man riding over snakes an' things—and the arnicky, and ev'ry kind the drug-store keeps. I've wore salt in my shoes tell they turned white all over; and I kep' a buckeye in my pocket tell it wore a hole and fell out. But I never get red o' the rheumatiz."

Mrs. Wincoop took two or three stitches in silence; then she said—"Patience, now, she *can* talk o' having rheumatiz. She's most bent in two with it when she has it—and that's near all the time."

The rocking ceased abruptly. Mrs. Willis's brows met, giving a look of sternness to her face.

"That's a good piece o' cotton flannel," she said. "Hefty! Fer pitty's sake! D'you put ruffles on the bottom o' Mr. Wincoop's night-shirt? Whatever d'you do that fer?"

"Because he likes 'em that way," responded Mrs. Wincoop, tartly. "There's no call fer remarks as I see, Mis' Willis. You put a pocket 'n Mr. Willis's, and paw never'd have that—never!" firmly.

"Well, I never see ruffles on a man's night-shirt before," said Mrs. Willis, laughing rather aggravatingly. "But they do look reel pretty, anyways."

"The longer you live the more you learn." Mrs. Wincoop spoke condescendingly. "But talking about Patience—have you see her lately?"

"No, I ain't." Mrs. Willis got up suddenly and commenced rummaging about on the table; there were two red spots on her thin face. "I'd most fergot to show you my new winter underclo's. Ain't them nice and warm, though? They feel so good to my rheumatiz. I keep thinking about them that can't get any. My, such hard times! All the banks broke, and no more prospect of good times than of a hen's being hatched with teeth! It puts me all of a trimble to think o' the winter here and ev'rybody so hard up. It's a pretty pass we've come to."

"I should say so. I don't see what Patience is a-going to live on this winter. She ain't fit to do anything; her rheumatiz is awful. She ain't got any fine wool underclo's."

Mrs. Willis sat down again, but she did not rock; she sat upright, holding her back stiff and her thin shoulders high and level.

"I guess this tight spell 'll learn folks to lay by money when they got it," she said, sternly. "I notice we ain't got any mortgage on our place, and I notice we got five thousand dollars invested. We got some cattle besides. We ain't frittered ev'rything we made away on foolishness, like some that I know of. We have things good and comf'terble, but we don't put on any style. Look at that Mis' Abernathy! I caught her teeheeing behind my back when I was buying red checked table clo's. Her husband a bookkeeper! And her a-putting on airs over me that could buy her up any day in the week! Now, he's lost his place, and I reckon she'll come down a peg or two."

"She's been reel good to Patience, anyways," said Mrs. Wincoop.

Mrs. Willis knitted so fast her needles fairly rasped together.

"She takes her in jell and perserves right frequent. You mind Patience always liked sweet things even when her 'n' Lizy was girls together, Eunice."

It was so unusual for one of these two women to speak the other's name that they now exchanged quick looks of surprise. Indeed, Mrs. Wincoop seemed the more surprised of the two. But the hard, matter-of-fact expression returned at once to each face. If possible, Mrs. Willis looked more grim and sour than before the unwonted address had startled her out of her composure.

"Well," she said, scarcely unclosing her thin lips, "I reckon she had all the sweet things she was a-hankering after when she was a girl. I reckon she had a plenty and to spare, and I expect they got to tasting pretty bitter a good spell ago. Too much sweet always leaves a bit'rish taste in the mouth. My religion is—do what's right, and don't wink at them that does wrong. I've stuck to my religion. I reckon you can't get anybody to stand up and put their finger on anything wrong I've done— nor any of my fambly, either." Mrs. Wincoop put her hand on her chest and coughed mournfully. "Let them that's *sinned*," went on Mrs. Willis, lifting her pale, cold eyes and setting them full on her visitor, "make allowance fer sinners, say I. Mis' Abernathy, or Mis' Anybody Else, can pack all the clo's and all the sweet things they've got a mind to over to Patience Appleby; mebbe they've sinned, too—*I* don't know! But I do know that I ain't, and so I don't pack things over to her, even if she is all doubled up with the rheumatiz," unconsciously imitating Mrs. Wincoop's tone. "And I don't make no allowance for her sins, either, Mis' Wincoop."

A faint color came slowly, as if after careful consideration, to Mrs. Wincoop's face.

"There wa'n't no call fer you a-telling that," she said, with a great calmness. "The whole town knows you wouldn't fergive a sin, if your fergiving it 'u'd save the sinner hisself from being lost! The whole town knows what your religion is, Mis' Willis. You set yourself up and call yourself perfeck, and wrap yourself up in yourself—"

"There come the men—sh!" said Mrs. Willis. Her face relaxed, but with evident reluctance. She began to knit industriously. But the temptation to have the last word was strong.

"It ain't my religion, either," she said, her voice losing none of its determination because it was lowered. "I'd of fergive her if she'd a-confessed up. We all tried to get her to. I tried more 'n anybody. I told her"—in a tone of conviction—"that nobody but a brazen thing 'u'd do what she'd done and not confess up to 't—and it never fazed her. She *wouldn't* confess up."

The men were scraping their feet noisily now on the porch, and Mrs. Willis leaned back with a satisfied expression, expecting no reply. But Mrs. Wincoop surprised her. She was sewing the last pearl button on Mr. Wincoop's night-shirt, and as she drew the thread through and fastened it with scrupulous care, she said, without looking up—"I don't take much stock in confessings myself, Mis' Willis. I don't see just how confessings is good for the soul when they hurt so many innocent ones as well

"Patience Appleby's Confessing-Up"

as the guilty ones. Ev'ry confessing affex somebody else; and so I say if you repent and want to atone you can do 't without confessing and bringing disgrace on others. It's nothing but curiosity that makes people holler out—'Confess-up now! Confess-up now.' It ain't anybody's business but God's—and I reckon *He* knows when a body's sorry he's sinned and wants to do better, and I reckon He helps him just as much as if he got up on a church tower and kep' a-hollering out—'Oh, good grieve, I've sinned! I've sinned!'—so 's the whole town could run and gap' at him! Mis' Willis, if some confessing-ups was done in this town that I know of, some people 'u'd be affected that 'u'd surprise you." Then she lifted up her voice cheerfully—"That you, father? Well, d' you bring the lantern? I reckon we'd best go right home; it's getting latish, and Mis' Willis thinks, from the way her arm aches her, that it's going to rain."

Mrs. Willis sat knitting long after Mr. Willis had gone to bed. Her face was more stern even than usual. She sat uncomfortably erect and did not rock. When the clock told ten, she arose stiffly and rolled the half finished stocking around the ball of yarn, fastening it there with the needles. Then she laid it on the table and stood looking at it intently, without seeing it. "I wonder," she said, at last, drawing a deep breath, "what she was a-driving at! I'd give a pretty to know."

...

"Mother, where's my Sund'y pulse-warmers at?"

"*I* don't know where your Sund'y pulse-warmers are at. Father, you'd aggravate a body into her grave! You don't half look up anything—and then begin asking me where it's at. What's under that bunch o' collars in your drawer? Looks some like your Sund'y pulse-warmers, don't it? This ain't Sund'y, anyways. Wa'n't your ev'ryday ones good enough to wear just to a church meeting?"

Mr. Willis had never been known to utter an oath; but sometimes he looked as if his heart were full of them.

"I reckon you don't even know where your han'ke'cher's at, father."

"Yes, I do, mother. I guess you might stop talking, an' come on now—I'm all ready."

He preceded his wife, leaving the front door open for her to close and lock. He walked stiffly, holding his head straight, lest his collar should cramp his neck or prick his chin. He had a conscious, dressed-up air. He carried in one hand a lantern, in the other an umbrella. It was seven o'clock of a Thursday evening and the bell was ringing for prayer-meeting. There was to be a church meeting afterward, at which the name of Patience Appleby was to be brought up for membership. Mrs. Willis breathed hard and deep as she thought of it.

She walked behind her husband to receive the full light of the lantern, holding her skirts up high above her gaiter-tops which were so large and so worn as to elastic, that they fairly ruffled around her spare, flat ankles. Her shadow danced in piece-meal on the picket fence. After a while she said—

"Father, I wish you wouldn't keep swinging that lantern so! A body can't see where to put their feet down. Who's that ahead o' us?"

"I can't make out yet."

"No wonder—you keep swinging that lantern so! Father, what does *possess* you to be so aggravating? If I'd of asked you to swing it, you couldn't of b'en *drug* to do it!"

Mrs. Willis was guiltless of personal vanity, but she did realize the importance of her position in village society, and something of this importance was imparted to her carriage as she followed Mr. Willis up the church aisle. She felt that every eye was regarding her with respect, and held her shoulders so high that her comfortable shawl fell therefrom in fuller folds than usual. She sat squarely in the pew, looking steadily and unwinkingly at the wonderful red velvet cross that hung over the spindle-legged pulpit, her hands folded firmly in her lap. She had never been able to understand how Sister Wirth who sat in the pew in front of the Willises, could always have her head a-lolling over to one side like a giddy, sixteen-year-old. Mrs. Willis abominated such actions in a respectable, married woman of family.

Mr. Willis crouched down uneasily in the corner of the seat and sat motionless, with a self-conscious blush across his weak eyes. His umbrella, banded so loosely that it bulged like a soiled-clothes bag, stood up against the back of the next pew.

At the close of prayer-meeting no one stirred from his seat. An ominous silence fell upon the two dozen people assembled there. The clock ticked loudly, and old lady Scranton, who suffered of asthma, wheezed with every breath and whispered to her neighbor that she was getting so phthisicy she wished to mercy they'd hurry up or she'd have to go home without voting. At last one of the deacons arose and said with great solemnity that he understood sister Wincoop had a name to propose for membership.

When Mrs. Wincoop stood up she looked pale but determined. Mrs. Willis would not turn to look at her, but she caught every word spoken.

"Yes," said Mrs. Wincoop, "I want to bring up the name of Patience Appleby. I reckon you all know Patience Appleby. She was born here, and she's always lived here. There's them that says she done wrong onct, but I guess she's about atoned up for that—if any mortal living has. I've know her fifteen year, and I don't know any better behaving woman anywheres. She never talks about anybody"—her eyes went to Mrs. Willis's rigid back—"and she never complains. She's alone and poor, and all crippled up with the rheumatiz. She wants to join church and live a Christian life, and I, fer one, am in favor o' us a-holding out our hand to her and helping her up."

"Amen!" shrilled out the minister on one of his upper notes. There was a general rustle of commendation—whispers back and forth, noddings of heads, and many encouraging glances directed toward sister Wincoop.

But of a sudden silence fell upon the small assembly. Mrs. Willis had arisen. Her expression was grim and uncompromising. At that moment sister Shidler's baby choked in its sleep, and cried so loudly and so gaspingly that every one turned to look at it.

In the momentary confusion Mr. Willis caught hold of his wife's dress and tried to pull her down; but the unfortunate man only succeeded in ripping a handful of gathers from the band. Mrs. Willis looked down at him from her thin height.

"You let my gethers be," she said, fiercely. "You might of knew you'd tear 'em, a-taking holt of 'em that way!"

Then quiet was restored and the wandering eyes came back to Mrs. Willis. "Brothers and sisters," she said, "it ain't becoming in me to remind you all what Mr. Willis and me have done fer this church. It ain't becoming in me to remind you about the organ, and the new bell, and the carpet fer the aisles—let alone our paying twenty dollars more a year than any other member. I say it ain't becoming in me, and I never 'd mention it if it wa'n't that I don't feel like having Patience Appleby in this church. If she does come in, *I* go out."

A tremor passed through the meeting. The minister turned pale and stroked his meagre whiskers nervously. He was a worthy man, and he believed in saving souls. He had prayed and plead with Patience to persuade her to unite with the church, but he had not felt the faintest presentiment that he was quarreling with his own bread and butter in so doing. One soul scarcely balances a consideration of that kind—especially when a minister has six children and a wife with a chronic disinclination to do anything but look pretty and read papers at clubs and things. It was small wonder that he turned pale.

"I want that you all should know just how I feel about it," continued Mrs. Willis. "I believe in doing what's right yourself and not excusing them that does wrong. I don't believe in having people like Patience Appleby in this church; and she don't come in while *I'm* in, neither. That's all I got to say. I want that you all should understand plain that her coming in means my going out."

Mrs. Willis sat down, well satisfied. She saw that she had produced a profound sensation. Every eye turned to the minister with a look that said, plainly—"What have you to say to *that!*"

But the miserable man had not a word to say to it. He sat helplessly stroking his whiskers, trying to avoid the eyes of both Mrs. Wincoop and Mrs. Willis. At last Deacon Berry said—"Why, sister Willis, I think if a body repents and wants to do better, the church 'ad ort to help 'em. That's what churches are for."

Mrs. Willis cleared her throat.

"I don't consider that a body's repented, Deacon Berry, tell he confesses-up. Patience Appleby's never done that to this day. When she does, I'm willing to take her into this church."

"Brothers and sisters," said Mrs. Wincoop, in a voice that held a kind of cautious triumph, "I fergot to state that Patience Appleby reckoned mebbe somebody 'u'd think she'd ort to confess before she come into the church; and she wanted I should ask the meeting to a'point Mis' Willis a committee o' one fer her to confess up to. Patience reckoned if she could satisfy Mis' Willis, ev'rybody else 'u'd be satisfied."

"Why—yes," cried the minister, with cheerful eagerness.

"That's all right—bless the Lord!" he added, in that jaunty tone with which so many ministers daily insult our God. "I know Mrs. Willis and Patience will be able to smooth over all difficulties. I think we may now adjourn."

"Whatever did she do that fer?" said Mrs. Willis, following the lantern homeward. "She's got something in her mind, *I* know, or she'd never want me a'p'inted. Father, what made you pull my gethers out? D'you think you could make me set down when I'd once made up my mind to stand up? You'd ought to know me better by this time. This is my secon'-best dress, and I've only wore it two winters—and now look at all these gethers tore right out!"

"You hadn't ought to get up and make a fool o' yourself, mother. You'd best leave Patience Appleby be."

"You'd ort to talk about anybody a-making a fool o' hisself! After you a-pulling my gethers clean out o' the band—right in meeting! You'd ort to tell me I'd best leave Patience Appleby be! I don't mean to leave her be. I mean to let her know she can't ac' scandalous, and then set herself up as being as good's church folks and Christians. *I'll* give her her come-uppings!"

For probably the first time in his married life Mr. Willis yielded to his feelings. "God-a'mighty, mother," he said; "sometimes you don't seem to have common sense! I reckon you'd best leave Patience Appleby be, if you know when you're well off." Then, frightened at what he had said, he walked on, hurriedly, swinging the lantern harder than ever.

Mrs. Willis walked behind him, dumb.

...

The day was cold and gray. Mrs. Willis opened with difficulty the broken-down gate that shut in Patience Appleby's house. "And no wonder," she thought, "it swags down so!"

"Patience Appleby's Confessing-Up"

There was a foot of snow on the ground. The path to the old, shabby house was trackless. Not a soul had been there since the snow fell—and that was two days ago! Mrs. Willis shivered under her warm shawl.

Patience opened the door. Her slow, heavy steps on the bare floor of the long hall affected Mrs. Willis strangely.

Patience was very tall and thin. She stooped, and her chest was sunken. She wore a dingy gray dress, mended in many places. There was a small, checked shawl folded in a "three-cornered" way about her shoulders. She coughed before she could greet her visitor.

"How d'you do, Mis' Willis," she said, at last. "Come in, won't you?"

"How are you, Patience?" Mrs. Willis said, and, to her own amazement, her voice did not sound as stern as she had intended it should.

She had been practicing as she came along, and this voice bore no resemblance whatever to the one she had been having in her mind. Nor, as she preceded Patience down the bare, draughty hall to the sitting-room, did she bear herself with that degree of frigid dignity which she had always considered most fitting to her position, both socially and morally.

Somehow, the evidences of poverty on every side chilled her blood. The sitting-room was worse, even, than the hall. A big, empty room with a small fire-place in one corner, wherein a few coals were turning gray; a threadbare carpet, a couple of chairs, a little table with the Bible on it, ragged wall-paper, and a shelf in one corner filled with liniment bottles.

Mrs. Willis sat down in one of the rickety chairs, and Patience, after stirring up the coals, drew the other to the hearth.

"I'm afraid the room feels kind o' coolish," she said. "I've got the last o' the coal on."

"D'you mean," said Mrs. Willis—and again her voice surprised her—"that you're all out o' coal?"

"All out." She drew the tiny shawl closer to her throat with trembling, bony fingers. "But Mis' Abernathy said she'd send me a scuttleful over today. I hate to take it from her, too; her husband's lost his position and they ain't overly well off. But sence my rheumatiz has been so bad I can't earn a thing."

Mrs. Willis stared hard at the coals. For the life of her she could think of nothing but her own basement filled to the ceiling with coal.

"I reckon," said Patience, "you've come to hear my confessing-up?"

"Why—yes." Mrs. Willis started guiltily.

"What's the charges agen me, Mis' Willis?"

Mrs. Willis's eyelids fell heavily.

"Why, I reckon you know, Patience. You done wrong onct when you was a girl, and I don't think we'd ort to take you into the church tell you own up to it."

There was a little silence. Then Patience said, drawing her breath in heavily—"Mebbe I did do wrong onct when I was a little girl—only fourteen, say. But that's thirty year ago, and that's a long time, Mis' Willis. I don't think I'd ort to own up to it."

"*I* think you'd ort."

"Mis' Willis,"—Patience spoke solemnly. "D'you think I'd ort to own up if it 'u'd affec' somebody else thet ain't never b'en talked about?"

"Yes, I do," said Mrs. Willis, firmly. "If they deserve to be talked about, they'd *ort* to be talked about."

"Even if it was about the best folks in town?"

"Yes." Mrs. Willis thought of the minister.

"Even if it was about the best-off folks? Folks that hold their head the highest, and give most to churches and mission-

"Patience Appleby's Confessing-Up"

ary; and thet ev'rybody' looks up to?"

"Ye-es," said Mrs. Willis. That did not describe the minister, certainly. She could not have told you why her heart began to beat so violently. Somehow, she had been surprised out of the attitude she had meant to assume. Instead of walking in boldly and haughtily, and giving Patience her "come-uppings," she was finding it difficult to conquer a feeling of pity for the enemy because she was so poor and so cold. She must harden her heart.

"Even"—Patience lowered her eyes to the worn carpet—"if it was folks thet had b'en loudest condemin' other folks's sins, and that had bragged high and low thet there wa'n't no disgrace in their fambly, and never had b'en none, and who'd just be about killed by my confessing-up?"

"Yes," said Mrs. Willis, sternly. But she paled to the lips.

"I don't think so," said Patience, slowly. "I think a body'd ort to have a chance if they want to live better, without havin' anybody a-pryin' into their effairs exceptin' God. But if you don't agree with me, I'm ready to confess-up all *I've* done bad. I guess you recollect, Mis' Willis, thet your 'Lizy and me was just of an age, to a day?"

Mrs. Willis's lips moved, but the words stuck in her throat.

"And how we ust to play together and stay nights with each other. We *loved* each other, Mis' Willis. You ust to give us big slices o' salt-risin' bread, spread thick with cream and sprinkled with brown sugar—I can just see you now, a-goin' out to the spring-house to get the cream. And I can just taste it, too, when I get good and hungry."

"What's all this got to do with your a-owning up?" demanded Mrs. Willis, fiercely. "What's my 'Lizy got to do with your going away that time? Where was you at, Patience Appleby?"

"I'm comin' to that," said Patience, calmly; but a deep flush came upon her face. "I've attoned-up fer that time, if any mortal bein' ever did, Mis' Willis. I've had a hard life, but I've never complained, because I thought the Lord was a-punishin' me. But I have suffered... Thirty year, Mis' Willis, of prayin' to be fergive fer one sin! But I ain't ever see the day I could confess-up to 't—and I couldn't now, except to 'Lizy's mother."

An awful trembling shook Mrs. Willis's heart. She looked at Patience with straining eyes. "Go on," she said, hoarsely.

"'Lizy and me was fourteen on the same day. She was goin' to Four Corners to visit her a'nt, but I had to stay at home and work. I was cryin' about it when, all of a sudden, 'Lizy says—'Patience, let's up and have a good time on our birthday!'"

"'Well, let's,'" I says, "'but how?'"

"'I'll start fer Four Corners and then you run away, and I'll meet you, and we'll go to Springville to the circus and learn to ride bareback'"—

Mrs. Willis leaned forward in her chair. Her face was very white; her thin hands were clenched so hard the knuckles stood out half an inch.

"Patience Appleby," she said, "you're a wicked, sinful liar! May the Lord A'mighty fergive you—*I* won't."

"I ain't askin' you to take my word; you can ask Mr. Willis hisself. He didn't go to Springville to buy him a horse, like he told you he did. 'Lizy and me had been at the circus two days when she tuk sick, and I sent fer Mr. Willis unbeknownst to anybody. He come and tuk her home and fixed it all up with her a'nt at Four Corners, and give out thet she'd been a-visitin' there. But I had to sneak home alone and live an outcast's life ever sence, and see her set up above me—just because Mr. Willis got down to beg me on his knees never to tell she was with me. And I never did tell a soul, Mis' Willis, tell last winter I was sick with a fever and told Mis' Wincoop when I was out o' my head. But she's never told anybody, either, and neither

"Patience Appleby's Confessing-Up"

of us ever will. Mr. Willis has helped me as much as he could without your a-findin' it out, but I know how it feels to be hungry and cold, and I know how it feels to see 'Lizy set up over me, and marry rich, and have nice children; and ride by me 'n her kerriage without so much as lookin' at me—and me a-chokin' with the dust off o' her kerriage wheels. But I never complained none, and I ain't a-complainin' now, Mis' Willis; puttin' 'Lizy down wouldn't help me any. But I do think it's hard if I can't be let into the church."

Her thin voice died away and there was silence. Patience sat staring at the coals with the dullness of despair on her face. Mrs. Willis's spare frame had suddenly taken on an old, pathetic stoop. What her haughty soul had suffered during that recital, for which she had been so totally unprepared, Patience would never realize. The world seemed to be slipping from under the old woman's trembling feet. She had been so strong in her condemnation of sinners because she had felt so sure she should never have any trading with sin herself. And lo! all these years her own daughter—her one beloved child, dearer than life itself—had been as guilty as this poor outcast from whom she had always drawn her skirts aside, as from a leper. Ay, her daughter had been the guiltier of the two. She was not spared that bitterness, even. Her harsh sense of justice forced her to acknowledge, even in that first hour, that this woman had borne herself nobly, while her daughter had been a despicable coward.

It had been an erect, middle-aged woman who had come to give Patience Appleby her "come-uppings"; it was an old, broken-spirited one who went stumbling home in the early, cold twilight of the winter day. The fierce splendor of the sunset had blazed itself out; the world was a monotone in milky blue—save for one high line of dull crimson clouds strung along the horizon.

A shower of snow-birds sunk in Mrs. Willis's path, but she did not see them. She went up the path and entered her comfortable home; and she fell down upon her stiff knees beside the first chair she came to—and prayed as she had never prayed before in all her hard and selfish life.

...

When Mr. Willis came home to supper he found his wife setting the table as usual. He started for the bedroom, but she stopped him.

"We're a-going to use the front bedroom after this, father," she said.

"Why, what are we going to do that fer, mother?"

"I'm a-going to give our'n to Patience Appleby."

"You're a-going to—*what*, mother?"

"I'm a-going to give our'n to Patience Appleby, I say. I'm a-going to bring her here to live, and she's got to have the warmest room in the house, because her rheumatiz is worse 'n mine. I'm a-going after her myself to-morrow in the kerriage." She turned and faced her husband sternly. "She's confessed-up ev'rything. I was dead set she should, and she has. I know where she was at, that time, and I know who was with her. I reckon I'd best be attoning up as well as Patience Appleby; and I'm going to begin by making her comf'terble and taking her into the church."

"Why, mother," said the old man, weakly. His wife repressed him with one look.

"Now, don't go to talking back, father," she said, sternly. "I reckon you kep' it from me fer the best, but it's turrable hard on me now. You get and wash yourself. I want that you should hold this candle while I fry the apple-fritters."

HIGGINSON'S AWARD-WINNING "Patience Appleby's Confessing-Up" appeared in *Peterson's Magazine* in October 1894. It was reprinted in Higginson's collections *The Flower That Grew in the Sand and Other Stories* (1896) and *From The Land of the Snow-Pearls: Tales From Puget Sound* (1897).

In "Patience Appleby's Confessing-Up," Higginson tells a tale of conflict between two women in a small village. The subject of friction between an older woman and a younger woman is one that Higginson often considered in her writing. In this story, older Mrs. Willis has harshly condemned younger Patience Appleby whose behavior in the past has been deemed immoral. Now Patience Appleby, who is alone, poor, and in ill health, wishes to join the church. Mrs. Willis will only agree to Patience Appleby's church membership if Patience publicly admits the details of her past transgressions. In "Patience Appleby's Confessing-Up," Higginson explores issues of Christian charity, kindness, and the consequences of restrictive social rules that governed women's behavior.

"The Takin' In of Old Mis' Lane"
• 1894 •

"Huhy! Huhy! Pleg take that muley cow! Huhy!"

"What she doin', maw?"

"Why, she's just a-holdin' her head over the bars, an' a-bawlin'! Tryin' to get into the little correll where her ca'f is! I wish paw'd of done as I told him an' put her into the up meadow. If there's anything on earth I abominate it's to hear a cow bawl."

Mrs. Bridges gathered up several sticks of wood from the box in the corner by the stove, and going out into the yard, threw them with powerful movements of her bare arm in the direction of the bars. The cow lowered her hornless head and shook it defiantly at her, but held her ground. Isaphene stood in the open door, laughing. She was making a cake. She beat the mixture with a long-handled tin spoon while watching the fruitless attack. She had reddish brown hair that swept away from her brow and temples in waves so deep you could have lost your finger in any one of them; and good, honest gray eyes, and a mouth that was worth kissing. She wore a blue cotton gown that looked as if it had just left the ironing-table. Her sleeves were rolled to her elbows.

"It don't do any good, maw," she said, as her mother returned with a defeated air. "She just bawls an' shakes her head right in your face. Look at her!"

"Oh, I don't want to look at her. It seems to me your paw might of drove her to the up meadow, seein's he was goin' right up by there. It ain't like as if he'd of had to go out o' his way. It aggravates me offul."

She threw the last stick of wood into the box, and brushed

the tiny splinters off her arm and sleeves.

"Well, I guess I might as well string them beans for dinner before I clean up."

She took a large milk pan, filled with beans, from the table and sat down near the window.

"Isaphene," she said, presently, "what do you say to an organ, an' a horse an' buggy? A horse with some style about him, that you could ride or drive, an' that 'u'd always be up when you wanted to go to town!"

"What do I say?" The girl turned and looked at her mother as if she feared one of them had lost her senses; then she returned to her cake-beating with an air of good-natured disdain.

"Oh, you can smile an' turn your head on one side, but you'll whistle another tune before long—or I'll miss my guess. Isaphene, I've been savin' up chicken an' butter money ever since we come to Puget Sound; then I've always got the money for the strawberry crop, an' for the geese an' turkeys, an' the calves, an' so on. Your paw's been real good about such things."

"I don't call it bein' good," said Isaphene. "Why shouldn't he let you have the money? You planted, an' weeded, an' picked the strawberries; an' you fed an' set the chickens, an' gethered the eggs; an' you've had all the tendin' of the geese an' turkeys an' calves—to say nothin' of the cows bawlin' over the bars," she added, with a sly laugh. "I'd say you only had your rights when you get the money for such things."

"Oh, yes, that's fine talk." Mrs. Bridges nodded her head with an air of experience. "But it ain't all men-folks that gives you your rights; so when one does, I say he deserves credit."

"Well, I wouldn't claim anybody'd been good to me just because he give me what I'd worked for an' earned. Now, if he'd give you all the money from the potato patch every year, or the hay meadow, or anything he'd done all the workin' with himself—I'd call that good in him. He never done anything like that, did he?"

"No, he never," replied Mrs. Bridges, testily. "An' what's more, he ain't likely to—nor any other man I know of! If you get a man that gives you all you work for an' earn, you'll be lucky—with all your airs!"

"Well, I guess I'll manage to get my rights, somehow," said Isaphene, beginning to butter the cake-pan.

"Somebody's comin'!" exclaimed her mother, lowering her voice to a mysterious whisper.

"Who is it?" Isaphene stood up straight, with that little quick beating of mingled pleasure and dismay that the cry of company brings to country hearts.

"I can't see. I don't want to be caught peepin'. I can see it's a woman, though; she's just passin' the row of hollyhocks. Can't you stoop down an' peep? She won't see you 'way over there by the table."

Isaphene stooped and peered cautiously through the wild cucumber vines that rioted over the kitchen window.

"Oh, it's Mis' Hanna!"

"My goodness! An' the way this house looks! You'll have to bring her out here 'n the kitchen, too. I s'pose she's come to spend the day—she's got her bag with her, ain't she?"

"Yes. What'll we have for dinner? I ain't goin' to cut this cake for her. I want this for Sund'y."

"Why, we've got corn beef to boil, an' a head o' cabbage; an' these here beans; an', of course, potatoes; an' watermelon preserves. An' you can make a custerd pie. I guess that's a good enough dinner for her. There! She's knockin'. Open the door, can't you? Well, if I ever! Look at that grease-spot on the floor!"

"Well, I didn't spill it."

"Who did, then, missy?"

"Well, *I* never."

Isaphene went to the front door, returning presently with a tall, thin lady.

"Here's Mis' Hanna, maw," she said, with the air of having made a pleasant discovery. Mrs. Bridges got up, greatly surprised, and shook hands with her visitor with exaggerated delight.

"Well, I'll declare! It's really you, is it? At last! Well, set right down an' take off your things. Isaphene, take Mis' Hanna's things. My! ain't it warm, walkin'?"

"It is so." The visitor gave her bonnet to Isaphene, dropping her black mitts into it after rolling them carefully together. "But it's always nice an' cool in your kitchen." Her eyes wandered about with a look of unabashed curiosity that took in everything. "I brought my crochet with me."

"I'm glad you did. You'll have to excuse the looks o' things. Any news?"

"None perticular." Mrs. Hanna began to crochet, holding the work close to her face. "Ain't it too bad about poor, old Mis' Lane?"

"What about her?" Mrs. Bridges snapped a bean-pod into three pieces, and looked at her visitor with a kind of pleased expectancy—as if almost any news, however dreadful, would be welcome as a relief to the monotony of existence. "Is she dead?"

"No, she ain't dead; but the poor, old creature 'd better be. She's got to go to the poor-farm, after all."

There was silence in the big kitchen, save for the rasp of the crochet needle through the wool and the snapping of the beans. A soft wind came in the window and drummed with the lightest of touches on Mrs. Bridges's temples. It brought all the sweets of the old-fashioned flower-garden with it—the mingled breaths of mignonette, stock, sweet lavender, sweet peas and clove pinks. The whole kitchen was filled with the fragrance. And what a big, cheerful kitchen it was! Mrs. Bridges contrasted it unconsciously with the poor-farm kitchen, and almost shivered, warm though the day was.

"What's her childern about?" she asked, sharply.

"Oh, her childern!" replied Mrs. Hanna, with a contemptuous air. "What does her childern amount to, I'd like to know."

"Her son's got a good, comf'table house an' farm."

"Well, what if he has? He got it with his wife, didn't he? An' M'lissy won't let his poor, old mother set foot inside the house! I don't say she is a pleasant body to have about—she's cross an' sick most all the time, an' childish. But that ain't sayin' her childern oughtn't to put up with her disagreeableness."

"She's got a married daughter, ain't she?"

"Yes, she's got a married daughter." Mrs. Hanna closed her lips tightly together and looked as if she might say something, if she chose, that would create a sensation.

"Well, ain't she got a good enough home to keep her mother in?"

"Yes, she has. But she got *her* home along with her husband, an' he won't have the old soul any more 'n M'lissy would."

There was another silence. Isaphene had put the cake in the oven. She knelt on the floor and opened the door very softly now and then, to see that it was not browning too fast. The heat of the oven had crimsoned her face and arms.

"Guess you'd best put a piece o' paper on top o' that cake," said her mother. "It smells kind o' burny like."

"It's all right, maw."

Mrs. Bridges looked out the window.

"Ain't my flowers doin' well, though, Mis' Hanna?"

"They are that. When I come up the walk I couldn't help thinkin' of poor, old Mis' Lane."

"What's that got to do with her?" Resentment bristled in Mrs. Bridges's tone and look.

Mrs. Hanna stopped crocheting, but held her hands stationary, almost level with her eyes, and looked over them in surprise at her questioner.

"Why, she ust to live here, you know."

"She did! In this house?"

"Why, yes. Didn't you know that? Oh, they ust to be right well off in her husband's time. I visited here consid'rable. My! the good things she always had to eat. I can taste 'em yet."

"Hunh! I'm sorry I can't give you as good as she did," said Mrs. Bridges, stiffly.

"Well, as if you didn't! You set a beautiful table, Mis' Bridges, an', what's more, that's your reputation all over. Everybody says that about you."

Mrs. Bridges smiled deprecatingly, with a slight blush of pleasure.

"They do, Mis' Bridges. I just told you about Mis' Lane because you'd never think it now of the poor, old creature. An' such flowers as she ust to have on both sides that walk! Larkspurs, an' sweet-williams, an' bach'lor's-buttons, an' mournin'-widows, an' pumgranates, an' all kinds. Guess you didn't know she set out that pink cabbage-rose at the north o' the front porch, did you? An' that hop-vine that you've got trained over your parlor window—set that out, too. An' that row o' young alders between here an' the barn—she set 'em all out with her own hands; dug the holes herself, an' all. It's funny she never told you she lived here."

"Yes, it is," said Mrs. Bridges, slowly and thoughtfully.

"It's a wonder to me she never broke down an' cried when she was visitin' here. She can't so much as mention the place without cryin'."

A dull red came into Mrs. Bridges's face.

"She never visited here."

"Never visited here!" Mrs. Hanna laid her crochet and her hands in her lap, and stared. "Why, she visited ev'rywhere.

That's how she managed to keep out o' the poor-house so long. Ev'rybody was reel consid'rate about invitin' her. But I expect she didn't like to come here because she thought so much o' the place."

Isaphene looked over her shoulder at her mother, but the look was not returned. The beans were sputtering nervously into the pan.

"Ain't you got about enough, maw?" she said. "That pan seems to be gettin' hefty."

"Yes, I guess." She got up, brushing the strings off her apron, and set the pan on the table. "I'll watch the cake now, Isaphene. You put the beans on in the pot to boil. Put a piece o' that salt pork in with 'em. Better get 'em on right away. It's pretty near eleven. Ain't this oven too hot with the door shet?"

Then the pleasant preparations for dinner went on. The beans soon commenced to boil, and an appetizing odor floated through the kitchen. The potatoes were pared—big, white fellows, smooth and long—with a sharp, thin knife, round and round and round, each without a break until the whole paring had curled itself about Isaphene's pretty arm almost to the elbow. The cabbage was chopped finely for the cold-slaw, and the vinegar and butter set on the stove in a saucepan to heat. Then Mrs. Bridges "set" the table, covering it first with a red cloth having a white border and fringe. In the middle of the table she placed an uncommonly large, six-bottled caster.

"I guess you'll excuse a red table-cloth, Mis' Hanna. The men-folks get their shirt-sleeves so dirty out in the fields that you can't keep a white one clean no time."

"I use red ones myself most of the time," replied Mrs. Hanna, crocheting industriously. "It saves washin'. I guess poor Mis' Lane 'll have to see the old place after all these years, whether she wants or not. They'll take her right past here to the poor-farm."

Mrs. Bridges set on the table a white plate holding a big square of yellow butter, and stood looking through the open door, down the path with its tall hollyhocks and scarlet poppies on both sides. Between the house and the barn some wild mustard had grown, thick and tall, and was now drifting, like a golden cloud, against the pale blue sky. Butterflies were throbbing through the air, and grasshoppers were crackling everywhere. It was all very pleasant and peaceful; while the comfortable house and barns, the wide fields stretching away to the forest, and the cattle feeding on the hillside added an appearance of prosperity. Mrs. Bridges wondered how she herself would feel—after having loved the place—riding by to the poor-farm. Then she pulled herself together and said, sharply:

"I'm afraid you feel a draught, Mis' Hanna, a-settin' so clost to the door."

"Oh, my, no; I like it. I like lots o' fresh air. Can't get it any too fresh for me. If I didn't have six children an' my own mother to keep, I'd take her myself."

"Take who?" Mrs. Bridges's voice rasped as she asked the question. Isaphene paused on her way to the pantry, and looked at Mrs. Hanna with deeply thoughtful eyes.

"Why, Mis' Lane—who else?—before I'd let her go to the poor-farm."

"Well, I think her children ought to be *made* to take care of her!" Mrs. Bridges went on setting the table with brisk, angry movements. "That's what I think about it. The law ought to take holt of it."

"Well, you see the law *has* took holt of it," said Mrs. Hanna, with a grim smile. "It seems a shame that there ain't somebody in the neighborhood that 'u'd take her in. She ain't much expense, but a good deal o' trouble. She's sick, in an' out o' bed, nigh onto all the time. My opinion is she's been soured by all her troubles; an' that if somebody 'u'd only take her in an' be kind to her, her temper'ment 'u'd emprove up wonderful. She's always mighty grateful for ev'ry little chore you do her. It just makes my heart ache to think o' her a-havin' to go to the poor-house!"

Mrs. Bridges lifted her head; all the softness and irresolution went out of her face.

"Well, I'm sorry for her," she said, with an air of dismissing a disagreeable subject; "but the world's full o' troubles, an' if you cried over all o' them you'd be a-cryin' all the time. Isaphene, you go out an' blow that dinner-horn. I see the men-folks 'av' got the horses about foddered. What did you do?" she cried out, sharply. "Drop a smoothin'-iron on your hand? Well, my goodness! Why don't you keep your eyes about you? You'll go an' get a cancer yet!"

"I'm thinkin' about buyin' a horse an' buggy," she announced, with stern triumph, when the girl had gone out. "An' an organ. Isaphene's been wantin' one most offul. I've give up her paw's ever gettin' her one. First a new harrow, an' then a paten' rake, an' then a seed-drill—an' then my mercy"—imitating a masculine voice—"he ain't got any money left for silliness! But I've got some laid by. I'd like to see his eyes when he comes home an' finds a bran new buggy with a top an' all, an' a horse that he can't hetch to a plow, no matter how bad he wants to! I ain't sure but I'll get a phaeton."

"They ain't so strong, but they're handy to get in an' out of—'specially for old, trembly knees."

"I ain't so old that I'm trembly!"

"Oh, my—no," said Mrs. Hanna, with a little start. "I was just thinkin' mebbe sometimes you'd go out to the poor-farm an' take poor, old Mis' Lane for a little ride. It ain't more'n five miles from here, is it? She ust to have a horse an' buggy o' her own. Somehow, I can't get her off o' my mind at all to-day. I just heard about her as I was a-startin' for your house."

The men came to the house. They paused on the back porch to clean their boots on the scraper and wash their hands and faces with water dipped from the rain-barrel. Their faces shone like brown marble when they came in.

...

It was five o'clock when Mrs. Hanna, with a sigh, began rolling the lace she had crocheted around the spool, preparatory to taking her departure.

"Well," she said, "I must go. I had no idy it was so late. How the time does go, a-talkin'. I've had a right nice time. Just see how well I've done—crocheted full a yard since dinner-time! My! how pretty that hop-vine looks. It makes awful nice shade, too. I guess when Mis' Lane planted it she thought she'd be settin' under it herself to-day—she took such pleasure in it."

The ladies were sitting on the front porch. It was cool and fragrant out there. The shadow of the house reached almost to the gate now. The bees had been drinking too many sweets—greedy fellows!—and were lying in the red poppies, droning stupidly. A soft wind was blowing from Puget Sound and turning over the clover leaves, making here a billow of dark green and there one of light green; it was setting loose the perfume of the blossoms, too, and sifting silken thistle-needles through the air. Along the fence was a hedge, eight feet high, of the beautiful ferns that grow luxuriantly in western Washington. The pasture across the lane was a tangle of royal color, being massed in with golden-rod, fire-weed, steeple-bush, yarrow, and large field-daisies; the cotton-woods that lined the creek at the side of the house were snowing. Here and there the sweet twin-sister of the steeple-bush lifted her pale and fluffy plumes; and there was one lovely, lavender company of wild asters.

Mrs. Bridges arose and followed her guest into the spare bedroom.

"When they goin' to take her to the poor-farm?" she asked, abruptly.

"Day after to-morrow. Ain't it awful? It just makes me sick. I couldn't of eat a bite o' dinner if I'd stayed at home, just for thinkin' about it. They say the poor, old creature ain't done nothin' but cry an' moan ever since she knowed she'd got to go."

"Here's your bag," said Mrs. Bridges. "Do you want I should tie your veil?"

"No, thanks; I guess I won't put it on. If I didn't have such a big fam'ly an' my own mother to keep, I'd take her in myself before I'd see her go to the poor-house. If I had a small fam'ly an' plenty o' room, I declare my conscience wouldn't let me sleep nights."

A deep red glow spread over Mrs. Bridges's face.

"Well, I guess you needn't to keep a-hintin' for me to take her," she said, sharply.

"*You!*" Mrs. Hanna uttered the word in a tone that was an unintentional insult; in fact, Mrs. Bridges affirmed afterward that her look of astonishment, and, for that matter, her whole air of dazed incredulity were insulting. "I never once thought o' *you*," she said, with an earnestness that could not be doubted.

"Why not o' me?" demanded Mrs. Bridges, showing something of her resentment. "What you been talkin' an' harpin' about her all day for, if you wasn't hintin' for me to take her in?"

"I never thought o' such a thing," repeated her visitor, still looking rather helplessly dazed. "I talked about it because it was on my mind, heavy, too; an', I guess, because I wanted to talk my conscience down."

Mrs. Bridges cooled off a little and folded her hands over the bedpost.

"Well, if you wasn't hintin'," she said, in a conciliatory tone, "it's all right. You kep' harpin' on the same string till I thought you was; an' it riles me offul to be hinted at. I'll take anything right out to my face, so's I can answer it, but I won't be hinted at. But why"—having rid herself of the grievance she at once swung around to the insult—"why *didn't* you think o' me?"

Mrs. Hanna cleared her throat and began to unroll her mitts.

"Well, I don't know just why," she replied, helplessly. She drew the mitts on, smoothing them well up over her thin wrists. "I don't know why, I'm sure. I'd thought o' most ev'rybody in the neighborhood—but you never come into my head *onct*. I was as innocent o' hintin' as a babe unborn."

Mrs. Bridges drew a long breath noiselessly.

"Well," she said, absent-mindedly, "come again, Mis' Hanna. An' be sure you always fetch your work an' stay the afternoon."

"Well, I will. But it's your turn to come now. Where's Isaphene?"

"I guess she's makin' a fire 'n the cook-stove to get supper by."

"Well, tell her to come over an' stay all night with Julia some night."

"Well—I will."

Mrs. Bridges went into the kitchen and sat down, rather heavily, in a chair. Her face wore a puzzled expression.

"Isaphene, did you hear what we was a-sayin' in the bedroom?"

"Yes, most of it, I guess."

"Well, what do you s'pose was the reason she never thought o' me a-takin' Mis' Lane in? Says she'd thought o' ev'rybody else."

"Why, you never thought o' takin' her in yourself, did you?" said Isaphene, turning down the damper of the stove with a clatter. "I don't see how anybody else 'u'd think of it when you didn't yourself."

"Well, don't you think it was offul impudent in her to say that, anyhow?"

"No, I don't. She told the truth."

"Why ought they to think o' ev'rybody takin' her exceptin' me, I'd like to know."

"Because ev'rybody else, I s'pose, has thought of it theirselves. The neighbors have all been chippin' in to help her for years. You never done nothin' for her, did you? You never invited her to visit here, did you?"

"No, I never. But that ain't no sayin' I wouldn't take her as quick's the rest of 'em. They ain't none of 'em takin' her in very fast, be they?"

"No, they ain't," said Isaphene, facing her mother with a steady look. "They ain't a one of 'em but's got their hands full—no spare room, an' lots o' children or their folks to take care of."

"Hunh!" said Mrs. Bridges. She began chopping cold boiled beef for hash.

"I don't believe I'll sleep to-night for thinkin' about it," she said, after a while.

"I won't neither, maw. I wish she wasn't goin' right by here."

"So do I."

After a long silence Mrs. Bridges said—"I don't suppose your paw'd hear to us a-takin' her in."

"I guess he'd hear to 't if we would," said Isaphene, dryly.

"Well, we can't do 't; that's all there is about it," announced Mrs. Bridges, with a great air of having made up her mind. Isaphene did not reply. She was slicing potatoes to fry, and she seemed to agree silently with her mother's decision. Presently, however, Mrs. Bridges said, in a less determined tone—"There's no place to put her in, exceptin' the spare room—an' we can't get along without that, noways."

"No," said Isaphene, in a non-committal tone.

Mrs. Bridges stopped chopping and looked thoughtfully out of the door.

"There's this room openin' out o' the kitchen," she said, slowly. "It's nice an' big an' sunny. It 'u'd be handy 'n winter, bein' right off o' the kitchen. But it ain't furnished up."

"No," said Isaphene, "it ain't."

"An' I know your paw'd never furnish it."

Isaphene laughed. "No, I guess not," she said.

"Well, there's no use a-thinkin' about it, Isaphene; we just can't take her. Better get them potatoes on; I see the men-folks comin' up to the barn."

The next morning after breakfast Isaphene said suddenly, as she stood washing dishes—"Maw, I guess you'd better take the organ money an' furnish up that room."

Mrs. Bridges turned so sharply she dropped the turkey-wing with which she was polishing the stove.

"You don't never mean it," she gasped.

"Yes, I do. I know we'd both feel better to take her in than to take in an organ"—they both laughed rather foolishly at the poor joke. "You can furnish the room real comf'table with what it 'u'd take to buy an organ; an' we can get the horse an' buggy, too."

"Oh, Isaphene, I've never meant but what you should have an organ. I know you'd learn fast. You'd soon get so's you could play 'Lilly Dale' an' 'Hazel Dell'; an' you might get so's you could play 'General Persifor F. Smith's Grand March.' No, I won't never spend that money for nothin' but an organ—so you can just shet up about it."

"I want a horse an' buggy worse, maw," said Isaphene, after a brief but fierce struggle with the dearest desire of her heart. "We can get a horse that I can ride, too. An' we'll get a phaeton, so's we can take Mis' Lane to church an' around." Then she added, with a regular masterpiece of diplomacy—"We'll show the neighbors that when we do take people in, we take 'em in all over!"

"Oh, Isaphene," said her mother, weakly, "wouldn't it just astonish 'em!"

...

It was ten o'clock of the following morning when Isaphene ran in and announced that she heard wheels coming up the lane. Mrs. Bridges paled a little and breathed quickly as she put on her bonnet and went out to the gate.

A red spring-wagon was coming slowly toward her, drawn by a single, bony horse. The driver was half asleep on the front seat. Behind, in a low chair, sat old Mrs. Lane; she was stooping over, her elbows on her knees, her gray head bowed.

Mrs. Bridges held up her hand, and the driver pulled in the unreluctant horse.

"How d'you do, Mis' Lane? I want you should come in an' visit me a while."

The old creature lifted her trembling head and looked at Mrs. Bridges; then she saw the old house, half hidden by vines and flowers, and her dim eyes filled with bitter tears.

"We ain't got time to stop, ma'am," said the driver, politely. "I'm a takin' her to the county," he added, in a lower tone, but not so low that the old woman did not hear.

"You'll have to make time," said Mrs. Bridges, bluntly. "You get down an' help her out. You don't have to wait. When I'm ready for her to go to the county, I'll take her myself."

Not understanding in the least, but realizing, as he said afterwards, that she "meant business" and wasn't the kind to be fooled with, the man obeyed with alacrity.

"Now, you lean all your heft on me," said Mrs. Bridges,

kindly. She put her arm around the old woman and led her up the hollyhock path, and through the house into the pleasant kitchen.

"Isaphene, you pull that big chair over here where it's cool. Now, Mis' Lane, you set right down an' rest."

Mrs. Lane wiped the tears from her face with an old cotton handkerchief. She tried to speak, but the sobs had to be swallowed down too fast. At last she said, in a choked voice—"It's awful good in you—to let me see the old place—once more. The Lord bless you—for it. But I'm most sorry I stopped—seems now as if I—just *couldn't* go on."

"Well, you ain't goin' on," said Mrs. Bridges, while Isaphene went to the door and stood looking toward the hill with drowned eyes. "This is our little joke—Isaphene's an' mine. This'll be your home as long it's our'n. An' you're goin' to have this nice big room right off o' the kitchen, as soon 's we can furnish it up. An' we're goin' to get a horse an' buggy—a *low* buggy, so's you can get in an' out easy like—an' take you to church an' all around."

...

That night, after Mrs. Bridges had put Mrs. Lane to bed and said good-night to her, she went out on the front porch and sat down; but presently, remembering that she had not put a candle in the room, she went back, opening the door noiselessly, not to disturb her. Then she stood perfectly still. The old creature had got out of bed and was kneeling beside it, her face buried in her hands.

"Oh, Lord God," she was saying aloud, "bless these kind people—bless 'em, oh, Lord God! Hear a poor, old mis'rable soul's prayer, an' bless 'em! An' if they've ever done a sinful thing, oh, Lord God, forgive 'em for it, because they've kep' me out o' the poor-house—"

Mrs. Bridges closed the door, and stood sobbing as if her heart must break.

"What's the matter, maw?" said Isaphene, coming up suddenly.

"Never you mind what's the matter," said her mother, sharply, to conceal her emotion. "You get to bed, an' don't bother your head about what's the matter of me."

Then she went down the hall and entered her own room; and Isaphene heard the key turned in the lock.

"The Takin' In of Old Mis' Lane" won the $500 first prize in *McClure's Magazine's* fiction contest. It was published in *McClure's* in December 1894 and reprinted in Higginson's collections *The Flower That Grew in the Sand And Other Stories* (1896) and *From The Land of the Snow-Pearls: Tales From Puget Sound* (1897).

The focus of "The Takin' In of Old Mis' Lane" is characteristic of Higginson's emphasis on the lush natural beauty of the Pacific Northwest as well as the economically precarious position of Pacific Northwest white women in the late nineteenth-century United States. Mrs. Bridges, the story's main character, lives comfortably with her husband and daughter in their handsome house with its luxuriant garden. She unexpectedly learns from a visiting neighbor that years ago her house had belonged to old Mrs. Lane who had planted much of the garden and many of the trees. Since that time, Mrs. Lane has been widowed: she is now poor, old, and neglected by her adult children. She is soon to be taken to the poor-farm. In this story, Higginson dramatizes the moral struggles of Mrs. Bridges as she gradually realizes that Mrs. Lane's transformation from well-off to destitute might happen to any woman, including Mrs. Bridges herself.

"Mrs. Risley's Christmas Dinner"
• 1895 •

SHE WAS AN OLD, OLD WOMAN. She was crippled with rheumatism and bent with toil. Her hair was gray,—not that lovely white that softens and beautifies her face, but harsh, grizzled gray. Her shoulders were round, her chest was sunken, her face had many deep wrinkles. Her feet were large and knotty; her hands were large, too, with great hollows running down their backs. And how painfully the cords stood out in her old, withered neck!

For the twentieth time she limped to the window and flattened her face against the pane. It was Christmas day. A violet sky sparkled coldly over the frozen village. The ground was covered with snow; the roofs were white with it. The chimneys looked redder than usual as they emerged from its pure drifts and sent slender curls of electric-blue smoke into the air.

The wind was rising. Now and then it came sweeping down the hill, pushing a great sheet of snow, powdered like dust, before it. The window-sashes did not fit tightly, and some of it sifted into the room and climbed into little cones on the floor. Snow-birds drifted past, like soft, dark shadows; and high overhead wild geese went sculling through the yellow air, their mournful "hawnk-e-hawnk-hawnks" sinking downward like human cries.

As the old woman stood with her face against the window and her weak eyes strained down the street, a neighbor came to the door.

"Has your daughter an' her fambly come yet, Mis' Risley?" she asked, entering sociably.

"Not yet," replied Mrs. Risley, with a good attempt at cheerfulness; but her knees suddenly began shaking, and she sat down.

"Why, she'd ought to 'a' come on the last train, hadn't she?"

"Oh, I do' know. There's a plenty o' time. Dinner won't be ready tell two past."

"She ain't b'en to see you fer five year, has she?" said the neighbor. "I reckon you'll have a right scrumptious set-out fer 'em?"

"I will so," said Mrs. Risley, ignoring the other question. "Her husband's comin'."

"I want to know! Why, he just thinks he's some punkins, I hear."

"Well, he's rich enough to think hisself anything he wants to." Mrs. Risley's voice took on a tone of pride.

"I sh'u'd think you'd want to go an' live with 'em. It's offul hard fer you to live here all alone, with your rheumatiz."

Mrs. Risley stooped to lay a stick of wood on the fire.

"I've worked nigh onto two weeks over this dinner," she said, "a-seed'n' raisins an' cur'nts, an' things. I've hed to skimp harrable, Mis' Tomlinson, to get it; but it's just—*perfec'*. Roast goose an' cranberry sass, an' cel'ry soup, an' mince an' punkin pie,—to say nothin' o' plum-puddin'! An' cookies an' cur'nt-jell tarts fer the children. I'll hev to wear my old underclo's all winter to pay fer 't; but I don't care."

"I sh'u'd think your daughter'd keep you more comf'terble, seein' her husband's so rich."

There was a silence. Mrs. Risley's face grew stern. The gold-colored cat came and arched her back for a caress. "My bread riz beautiful," Mrs. Risley said then. "I worried so over 't. An' my fruit-cake smells that good when I open the stun crock! I put a hull cup o' brandy in it. Well, I guess you'll hev to excuse me. I've got to set the table."

When Mrs. Tomlinson was gone, the strained look came back to the old woman's eyes. She went on setting the table, but at the sound of a wheel, or a step even, she began to tremble and put her hand behind her ear to listen.

"It's funny they *didn't* come on that last train," she said. "I w'u'dn't tell her, though. But they'd ort to be here by this time."

She opened the oven door. The hot, delicious odor of its precious contents gushed out. Did ever goose brown so perfectly before? And how large the liver was! It lay in the gravy in one corner of the big dripping-pan, just beginning to curl at the edges. She tested it carefully with a little three-tined iron fork.

The mince-pie was on the table, waiting to be warmed, and the pumpkin-pie was out on the back porch,—from which the cat had been excluded for the present. The cranberry sauce, the celery in its high, old-fashioned glass, the little bee-hive of hard sauce for the pudding and the thick cream for the coffee, bore the pumpkin-pie company. The currant jelly in the tarts glowed like great red rubies set in circles of old gold; the mashed potatoes were light and white as foam.

For one moment, as she stood there in the savory kitchen, she thought of the thin, worn flannels, and how much better her rheumatism would be with the warm ones which could have been bought with the money spent for this dinner. Then she flushed with self-shame.

"I must be gittin' childish," she exclaimed, indignantly; "to begredge a Chris'mas dinner to 'Lizy. 'S if I hedn't put up with old underclo's afore now! But I will say there ain't many women o' my age thet c'u'd git up a dinner like this 'n',—rheumatiz an' all."

A long, shrill whistle announced the last train from the city. Mrs. Risley started and turned pale. A violent trembling seized her. She could scarcely get to the window, she stumbled so. On the way she stopped at the old walnut bureau to put a lace cap on her white hair and to look anxiously into the mirror.

"Five year!" she whispered. "It's an offul spell to go without seein' your only daughter! Everything'll seem mighty poor an' shabby to her, I reckon,—her old mother worst o' all. I never sensed how I'd changed tell now. My! how no-account I'm a gittin'! I'm all of a trimble!"

Then she stumbled on to the window and pressed her cheek against the pane.

"They'd ort to be in sight now," she said. But the minutes went by, and they did not come.

"Mebbe they've stopped to talk, meetin' folks," she said, again. "But they'd ort to be in sight now." She trembled so she had to get a chair and sit down. But still she wrinkled her cheek upon the cold pane and strained her dim eyes down the street.

After a while a boy came whistling down from the corner. There was a letter in his hand. He stopped and rapped, and when she opened the door with a kind of frightened haste, he gave her the letter and went away, whistling again.

A letter! Why should a letter come? Her heart was beating in her throat now,—that poor old heart that had beaten under so many sorrows! She searched in a dazed way for her glasses. Then she fell helplessly into a chair and read it:

> "DEAR MOTHER,—I am so sorry we cannot come, after all. We just got word that Robert's aunt has been expecting us all the time, because we've spent every Christmas there. We feel as if we *must* go there, because she always goes to so much trouble to get up a fine dinner; and we knew you wouldn't do that. Besides, she is so rich; and one has to think of one's children, you know. We'll come, *sure*, next year. With a merry, merry Christmas from all,—ELIZA."

It was hard work reading it, she had to spell out so many of the words. After she had finished, she sat for a long, long time motionless, looking at the letter. Finally the cat came and rubbed against her, "myowing" for her dinner. Then she saw that the fire had burned down to a gray, desolate ash.

She no longer trembled, although the room was cold. The wind was blowing steadily now. It was snowing, too. The bleak Christmas afternoon and the long Christmas night stretched before her. Her eyes rested upon the little fir-tree on a table in one corner, with its gilt balls and strings of popcorn and colored candles. She could not bear the sight of it. She got up stiffly.

"Well, kitten," she said, trying to speak cheerfully, but with a pitiful break in her voice, "let's go out an' eat our Christmas dinner."

"Mrs. Risley's Christmas Dinner" was published in *Lippincott's* in January 1895. It was reprinted in Higginson's collections *The Flower That Grew in the Sand and Other Stories* (1896) and *From The Land of the Snow-Pearls: Tales From Puget Sound* (1897), and in other magazines and collections.

"Mrs. Risley's Christmas Dinner" features an impoverished elderly woman who lives alone in a remote town on Puget Sound. The story takes place on a cold, snowy Christmas Day. Mrs. Risley has practiced a severe economy in order to afford the ingredients to prepare a perfect holiday dinner for her only daughter, Lizy, who has not visited for five years. Lizy and her rich husband are due in that day on the train. In "Mrs. Risley's Christmas Dinner," Higginson returns to questions of mothers and daughters and the ways and reasons that their family ties alter over time.

"The Arnspiker Chickens"
• 1895 •

"Well, if there ain't them Arnspiker chickens in the strawberry patch *ag'in!* Oh-*oh!* that's the fifth time this mornin', an' I've druv 'em out with stove-wood every time. It don't do a bit o' good. They just git into a nice hill an' go to wallerin' an' scratchin' an' cluckin'! The cluckin' makes me almost as aggravated as the scratchin'—it sounds just as if they was *darin'* me, because they know I durs'n't kill 'em. Oh, just look at 'em! A-flound'rin' right in the middle of that nicest hill! It's enough to distract a saint! Father! Father! For pity's sake—can't you go an' scare 'em out with stove-wood?"

Mr. Webster got up stiffly from the dinner-table. He was a patient-faced old gentleman with blue, dreamy eyes. He had a stoop in his shoulders—from overmuch hoeing in great potato fields, he always explained with his gentle smile; but some of his neighbors were wont to declare among themselves that "livin' all them years with Mis' Webster's tongue was enough to give him a stoop in his shoulders without ever tetchin' a hoe."

"Why, mother," he said, going hesitatingly to the kitchen door, "I don't like to throw stove-wood at 'em. I might hurt 'em."

"You might *hurt* 'em, aigh? Well, I want that you should *hurt* 'em. I want that you should *kill* 'em if they don't stay out o' that strawberry patch! What was the sense in our movin' into town to spend the rest o' our days if we're to have the life clucked an' scratched out o' us by our neighbor's chickens? You ain't got any answer to that, have you? Aigh?"

Evidently Mr. Webster had not. He took two or three

sticks of wood from the well-filled box, and started again, in a half-hearted way, for the door.

"Oh, my land!" exclaimed Mrs. Webster, contemptuously. She ran after him and snatched the wood from him. "Why don't you wait a coon's age? Why don't you wait till they scratch the strawberries up by the *roots*? I never see! I notice you like to eat the berries as well as anybody, but you ain't willin' to turn your hand over to take care of 'em."

She rushed down the steps and out into the yard, throwing the sticks of wood with fierce strength.

Mr. Webster watched her with anxiety. "Oh, mother, look out!" he called deprecatingly. "You 'most hit that little pullet."

"*I want* to hit that little pullet!"

The chickens flew, cackling, over the low fence and down the hill.

Mrs. Webster stood watching them in grim satisfaction. When they had disappeared among the ferns she came back slowly. Her face was flushed with triumph. She was breathing hard. "I'll pullet 'em!" she said.

"You hadn't ought to throw at 'em, mother." Mr. Webster spoke gently. "You might hurt one of 'em. There's Mis' Arnspiker a-standin' in the door, a-watchin' you, too."

"Well, I'm glad she saw me. Where's my sunbunnit at? I'm goin' right down to give her a talkin' to. I've tell her three times now that her chickens is the ruination of my strawberries. All she ever says is, well, she's offul sorry, an' she thinks it's that old speckled hen's fault, an' she'll drive 'em down towards Burmeister's! I wonder if she thinks the Burmeisters want 'em any worse 'n I do! She's got to git red of them chickens, an' that's all there is about it. There's a law ag'in havin' em in town an' I ain't a-goin' to stand it another day. I'll let her know I ain't a Corbett an' a Fitzsimmons to stand up an' be knocked down a dozen times!"

"Now, mother, if you go down there, you'll be sorry—"

"You 'tend to your own effairs, father, will you? I won't be set upon! There can't *anybody* set upon me—let alone that Mis' Arnspiker!"

Mr. Webster went into the kitchen and sat down. "There's no use in argy'n' with Mari'," he said, with a sigh of resignation.

Mr. and Mrs. Webster had crossed the plains in the sixties and settled on a ranch in what was then the territory of Washington. Here they lived a life of toil and privation—a hard, narrow, joyless life—until the "boom" came along in 1888 and made them wealthy.

Then they moved "to town" and built a comfortable home and settled down to the difficult occupation of finding content and peace.

Unfortunately they built upon a hill. There is something about a hill that attracts the large end of a spy-glass as a red rag attracts a bull. Soon after Mrs. Webster had laboriously and patiently climbed her hill and founded her home upon a beautiful height, the iron came into her soul and rusted there.

It was bad enough, she thought, in all mercy, to learn that her neighbors down below gossiped about her leaving her wash a-switching out on the line, all wet and dripping with rain, three days an' nights at a time; and about her using table-cloths with red borders when she could easy afford white ones; and about the unmended holes in the knees of poor Mr. Webster's undergarments; and about their only using three towels an' two napkins a week—but for them to figure out that she and her husband did not live harmoniously together, solely because four sheets and four pillow-slips were hung on the line every wash-day, turned her soul sick within her.

At first she bore it meekly. But one morning about ten o'clock while she was stooping over the colored clothes in the wash-tub, who should walk into the kitchen but Mrs. Peters in her afternoon dress and white apron. There was a frill of lace at her throat, and she carried her "crochet."

At sight of Mrs. Webster she stood still and threw up her hands.

"Have you got a preparation?"

"Have I got a—*what?*" said Mrs. Webster, through the steam.

"Have you got a preparation?"

"A—*preparation?*"

"Yaas. A preparation. W'y, a rule. Have you got a rule?"

"I don't know what you mean."

"W'y, a rule to make a washing preparation by. I'll lend you mine. I had my wash all out on the line, an' my kitching an' porches an' steps an' all scrubbed by nine o'clock. I come to spend the day—an' here you ain't near through."

Mrs. Webster cleared her throat. "I've only got one rule," she said, "an' that is to do my visitin' on some day besides washday; an' I ain't got any preparation—for visitors *on* washday."

And she bent into the steam again and was lost to view. But now, of course, she had an enemy.

A few days later Mrs. Gunn came in to "set a spell." "I come to tell you about his brother-in-law's cousin, his wife," she said. "She's got creepin' paralysis in her arm. Creep—*my!* It'll more likely *run*. He was over to his brother's this morning and his brother says his cousin is all worked up. He wants I should go and make a visit on her to-morrow. I ain't suffering to—she's always been thinking herself so exalted, and so anumated over it. Maybe this'll take her down a peg. She won't go a-silking by quite so big—with creepin' paralysis in her arm! He says he's see the grocery wagon go there as high as three times a day. Has she ever made a call on you?"

"No, ma'am," said Mrs. Webster, politely.

"Well, it wouldn't of hurt her. I guess you don't feel bad.

She's perfectly frivulous. I can't abide her, but he says, well, never mind—she's in the fambly. I don't like the way her forehead protrudes back, anyhow. W'y, there goes Mis' Brun down town with a white petticoat on in all this rain! Did you ever hear tell? Oh, that makes me think! Mis' Brun told me she see a new cupboard a-coming up the alley, an' she thought it must be a-coming here. May I ask if it was Mis' Fiske's? She's selling out, an' we know where everything went to but the cupboard."

All these things and heavier Mrs. Webster endured; but they gradually embittered her. When Mrs. Arnspiker turned her hens out and they came strutting and clucking up the hill to her strawberry patch, her patience went out the window. The worm turned; and being of the long-suffering sex, it turned with unexpected vigor.

Mrs. Webster went down the narrow path among the ferns. She held her skirts up high on both sides.

The Arnspiker home was a small, unpainted shack. It had a dingy, spiritless look. Mrs. Arnspiker was a widow and she was very poor. She had no children and few friends. She took in washing, and she sold eggs.

She was standing on the back porch when Mrs. Webster opened the gate. She was a small, pale woman. Her face had many deep lines of care. There was a kind of entreaty in her faded eyes as she greeted her visitor. It did not move Mrs. Webster.

"How-d'you-do, Mis' Arnspiker?" she said, hostilely.

"How-r-you, Mis' Webster?" Mrs. Arnspiker's heart was beating fast and hard. "Won't you step in an' set down a spell? Or 'd you ruther set down here 'n the sun? Here's a chair—excuse me! It ain't overly clean." She wiped it carefully with the wrong side of her apron. "You're looking reel well, Mis' Webster," she went on, diplomatically. It is better to be born diplomatic than rich. "I never see you looking better. My! the color 'n that calico *is* becoming to you. Where'd you git it at?"

"Cam'ellses." Mrs. Webster spoke icily.

"Go on! Well, you don't say! I didn't suppose they had anything so pretty in their store. It's offul becoming. That kind o' buff color alwus *is* becoming to a nice, *clear* complexion. There ain't many complected just like you, Mis' Webster, an' so there ain't many that can wear buff."

There was a silence. Mrs. Webster sat looking fixedly at the hard, cleanly swept dooryard. There was not a blade of grass in it. It had a look of desolation—of utter abandonment to despair. She was thinking that it was not so easy to begin about the chickens as she had imagined it would be. After all, Mis' Arnspiker did have some taste about her. It had been only two days since that uppish Mis' Lawrence had giggled right in her face and cried out—"W'y, Mis' Webster, the idy! *you* a-wearing *buff!*" Giddy, fool thing!

Then she pulled herself together, and said sternly—"Mis' Arnspiker, I come down—"

"I wonder now," interrupted Mrs. Arnspiker, with a flustered air, "if you'd just as live tell how much it were a yard."

"How much what were a yard?"

"Why, that buff calico you're a-wearing."

Mrs. Webster lifted her eyes and looked hard at her neighbor. Her thin lips unclosed. She spoke slowly and firmly. She was not to be propitiated. "It were seven cents. Mis' Arnspiker, I come down—"

"I wonder 'f you'd mind my having one like it, seein's we're neighbors. It wouldn't be becoming to me, though." Mrs. Arnspiker sighed. "There ain't a woman in town it 'u'd become as it does you. There ain't a one."

There was another silence. A faint, uncontrollable blush of pleasure had arisen to Mrs. Webster's thin cheek. She sat looking up at her big, green house on the hill. Her heart stirred pleasantly. She had never been told before that she had a clear complexion. Indeed, had Mrs. Arnspiker been a Catholic, she would have fasted a full week, in the hope of absolution for suggesting it now; being a Protestant, she meant to put a good sum in the missionary-box to ease her conscience.

"You can have a dress like it, if you want," said Mrs. Webster.

"You're offul clever. I don't believe I can wear it, though; but you're offul clever. Who is that a-going along the path?" She stretched out her thin neck like a chicken and peered out from under lowered lids. "Oh, it's Mis' Ballot! I feel condemned. I ain't been to see her since her baby died. She took it so hard, too. She's a-going out to the cemetry now with a callo lily. Don't she look mournful all in black! I do feel condemned."

There was quite a softened expression on Mrs. Webster's face and all might have been well; but at that critical moment three hens, having been safely delivered of their daily contributions to Mrs. Arnspiker's store, flew from their nests as one hen and, floundering clumsily over the fence, made straight for Mrs. Webster's strawberry patch on a run, cackling triumphantly, as much as to say—"Do we not deserve a berry?"

Mrs. Webster's face grew black. "Mis' Arnspiker," she said, sternly; and Mrs. Arnspiker drew a long breath and gave up. "Your chickens have been in my strawberry patch ag'in, an' been the ruination of it."

"Oh, my!" said Mrs. Arnspiker, collapsing weakly. Mrs. Webster regarded her steadfastly and pitilessly. "I'm offul sorry."

"Well, I'm sorry, too, Mis' Arnspiker. *I'm* sorry just about ten dollars' worth. Bein' sorry don't seem to keep them chickens—"

"It's that old speckled hen's fault!" exclaimed Mrs. Arnspiker, brightening as if with a sudden inspiration. "She coaxes the other 'ns up there. I'll have to drive 'em down towards—"

"Burmeister's," interrupted Mrs. Webster, dryly. "You've been a-doing that for a month past." She got up slowly. "I reckon you'll have to git red o' them hens, Mis' Arnspiker. I've had just about all of 'em I want. I ain't a Corbett or a Fitzsimmons—to stand up an' be knocked down a dozen times! I can't efford to set out berries for *hens*. How'd you like to have a nice place like our 'n, an' then go an' have everything ruined up by somebody's hens?"

"It seems to me," said Mrs. Arnspiker, with a sigh, "if I had a nice place like your 'n, I'd be so happy I wouldn't worry over little things like strawberries."

She did not mean to be impertinent. It did not occur to her that she was. She simply gave utterance to the thought as it came to her.

Mrs. Webster's face grew scarlet. She had been yearning for something at which she might take offence. It is not possible to give a piece of one's mind to a meek person. Now, this sounded like a challenge.

"Oh, you wouldn't, aigh? Well, I'll give you to know I've *slaved* for all I got, Mis' Arnspiker!"

"Well, so 've I," said Mrs. Arnspiker, with a simplicity that held unconscious pathos. "But, someways, Mis' Webster, some people slave an' git rich, an' other 'ns slave an' git poor."

This was a truth that had never presented itself to Mrs. Webster. For a full minute she was silent. Then she drew in her thin lips. "Well, this ain't got anything to do with the chickens," she said. "There's a law ag'in 'em, an' I reckon you'll have to either git red of 'em or keep 'em shet up."

"They won't lay if I keep 'em shet up," said Mrs. Arnspiker, helplessly. "I can't keep 'em shet up. I got to have my eggs."

"Well, an' I got to have my strawberries. I got the law. You can't git around that, can you? It ain't many as 'u'd come an' argy with you 's I've done."

There was a deep silence. A brown hen came strutting about Mrs. Arnspiker's feet. She had a pert and flaunting air that betrayed her habit of imposing upon that lady's affectionate regard for her. Mrs. Arnspiker looked at her. Her eyes filled suddenly with tears. "I don't believe I *could* part with that little brown hen," she said, brokenly.

"She's the wo'st of the hull of 'em!" exclaimed Mrs. Webster, fiercely. "I've said all I'm a-going to. You can do just as you want, Mis' Arnspiker. But if them hens git into my strawberry patch ag'in an' ruminate around them vines,—you'll have to stand the damage. I got the law!"

She turned abruptly and went out of the yard. She held one shoulder higher than the other, and walked with long, firm strides, swinging her arms.

...

It was a week later that Mrs. Worstel came to spend the afternoon with Mrs. Webster. She brought a towel which she was hemstitching. The two ladies sat on the back porch, because it was shaded by hop-vines. The cool, salt breeze from off Puget Sound swept through, rustling the harsh hop-leaves and swinging the scarlet clusters of bloom on the wild honeysuckle vine over the window.

It was June. The "yard" was in its fairest beauty. The rose-bushes were bending beneath their riot of bloom. One bed was a long flame of ruddy gold where the California poppies opened their hearts. Another was bordered with purple and yellow pansies. Some tardy gladioli were thrusting their pale green swords up through the rich earth. Velvet wallflowers still sweetened the air. Bees waded through their pollen, and lavender butterflies drifted down on spread wings to find them. Banks of "summer snow" still made the terraces white.

"My-O, my land!" said Mrs. Worstel, dropping her work in her lap. "How sweet it is!"

"The Arnspiker Chickens"

"It is so," said Mrs. Webster, pulling herself up with pride. "There ain't many yards furder along than mine, if I do say it. I never see such flowers in Peoria-'llinois."

"Oh, did you come from Peoria-'llinois? W'y, I'm from Quincy-'llinois, myself."

"I want to know."

"Yaas. I stopped in at Mis' Arnspiker's as I come along. She's feelin' turrable bad."

Mrs. Webster looked up coldly. "What she feeling bad about?"

"W'y, she's had to sell all her chickens. They was botherin' some o' her neighbors—that Mis' Burmeister, I guess! She never does have a speck o' mercy on poor people! Mis' Arnspiker didn't say it was her, but I don't b'lieve anybody else 'ud be so all-fired mean. Go an' complain of a poor widow's layin' hens!"

There was a scarlet spot on each of Mrs. Webster's high cheek-bones. She was sewing and she did not lift her eyes. When the silence became oppressive, she said, grimly—"Is Mis' Arnspiker so offul poor?"

"My, yaas. That's all she's had to make a livin' off of—them hens o' her'n. I don't see what she'll do. She does take in a little wash, but she ain't able to take in enough to keep a flea alive—little, sickly thing! She's alwus havin' a felon. I've see her up an' a-washin' at four o'clock in the mornin'—"

"Four o'clock in the morning!" Mrs. Webster would have grasped at any straw to turn the conversation. "*You!* For mercy's sake! D' you git up so early?"

"No, but I was awake. I see her out the window. Four o'clock's my coughin'-time. I feel offul sorry for her. The way she did set store by them chickens! I've see her call 'em up, one at a time, in her lap to eat out o' her hand. An' that little brown hen—she just *loved* her! The tears fairly run down her cheeks when she tell me about sellin' 'em."

"Hunh!" said Mrs. Webster, dryly.

"I should think that Mis' Burmeister 'u'd be ashamed o' herself," continued Mrs. Worstel. "A body with a fine house an' comf'table off! Them that don't have any mercy on the poor needn't to expect none."

"Hunh!" said Mrs. Webster. After a little she added, weakly—"Well, I guess that she didn't want her neighbor's chickens a-ruminating in her strawberry patch. I guess she didn't want that her berries should be all et up."

"Oh, my! She'd best be buyin' her berries from poor people's raisin', instid o' raisin' her own here in town, just to save a few cents—"

She stopped abruptly. A deep color spread over her face. Her wandering eyes had fallen upon Mrs. Webster's strawberry patch down in the corner of the yard.

"Pfew!" she said, moving her chair a little. "How warm it's a-gittin'!... Well, it's mighty hard to be a widow an' sickly at that, an' then have your only means o' support took away from you by a complainin' neighbor."

Mrs. Webster cleared her throat. Her face took on a hard look.

"Well," she said, slowly, "I don't just agree with you, Mis' Worstel. It's ag'in the law to keep chickens in town, unless you keep 'em shet up. I don't see 's Mis' Arnspiker has got any call to go around a-talking about her neighbors because she had to git red o' her 'n."

"Mercy! She wa'n't complainin', Mis' Webster. She never said a word—not a single, breathin' word—ag'in anybody. She never even told me who it were that made a fuss. That's what made me feel so—the meek way she took it in. She said she knew it were ag'in the law, an' it wa'n't right for her to be a bother an' a aggravation to her neighbors, anyhow—but that

"The Arnspiker Chickens"

didn't make her feel it any the lesser to give 'em up. Said she knew most people 'u'd *laff* at the idy o' her a-feelin' so about a passel o' hens, but that most people wa'n't all alone in the world, an' poor as Job's turkey at that, an' so they didn't git their affections set on dumb animals like her 'n had got. She cried as if her heart was broke. The tears just *run* down her cheeks. She kep' sayin' she didn't see how she could git along 'ithout her chickens, 'specially that little brown hen. She ust to follow Mis' Arnspiker all over... I must go. How the afternoon has went. I've enjoyed myself, I declare. Oh, has Mis' Riley's son got an ear?"

"Has he got a—*what?*"

"An ear—has he got an ear?"

"An *ear!*"

"Yes, an ear. Has he got an ear—for music?"

"Oh," said Mrs. Webster, solemnly. "I do' know."

"Well, I see his mother's got a teacher there givin' him lessons on his catarrh. I just wondered if he had an ear. Come over an' set the afternoon with your work. My, how sweet that mount'n ba'm smells!"

Mrs. Webster walked with her guest around the house. She replied in an absent-minded way to Mrs. Worstel's extravagant praises of her bleeding-hearts and bachelor's-buttons and mourning-widows. She was lost in thought.

At the gate Mrs. Worstel paused. "Well," she said, with a long breath, "seems to me you've got everything heart could ask for."

"Who'd she sell 'em to?" asked Mrs. Webster, suddenly.

"Who? What? Oh, Mis' Arnspiker? Why, she sell 'em to Mr. Jones, right down in the next block. He's got a reg'lar lot for keepin' 'em in. Well, good day."

When her guest was out of sight, Mrs. Webster put on her sunbonnet, and went out the gate. She gave a long look down at Mrs. Arnspiker's little shabby house, with its hard, white yard and the sun blazing into its unshaded windows.

Then she turned down the street in the opposite direction.

At dusk that evening Mrs. Webster walked into Mrs. Arnspiker's back yard. She carried a box with slats across the top. Between these slats arose the brown head of a hen with two very astonished and anxious eyes.

Mrs. Arnspiker sat alone on the porch, rocking slowly in a creaking chair. "Why, Mis' Webster!" she exclaimed. She stood up. Mrs. Webster set the box down at her feet.

"Here's your brown hen," she announced, without a change of countenance. "I've bought all your chickens back. The man'll bring the rest of 'em to-morrow. I had to pay once ag'in what you got for 'em, but I'd of paid three times ag'in but what I'd of had 'em!"

"Oh—Mis'—Webster—"

"Well, now, don't go to crying over a *hen!* You let your chickens run. We'll put some wire-netting atop o' our fence an' keep 'em out."

She half turned to go, and then stopped. "I'm sorry I acted up so over them chickens," she said, speaking very fast. "But the neighbors have just made a reg'lar Jezebel out o' me—a-prying an' a-spying."

She walked out of the yard before Mrs. Arnspiker could reply. Mr. Webster met her at the door. "W'y, Mari'," he said, mildly, "where you been?"

"Now, don't meddle," she retorted, sharply; but at once repented, and added in a conciliatory tone—"Mis' Worstel thinks Mis' Riley's little boy has got an ear. He's a-taking lessons on the catarrh."

"THE ARNSPIKER CHICKENS" was published in *The Outlook* in July 1895. It was reprinted in *A Forest Orchid and Other Stories* (1897) and in newspapers and magazines across the United States.

"The Arnspiker Chickens" is set in a small town on Puget Sound where everyone minds everyone else's business. In this story, Mrs. Webster is aggravated by the ways that the inquisitive women in the town scrutinize and gossip about her laundry, her purchases, her marriage, and other details of her life. Already frustrated, Mrs. Webster reaches her breaking point when the chickens belonging to her neighbor, Mrs. Arnspiker, begin to regularly raid her prized strawberry patch. "The Arnspiker Chickens" centers on small town life, friction among neighbors, and the struggle for women to achieve sympathy for other women.

"A Point of Knuckling-Down"
• 1895 •

Part I

Emarine went along the narrow hall and passed through the open door. There was something in her carriage that suggested stubbornness. Her small body had a natural backward sway, and the decision with which she set her heels upon the floor had long ago caused the readers of character in the village to aver that "Emarine Endey was contrairier than any mule."

She wore a brown dress, a gray shawl folded primly around her shoulders, and a hat that tried in vain to make her small face plain. There was a frill of white, cheap lace at her slender throat, fastened in front with a cherry ribbon. Heavy gold earrings with long, shining pendants reached almost to her shoulders. They quivered and glittered with every movement.

Emarine was pretty, in spite of many freckles and the tightness with which she brushed her hair from her face and coiled it in a sleek knot at the back of her head. "Now, be sure you get it just so slick, Emarine," her mother would say, watching her steadily while she combed and brushed and twisted her long tresses.

As Emarine reached the door her mother followed her down the hall from the kitchen. The house was old, and two or three loose pieces in the flooring creaked as she stepped heavily upon them.

"Oh, say, Emarine!"

"Well?"

"You get an' bring home a dollar's worth o' granylated sugar, will you?"

"Well."

"An' a box o' ball bluin'. Mercy, child! Your dress-skirt sags awful in the back. Why don't you run a tuck in it?"

Emarine turned her head over her shoulder with a birdlike movement, and bent backward, trying to see the offensive sag.

"Can't you pin it up, maw?"

"Yes, I guess. Have you got a pin? Why, Emarine Endey! If ever I see in all my born days! What are you a-doin' with a red ribbon on you—an' your Uncle Herndon not cold in his grave yet! A fine spectickle you'd make o' yourself, a-goin' the length an' the breadth o' the town with that thing a-flarin' on you. You'll disgrace this whole fambly yet! I have to keep watch o' you like a two-year-old baby. Now, you get an' take it right off o' you; an' don't you let me ketch you a-puttin' it on again till a respectful time after he's be'n dead. I never hear tell o' such a thing."

"I don't see what a red ribbon's got to do with Uncle Herndon's bein' dead," said Emarine.

"Oh, you don't, aigh? Well, *I* see. You act as if you didn't have no feelin'."

"Well, goin' without a red ribbon won't make me feel any worse, will it, maw?"

"No, it won't. Emarine, what does get into you to act so tantalizin'? I guess it'll look a little better. I guess the neighbors won't talk quite so much. You can see fer yourself how they talk about Mis' Henspeter because she wore a rose to church before her husband had be'n dead a year. All she had to say fer herself was that she liked flowers, an' didn't sense it 'u'd be any disrespect to her husband to wear it—seein's he'd always liked 'em, too. They all showed her 'n a hurry what they thought about it. She's got narrow borders on all her han'kachers, too, a'ready."

"Why don't you stay away from such people?" said Emarine. "Old gossips! You know I don't care what the neighbors say—or think, either."

"Well, *I* do. The land knows they talk a plenty even without givin''em anything to talk about. You get an' take that red ribbon off o' you."

"Oh, I'll take it off if you want I sh'u'd." She unfastened it deliberately and laid it on a little table. She had an exasperating air of being unconvinced and of complying merely for the sake of peace.

She gathered her shawl about her shoulders and crossed the porch.

"Emarine!"

"Well?"

"Who's that a-comin' over the hill path? I can't make out the dress. It looks some like Mis' Grandy, don't it?"

Emarine turned her head. Her eyelids quivered closer together in an effort to concentrate her vision on the approaching guest.

"Well, I never!" exclaimed her mother, in a subdued but irascible tone. "There you go—a-lookin' right square at her, when I didn't want that she sh'u'd know we saw her! It does seem to me sometimes, Emarine, that you ain't got good sense."

"I'd just as soon she knew we saw her," said Emarine, unmoved. "It's Miss Presley, maw."

"Oh, land o' goodness! That old sticktight? She'll stay all day if she stays a minute. Set an' set! An' there I've just got the washin' all out on the line, an' she'll tell the whole town we wear underclo's made out o' unbleached muslin! Are you sure it's her? It don't look overly like her shawl."

"Yes, it's her."

"Well, go on an' stop an' talk to her, so 's to give me a chance to red up some. Don't ferget the ball bluin', Emarine."

"A Point of Knuckling-Down"

Emarine went down the path and met the visitor just between the two tall lilac trees, whose buds were beginning to swell.

"Good mornin', Miss Presley."

"Why, good mornin', Emarine. Z' your maw to home?"

"Yes 'm."

"I thought I'd run down an' set a spell with her, an' pass the news."

Emarine smiled faintly and was silent.

"Ain't you goin' up town pretty early fer wash-day?"

"Yes 'm."

"I see you hed a beau home from church las' night."

Emarine's face flushed; even her ears grew rosy.

"Well, I guess he's a reel nice young man, anyways, Emarine. You needn't to blush so. Mis' Grandy was a-sayin' she thought you'd done offul well to git him. He owns the house an' lot they live in, an' he's got five hunderd dollars in the bank. I reckon he'll have to live with the ol' lady, though, when he gits married. They do say she's turrable hard to suit."

Emarine lifted her chin. The gold pendants glittered like diamonds.

"It don't make any difference to me whuther she's hard to suit or easy," she said. "I'll have to be goin' on now. Just knock at the front door, Miss Presley."

"Oh, I can go right around to the back, just as well, an' save your maw the trouble o' comin' to the door. If she's got her washin' out, I can stoop right under the clo's line."

"Well, we like to have our comp'ny come to the front door," said Emarine, dryly.

It was a beautiful morning in early spring. The alders and the maples along the hill were wrapped in reddish mist. The saps were mounting through delicate veins. Presently the mist would quicken to a pale green as the young leaves unfolded, but as yet everything seemed to be waiting. The brown earth had a fresh, woody smell that caused the heart to thrill with a vague sense of ecstasy—of some delight deep hidden and inexplicable. Pale lavender "spring beauties" stood shyly in groups or alone, in sheltered places along the path. There was even, here and there, a trillium—or white lily, as the children called it—shivering on its slender stem. There were old stumps, too, hollowed out by long-spent flames into rustic urns, now heaped to their ragged rims with velvet moss. On a fence near a meadow-lark was pouring out its few, but full and beautiful, notes of passion and desire. Emarine paused to listen. Her heart vibrated with exquisite pain to the ravishment of regret in those liquid tones.

"Sounds as if he was sayin'—'*Sweet—oh—Sweet—my heart is breaking!*' " she said; and then with a kind of shame of the sentiment in such a fancy, she went on briskly over the hill. Her heels clicked sharply on the hard road.

Before she reached the long wooden stairs which led from the high plateau down to the one street of Oregon City, Emarine passed through a beautiful grove of firs and cedars. Already the firs were taking on their little plushy tufts of pale green, and exuding a spicy fragrance. Occasionally a last year's cone drew itself loose and sunk noiselessly into a bed of its own brown needles. A little way from the path a woodpecker clung to a tree, hammering into the tough bark with its long beak. As Emarine approached, it flew heavily away, the undersides of its wings flashing a scarlet streak along the air.

As her eyes ceased following its flight, she became aware that some one was standing in the path, waiting. A deep, self-conscious blush swept over her face and throat. "Emarine never does anything up by halves," her mother was wont to declare. "When she blushes, she *blushes!*"

She stepped slowly toward him with a sudden stiff

awkwardness.

"Oh—you, is it, Mr. Parmer?" she said, with an admirable attempt—but an attempt only—at indifference.

"Yes, it's me," said the young fellow, with an embarrassed laugh. With a clumsy shuffle he took step with her. Both faces were flaming. Emarine could not lift her eyes from their contemplation of the dead leaves in her path—yet she passed a whole company of "spring beauties" playing hide-and-seek around a stump, without seeing them. Her pulses seemed full of little hammers, beating away mercilessly. Her fingers fumbled nervously with the fringes on her shawl.

"Don't choo want I sh'u'd pack your umberell fer yuh?" asked the young man, solemnly.

"Why—yes, if you want."

It was a faded thing she held toward him, done up rather baggily, too; but he received it as reverently as if it had been a twenty-dollar silk one with a gold handle.

"Does your mother know I kep' yuh comp'ny home from church last night?"

"Unh-hunh."

"What 'id she say?"

"She didn't say much."

"Well, what?"

"Oh, not much." Emarine was rapidly recovering her self-possession. "I went right in an' up an' told her."

"Well, why can't choo tell me what she said? Emarine, yuh can be the contrairiest girl when yuh want."

"Can I?" She flashed a coquettish glance at him. She was quite at her ease by this time, although the color was still burning deep in her cheeks. "I sh'u'dn't think you'd waste so much time on contrairy people, Mr. Parmer."

"Oh, Emarine, go on an' tell me!"

"Well"—Emarine laughed mirthfully—"she put the backs

of her hands on her hips—this way!" She faced him suddenly, setting her arms akimbo, the shawl's fringes quivering over her elbows; her eyes fairly danced into his. "An' she looked at me a long time; then she says—'Hunh! *You—leetle—heifer!* You think you're some pun'kins, don't you? A-havin' a beau home from meetin'.'"

Both laughed hilariously.

"Well, what else 'id she say?"

"I don't believe you want to know. Do you—sure?"

"I cross my heart."

"Well—she said it c'udn't happen more'n ev'ry once 'n so often."

"Pshaw!"

"She did."

The young man paused abruptly. A narrow, unfrequented path led through deeper woods to the right.

"Emarine, let's take this catecornered cut through here."

"Oh, I'm afraid it's longer—an' it's washday, you know," said Emarine, with feeble resistance.

"We'll walk right fast. Come on. George! But it's nice and sweet in here, though!"

They entered the path. It was narrow and the great trees bent over and touched above them.

There was a kind of soft lavender twilight falling upon them. It was very still, save for the fluttering of invisible wings and the occasional shrill scream of a blue-jay.

"It *is* sweet in here," said Emarine.

The young man turned quickly, and with a deep, asking look into her lifted eyes, put his arms about her and drew her to him. "Emarine," he said, with passionate tenderness. And then he was silent, and just stood holding her crushed against him, and looking down on her with his very soul in his eyes. Oh, but a man who refrains from much speech in such an hour

"A Point of Knuckling-Down"

has wisdom straight from the gods themselves!

After a long silence Emarine lifted her head and smiled trustfully into his eyes. "It's washday," she said, with a flash of humor.

"So it is," he answered her, heartily. "An' I promised yuh we'd hurry up—an' I alwus keep my promises. But first—Emarine—"

"Well?"

"Yuh must say somethin' first."

"Say what, Mr. Parmer?"

" '*Mr. Parmer!* ' " His tone and his look were reproachful. "Can't choo say Orville?"

"Oh, I can—if you want I sh'u'd."

"Well, I do want choo sh'u'd, Emarine. Now, yuh know what else it is I want choo sh'u'd say before we go on."

"Why, no, I don't—hunh-unh." She shook her head, coquettishly.

"Emarine"—the young fellow's face took on a sudden seriousness—"I want choo to say yuh'll marry me."

"Oh, my, no!" cried Emarine. She turned her head to one side, like a bird, and looked at him with lifted brows and surprised eyes. One would have imagined that such a thought had never entered that pretty head before.

"What, Emarine! Yuh won't?" There was consternation in his voice.

"Oh, my, no!" Both glance and movement were full of coquettishness. The very fringes of the demure gray shawl seemed to have taken on new life and vivacity.

Orville Palmer's face turned pale and stern. He drew a long breath silently, not once removing that searching look from her face.

"Well, then," he said, calmly, "I want to know what choo mean by up an' lettin' me kiss yuh—if yuh don't mean to marry me."

This was an instant quietus to the girl's coquetry. She gave him a startled glance. A splash of scarlet came into each cheek. For a moment there was utter silence. Then she made a soft feint of withdrawing from his arms. To her evident amazement, he made no attempt to detain her. This placed her in an awkward dilemma, and she stood irresolutely, with her eyes cast down.

Young Palmer's arms fell at his sides with a movement of despair. Sometimes they were ungainly arms, but now absence of self-consciousness lent them a manly grace.

"Well, Emarine," he said, kindly, "I'll go back the way I come. Goodby."

With a quick, spontaneous burst of passion—against which she had been struggling, and which was girlish and innocent enough to carry a man's soul with it into heaven—Emarine cast herself upon his breast and flung her shawl-entangled arms about his shoulders. Her eyes were earnest and pleading, and there were tears of repentance in them. With a modesty that was enchanting she set her warm, sweet lips tremblingly to his, of her own free will.

"I didn't mean it," she whispered. "I was only a—a-foolin'."

...

The year was older by a month when one morning Mrs. Endey went to the front door and stood with her body swaying backward, and one rough hand roofing the rich light from her eyes.

"Emarine 'ad ought to 'a' got to the hill path by this time," she said, in a grumbling tone. "It beats me what keeps her so! I reckon she's a-standin' like a bump on a lawg, watchin' a red ant or a tumble-bug, or some fool thing! She'd leave her dish-washin' any time an' stand at the door a-ketchin' cold in her bare arms, with the suds a-drippin' all over her apron an' the floor—a-listenin' to one o' them silly meadow-larks hollerin' the same noise over 'n over. Her paw's women-folks are all just such fools."

She started guiltily and lowered her eyes to the gate which had clicked sharply.

"Oh!" she said. "That you, Emarine?" She laughed rather foolishly. "I was lookin' right over you—lookin' *fer* you, too. Miss Presley's be'n here, an' of all the strings she had to tell! Why, fer pity's sake! Is that a dollar's worth o' coffee?"

"Yes, it is; an' I guess it's full weight, too, from the way my arm feels! It's just about broke."

"Well, give it to me, an' come on out in the kitching. I've got somethin' to tell you."

Emarine followed slowly, pinning a spray of lilac bloom in her bosom as she went.

"Emarine, where's that spring balance at? I'm goin' to weigh this coffee. If it's one grain short, I'll send it back a-flyin'. I'll show 'em they can't cheat this old hen!"

She slipped the hook under the string and lifted the coffee cautiously until the balance was level with her eyes. Then standing well back on her heels and drawing funny little wrinkles up around her mouth and eyes, she studied the figures earnestly, counting the pounds and the half-pounds down from the top. Finally she lowered it with a disappointed air. "Well," she said, reluctantly, "it's just it—just to a 't.' They'd ought to make it a leetle over, though, to allow fer the paper bag. Get the coffee-canister, Emarine."

When the coffee had all been jiggled through a tin funnel into the canister, Mrs. Endey sat down stiffly and began polishing the funnel with a cloth. From time to time she glanced at Emarine with a kind of deprecatory mystery. At last she said—"Miss Presley spent the day down't Mis' Parmer's yesterday."

"Did she?" said Emarine, coldly; but the color came into her cheeks. "Shall I go on with the puddin'?"

"Why, you can if you want. She told me some things I don't like."

Emarine shattered an egg-shell on the side of a bowl and released the gold heart within.

"Miss Presley says once Mis' Parmer had to go out an' gether the eggs an' shet up the chickens, so Miss Presley didn't think there'd be any harm in just lookin' into the drawers an' things to see what she had. She says she's awful short on table cloths—only got three to her name! An' only six napkeens, an' them coarse 's anything! When Mis' Parmer come back in, Miss Presley talked around a little, then she says—'I s'pose you're one o' them spic an' span kind, Mis' Parmer, that alwus has a lot o' extry table cloths put away in lavender.'"

Emarine set the egg-beater into the bowl and began turning it slowly.

"Mis' Parmer got mighty red all of a sudden; but she says right out—'No, I'm a-gettin' reel short on table cloths an' things, Miss Presley, but I ain't goin' to replenish. Orville's thinkin' o' gettin' married this year, an' I guess Emarine 'll have a lot o' extry things.' An' then she ups an' laughs an' says—'I'll let her stock up the house, seein's she's so anxious to get into it.'"

Emarine had turned pale. The egg-beater fairly flew round and round. A little of the golden foam slipped over the edge of the bowl and slid down to the white table.

"Miss Presley thinks a good deal o' you, Emarine, so that got her spunk up; an' she just told Mis' Parmer she didn't believe you was dyin' to go there an' stock up her drawers fer her. Says she— 'I don't think young people 'ad ought to live with mother-in-laws, any way.' Said she thought she'd let Mis' Parmer put that in her pipe an' smoke it when she got time."

There was a pulse in each side of Emarine's throat beating

hard and full. Little blue, throbbing cords stood out in her temples. She went on mixing the pudding mechanically.

"Then Mis' Parmer just up an' said with a tantalizin' laugh that if you didn't like the a-commodations at her house, you needn't to come there. Said she never did like you, anyways, ner anybody else that set their heels down the way you set your'n. Said she'd had it all out with Orville, an' he'd promised her faithful that if there was any knucklin'-down to be done, you'd be the one to do it, an' not her!"

Emarine turned and looked at her mother. Her face was white with controlled passion. Her eyes burned. But her voice was quiet when she spoke.

"I guess you'd best move your chair," she said, "so's I can get to the oven. This puddin''s all ready to go in."

When she had put the pudding in the oven she moved about briskly, clearing the things off the table and washing them. She held her chin high. There was no doubt now about the click of her heels; it was ominous.

"I won't marry him!" she cried at last, flinging the words out. "He can have his mother an' his wore-out table cloths!" Her voice shook. The muscles around her mouth were twitching.

"My mercy!" cried her mother. She had a frightened look. "Who cares what his mother says? I w'udn't go to bitin' off my nose to spite my face, if I was you!"

"Well, I care what he says. I'll see myself knucklin'-down to a mother-in-law!"

"Well, now, don't go an' let loose of your temper, or you'll be sorry fer it. You're alwus mighty ready a-tellin' me not to mind what folks say, an' to keep away from the old gossips."

"Well, you told me yourself, didn't you? I can't keep away from my own mother very well, can I?"

"Well, now, don't flare up so! You're worse 'n karosene with a match set to it."

"What 'id you tell me for, if you didn't want I sh'u'd flare up?"

"Why, I thought it 'u'd just put you on your mettle an' show her she c'u'dn't come it over you." Then she added, diplomatically changing her tone as well as the subject—"Oh, say, Emarine, I wish you'd go up in the antic an' bring down a bunch o' pennyrile. I'll watch the puddin'."

She laughed with dry humor when the girl was gone. "I got into a pickle that time. Who ever 'd 'a' thought she'd get stirred up so? I'll have to manage to get her cooled down before Orville comes to-night. They ain't many matches like him, if his mother *is* such an old scarecrow. He ain't so well off, but he'll humor Emarine up. He'd lay down an' let her walk on him, I guess. There's Mis' Grisley b'en a-tryin' fer months to get him to go with her Lily—*Lily*, with a complexion like sole-leather!—an' a-askin' him up there all the time to dinner, an' a-flatterin' him up to the skies. I'd like to know what they always name dark-complected babies Lily fer! Oh, did you get the pennyrile, Emarine? I was laughin' to myself, a-wond'rin' what Mis' Grisley's Lily 'll say when she hears you're goin' to marry Orville."

Emarine hung a spotless dish-cloth on two nails behind the stove, but did not speak.

Mrs. Endey turned her back to the girl and smiled humorously.

"That didn't work," she thought. "I'll have to try somethin' else."

"I've made up my mind to get you a second-day dress, too, Emarine. You can have it any color you want—dove-color 'd be awful nice. There's a hat down at Mis' Norton's milliner' store that 'u'd go beautiful with dove-color."

Emarine took some flat-irons off the stove, wiped them carefully with a soft cloth and set them evenly on a shelf. Still she did not speak. Mrs. Endey's face took on an anxious look.

"There's some beautiful artaficial orange flowers at Mis' Norton's, Emarine. You can be married in 'em, if you want. They're so reel they almost smell sweet."

She waited a moment, but receiving no reply, she added with a kind of desperation—"An' a veil, Emarine—a long, white one a-flowin' down all over you to your feet—one that 'u'd just make Mis' Grisley's Lily's mouth water. What do you say to that? You can have that, too, if you want."

"Well, I don't want!" said Emarine, fiercely. "Didn't I say I wa'n't goin' to marry him? I'll give him his walking-chalk when he comes to-night. I don't need any help about it, either."

She went out, closing the door as an exclamation point.

Oregon City kept early hours. The curfew ringing at nine o'clock on summer evenings gathered the tender-aged of both sexes off the street.

It was barely seven o'clock when Orville Palmer came to take Emarine out for a drive. He had a high top-buggy, rather the worse for wear, and drove a sad-eyed, sorrel horse.

She was usually ready to come tripping down the path, to save his tying the horse. To-night she did not come. He waited a while. Then he whistled and called—"Oh, Emarine!"

He pushed his hat back and leaned one elbow on his knee, flicking his whip up and down, and looking steadily at the open door. But she did not come. Finally he got out and, tying his horse, went up the path slowly. Through the door he could see Emarine sitting quietly sewing. He observed at once that she was pale.

"Sick, Emarine?" he said, going in.

"No," she answered, "I ain't sick."

"Then why under the sun didn't choo come when I hollowed?"

"I didn't want to." Her tone was icy.

He stared at her a full minute. Then he burst out laughing. "Oh, say, Emarine, yuh can be the contrariest girl I ever see! Yuh do love to tease a fellow so. Yuh'll have to kiss me fer that."

He went toward her. She pushed her chair back and gave him a look that made him pause.

"How's your mother?" she asked.

"My mother?" A cold chill went up and down his spine. "Why—oh, she's all right. Why?"

She took a small gold ring set with a circle of garnets from her finger and held it toward him with a steady hand.

"You can take an' show her this ring, an' tell her I ain't so awful anxious to stock her up on table cloths an' napkeens as she thinks I am. Tell her yuh'll get some other girl to do her knucklin'-down fer her. I ain't that kind."

The young man's face grew scarlet and then paled off rapidly. He looked like a man accused of a crime. "Why, Emarine," he said, feebly.

He did not receive the ring, and she threw it on the floor at his feet. A whole month she had slept with that ring against her lips—the bond of her love and his! Now, it was only the emblem of her "knuckling-down" to another woman.

"You needn't to stand there a-pretendin' you don't know what I mean."

"Well, I don't, Emarine."

"Yes, you do, too. Didn't you promise your mother that if there was any knucklin'-down to be did, I'd be the one to do it, an' not her?"

"Why—er—Emarine—"

She laughed scornfully.

"Don't go to tryin' to get out of it. You know you did. Well, you can take your ring, an' your mother, an' all her old duds. I don't want any o' you."

"Emarine," said the young man, looking guilty and honest

at the same time, "the talk I had with my mother didn't amount to a pinch o' snuff. It wa'n't anything to make yuh act this way. She don't like yuh just because I'm goin' to marry yuh"—

"Oh, but you ain't," interrupted Emarine, with an aggravating laugh.

"Yes, I am, too. She kep' naggin' at me day an' night fer fear yuh'd be sassy to her an' she'd have to take a back seat."

"I'll tell you what's the matter with her!" interrupted Emarine. "She's got the big-head. She thinks ev'rybody wants to rush into her old house, an' marry her son, an' use her old things! She wants to make ev'rybody toe *her* mark."

"Emarine! She's my mother."

"I don't care if she is. I w'u'dn't tech her with a ten-foot pole."

"She 'll be all right after we're married, Emarine, an' she finds out how—how nice yuh are."

His own words appealed to his sense of the ridiculous. He smiled. Emarine divined the cause of his reluctant amusement and was instantly furious. Her face turned very white. Her eyes burned out of it like two fires.

"You think I ain't actin' very nice now, don't you? I don't care what you think, Orville Parmer, good or bad."

The young man stood thinking seriously.

"Emarine," he said, at last, very quietly, "I love yuh an' yuh know it. An' yuh love me. I'll alwus be good to yuh an' see that choo ain't emposed upon, Emarine. An' I think the world an' all of yuh. That's all I got to say. I can't see what ails yuh, Emarine… When I think o' that day when I asked yuh to marry me… An' that night I give yuh the ring"—the girl's eyelids quivered suddenly and fell. "An' that moonlight walk we took along by the falls… Why, it seems as if this can't be the same girl."

There was such a long silence that Mrs. Endey, cramping her back with one ear pressed to the keyhole of the door, decided that he had won and smiled dryly.

At last Emarine lifted her head. She looked at him steadily. "Did you, or didn't you, tell your mother I'd have to do the knucklin'-down?"

He shuffled his feet about a little.

"Well, I guess I did, Emarine, but I didn't mean anything. I just did it to get a little peace."

The poor fellow had floundered upon an unfortunate excuse.

"Oh!" said the girl, contemptuously. Her lip curled. "An' so you come an' tell me the same thing for the same reason— just to get a little peace! A pretty time you'd have a-gettin' any peace at all, between the two of us! You're chickenish—an' I hate chickenish people."

"Emarine!"

"Oh, I wish you'd go." There was an almost desperate weariness in her voice.

He picked up the ring with its shining garnet stars, and went.

Mrs. Endey tiptoed into the kitchen.

"My back's about broke." She laughed noiselessly. "I swan I'm proud o' that girl. She's got more o' me in her 'n I give her credit fer. The idee o' her a-callin' him chickenish right out to his face! That done me good. Well, I don't care such an awful lot if she don't marry him. A girl with that much spunk deserves a *gov'nor!* An' that mother o' his'n's a case. I guess her an' me 'd 'a' fit like cats an' dogs, anyhow." Her lips unclosed with reluctant mirth.

...

The next morning Emarine arose and went about her work as usual. She had not slept. But there were no signs of relenting, or of regret, in her face. After the first surreptitious look at her, Mrs. Endey concluded that it was all settled unchangeably. Her aspiring mind climbed from a governor to a United States senator. There was nothing impossible to a girl who could break her own heart at night and go about the next morning setting her heels down the way Emarine was setting hers.

Mrs. Endey's heart swelled with triumph.

Emarine washed the dishes and swept the kitchen. Then she went out to sweep the porch. Suddenly she paused. A storm of lyric passion had burst upon her ear; and running through it she heard the words—"*Sweet—oh—Sweet—my heart is breaking!*"

The girl trembled. Something stung her eyes sharply.

Then she pulled herself together stubbornly. Her face hardened. She went on sweeping with more determined care than usual.

"Well, I reckon," she said, with a kind of fierce philosophy, "it 'u'd 'a' been breaking a good sight worse if I'd 'a' married him an' that mother o' his'n. That's some comfort."

But when she went in she closed the door carefully, shutting out that impassioned voice.

Part II

It was eight o'clock of a June morning. It had rained during the night. Now the air was sweet with the sunshine on the wet leaves and flowers.

Mrs. Endey was ironing. The table stood across the open window, up which a wild honeysuckle climbed, flinging out slender, green shoots, each topped with a cluster of scarlet spikes. The splendor of the year was at its height. The flowers were marching by in pomp and magnificence.

Mrs. Endey spread a checked gingham apron on the ironing

cloth. It was trimmed at the bottom with a ruffle, which she pulled and smoothed with careful fingers.

She selected an iron on the stove, set the wooden handle into it with a sharp, little click, and polished it on a piece of scorched newspaper. Then she moved it evenly across the starched apron. A shining path followed it.

At that moment some one opened the gate. Mrs. Endey stooped to peer through the vines.

"Well, 'f I ever 'n all my natcherl life!" she said, solemnly. She set the iron on its stand and lifted her figure erect. She placed one hand on her hip, and with the other rubbed her chin in perplexed thought. "If it ain't Orville Parmer, you may shoot me! That beats me! I wonder 'f he thinks Emarine 's a-dyin' o' love fer him!"

Then a thought came that made her feel faint. She fell into a chair, weakly. "Oh, my land!" she said. "I wonder 'f that *ain't* what's the matter of her! I never'd thought o' that. I'd thought o' ev'rything *but* that. I wonder! There she's lied flat o' her back ever sence she fell out with him a month ago. Oh, my mercy! I wonder 'f that is it. Here I've b'en rackin' my brains to find out what ails 'er."

She got up stiffly and went to the door. The young man standing there had a pale, anxious face.

"Good-mornin', Mis' Endey," he said. He looked with a kind of entreaty into her grim face. "I come to see Emarine."

"Emarine's sick." She spoke coldly.

"I know she is, Mis' Endey." His voice shook. "If it wa'n't fer her bein' sick, I w'u'dn't be here. I s'pose, after the way she sent me off, I ain't got any spunk or I w'u'dn't 'a' come anyway; but I heard—"

He hesitated and looked away.

"What 'id you hear?"

"I heard she wa'n't a-goin' to—get well."

There was a long silence.

"Is she?" he asked, then. His voice was low and broken.

Mrs. Endey sat down. "I do' know," she said, after another silence. "I'm offul worried about her, Orville. I can't make out what ails 'er. She won't eat a thing; even floatin' island turns agi'n 'er—an' she al'ays loved that."

"Oh, Mis' Endey, can't I see 'er?"

"I don't see 's it 'u'd be any use. Emarine's turrable set. 'F you hadn't went an' told your mother that if there was any knucklin'-down to be did between her an' Emarine, Emarine 'u'd have to do it, you an' her'd 'a' b'en married by this time. I'd bought most ha'f her weddin' things a'ready."

The young man gave a sigh that was almost a groan. He looked like one whose sin has found him out. He dropped into a chair, and putting his elbows on his knees, sunk his face into his brown hands.

"Good God, Mis' Endey!" he said, with passionate bitterness. "Can't choo ever stop harpin' on that? Ain't I cursed myself day an' night ever sence? Oh, I wish yuh'd help me!" He lifted a wretched face. "I didn't mean anything by tellin' my mother that; she's a-gettin' kind o' childish, an' she was afraid Emarine 'u'd run over 'er. But if she'll only take me back, she'll have ev'rything her own way."

A little gleam of triumph came into Mrs. Endey's face. Evidently the young man was rapidly becoming reduced to a frame of mind desirable in a son-in-law.

"Will you promise that, solemn, Orville Parmer?" She looked at him sternly.

"Yes, Mis' Endey, I will—solemn." His tone was at once wretched and hopeful. "I'll promise anything under the sun, 'f she'll only fergive me. I can't *live* without 'er—an' that's all there is about it. Won't choo ask her to see me, Mis' Endey?"

"Well, I do' know," said Mrs. Endey, doubtfully. She cleared her throat, and sat looking at the floor, as if lost in thought. He should never have it to say that she had snapped him up too readily. "I don't feel much like meddlin'. I must say I side with Emarine. I do think"—her tone became regretful—"a girl o' her spir't deserves a gov'nor."

"I know she does," said the young man, miserably. "I alwus knew *I* wa'n't ha'f good enough fer 'er. But Mis' Endey, I know she loves me. Won't choo—"

"Well!" Mrs. Endey gave a sigh of resignation. She got up very slowly, as if still undecided. "I'll see what she says to 't. But I'll tell you right out I sha'n't advise 'er, Orville."

She closed the door behind her with deliberate care. She laughed dryly as she went up stairs, holding her head high. "There's nothin' like makin' your own terms," she said, shrewdly.

She was gone a long time. When Orville heard her coming lumbering back down the stairs and along the hall, his heart stopped beating.

Her coming meant—everything to him; and it was so slow and so heavy it seemed ominous. For a moment he could not speak, and her face told him nothing. Then he faltered out— "Will she? Oh, don't choo say she won't!"

"Well," said Mrs. Endey, with a sepulchral sigh, "she'll see you, but I don't know 's anything 'll come of it. Don't you go to bracin' up on that idee, Orville Parmer. She's set like a strip o' calico washed in alum water."

The gleam of hope that her first words had brought to his face was transitory. "You can come on," said Mrs. Endey, lifting her chin solemnly.

Orville followed her in silence.

The little room in which Emarine lay ill was small and white, like a nun's chamber. The ceiling slanted on two sides. There was white matting on the floor; there was an oval blue rug of braided rags at the side of the bed, and another in front of the bureau. There was a small cane-seated and cane-backed rocker. By the side of the bed was a high, stiff wooden chair, painted very black and trimmed with very blue roses.

There were two or three pictures on the walls. The long curtains of snowy butter-cloth were looped high.

The narrow white bed had been wheeled across the open window, so Emarine could lie and look down over the miles of green valley, with the mellifluous Willamette winding through it like a broad silver-blue ribbon. By turning her head a little she could see the falls; the great bulk of water sliding over the precipice like glass, to be crushed into powdered foam and flung high into the sunlight, and then to go seething on down to the sea.

At sunrise and at sunset the mist blown up in long veils from the falls quickened of a sudden to rose and gold and purple, shifting and blending into a spectral glow of thrilling beauty. It was sweeter than guests to Emarine.

The robins were company, too, in the large cherry tree outside of her window; and sometimes a flight of wild canaries drifted past like a yellow, singing cloud. When they sank, swiftly and musically, she knew that it was to rest upon a spot golden with dandelions.

Outside the door of this room Mrs. Endey paused. "I don't see 's it 'u'd be proper to let you go in to see 'er alone," she said, sternly.

Orville's eyes were eloquent with entreaty. "Lord knows there w'u'dn't be any harm in 't," he said, humbly but fervently. "I feel jest as if I was goin' in to see an angel."

Mrs. Endey's face softened; but at once a smile came upon it—one of those smiles of reluctant, uncontrollable humor that take us unawares sometimes, even in the most tragic moments. "She's got too much spunk fer an angel," she said.

"Don't choo go to runnin' of her down!" breathed Orville,

with fierce and reckless defiance.

"I wa'n't a-runnin' of her down!" retorted Mrs. Endey, coldly. "You don't ketch me a-runnin' of my own kin down, Orville Parmer!" She glowered at him under drawn brows. "An' I won't stand anybody else's a-runnin' of 'em down or a-walkin' over 'em, either! There ain't no call fer *you* to tell me not to run 'em down." Her look grew blacker. "I reckon we'd best settle all about your mother before we go in there, Orville Parmer."

"What about 'er?" His tone was miserable; his defiance was short-lived.

"Why, there's no use 'n your goin' in there unless you're ready to promise that you'll give Emarine the whip-hand over your mother. You best make up your mind."

"It's *made* up," said the young fellow, desperately. "Lord Almighty, Mis' Endey, it's made up."

"Well." She turned the door-knob. "I know it ain't the thing, an' I'd die if Miss Presley sh'u'd come an' find out—the town w'u'dn't hold her, she'd talk so! Well! Now, don't stay too long. 'F I see anybody a-comin' I'll cough at the foot o' the stairs."

She opened the door and when he had passed in, closed it with a bitter reluctance. "It ain't the proper thing," she repeated; and she stood for some moments with her ear bent to the keyhole. A sudden vision of Miss Presley coming up the stairs to see Emarine sent her down to the kitchen with long, cautious strides, to keep guard.

Emarine was propped up with pillows. Her mother had dressed her in a white sacque, considering it a degree more proper than a nightdress. There was a wide ruffle at the throat, trimmed with serpentine edging. Emarine was famous for the rapidity with which she crocheted, as well as for the number and variety of her patterns.

Orville went with clumsy noiselessness to the white bed.

He was holding his breath. His hungry eyes had a look of rising tears that are held back. They took in everything—the girl's paleness and her thinness; the beautiful dark hair, loose upon the pillow; the blue veins in her temples; the dark lines under her languid eyes.

He could not speak. He fell upon his knees, and threw one arm over her with compelling passion, but carefully, too, as one would touch a flower, and laid his brow against her hand. His shoulders swelled. A great sob struggled from his breast. "Oh, Emarine, Emarine!" he groaned. Then there was utter silence between them.

After a while, without lifting his head, he pushed her sleeve back a very little and pressed trembling, reverent lips upon the pulse beating irregularly in her slim wrist.

"Oh, Emarine!" he said, still without lifting his head. "I love yuh—I love yuh! I've suffered—oh, to think o' you layin' here sick, night after night fer a whole month, an' me not here to do things fer yuh. I've laid awake imaginin' that yuh wanted a fresh drink an' c'u'dn't make anybody hear; or that yuh wanted a cool cloth on your forrid, or a little jell-water, or somethin'. I've got up 'n the middle o' the night an' come an' stood out at your gate tell I'd see a shado' on the curt'n an' know yuh wa'n't alone... Oh, Emarine, Emarine!"

She moved her hand; it touched his throat and curved itself there, diffidently. He threw up his head and looked at her. A rush of passionate, startled joy stung through him like needles, filling his throat. He trembled strongly. Then his arms were about her and he had gathered her up against his breast; their lips were shaking together, after their long separation, in those kisses but one of which is worth a lifetime of all other kisses.

Presently he laid her back very gently upon her pillow, and still knelt looking at her with his hand on her brow. "I've tired yuh," he said, with earnest self-reproach. "I won't do 't ag'in,

Emarine—I promise. When I looked 'n your eyes an' see that yuh'd fergive me; when I felt your hand slip 'round my neck, like it ust to, an' like I've b'en *starvin'* to feel it fer a month, Emarine—I c'u'dn't help it, nohow; but I won't do 't ag'in. Oh, to think that I've got choo back ag'in!"

He laid his head down, still keeping his arm thrown, lightly and tenderly as a mother's, over her.

The sick girl looked at him. Her face settled into a look of stubbornness; the exaltation that had transfigured it a moment before was gone. "You'll have to promise me," she said, "about your mother, you know. I'll have to be first."

"Yuh shall be, Emarine."

"You'll have to promise that if there's any knucklin'-down, she'll do 't, an' not me."

He moved uneasily. "Oh, don't choo worry, Emarine. It'll be all right."

"Well, I want it settled now. You'll have to promise solemn that you'll stand by ev'rything I do, an' let me have things my way. If you don't, you can go back the way you come. But I know you'll keep your word if you promise."

"Yes," he said, "I will."

But he kept his head down and did not promise.

"Well?" she said, and faint as she was, her voice was like steel.

But still he did not promise.

After a moment she lifted her hand and curved it about his throat again. He started to draw away, but almost instantly shuddered closer to her and fell to kissing the white lace around her neck.

"Well," she said, coldly, "hurry an' make your choice. I hear mother a-comin'."

"Oh, Emarine!" he burst out, passionately. "I promise—I promise yuh ev'rything. My mother's gittin' old an' childish, an' it ain't right, but I can't give you up ag'in—I *can't!* I promise—I swear!"

Her face took on a tenderness worthy a nobler victory. She slipped her weak, bare arm up around him and drew his lips down to hers.

An hour later he walked away from the house, the happiest man in Oregon City—or in all Oregon, for that matter. Mrs. Endey watched him through the vines. "Well, he's a-walkin' knee-deep in *promises*," she reflected, with a comfortable laugh, as she sent a hot iron hissing over a newly sprinkled towel. "I guess that mother o' his'n 'll learn a thing er two if she tries any o' her back-sass with Emarine."

Emarine gained strength rapidly. Orville urged an immediate marriage, but Mrs. Endey objected. "I won't hear to 't tell Emarine gits her spunk back," she declared. "When she gits to settin' her heels down the way she ust to before she got sick, she can git married. I'll know then she's got her spunk back."

Toward the last of July Emarine commenced setting her heels down in the manner approved by her mother; so, on the first of August they were married and went to live with Mrs. Palmer. At the last moment Mrs. Endey whispered grimly—"Now, you mind you hold your head high."

"Hunh!" said Emarine. She lifted her chin so high and so suddenly that her long ear-rings sent out flashes in all directions.

...

They had been married a full month when Mrs. Endey went to spend a day at the Palmer's. She had a shrewd suspicion that all was not so tranquil there as it might be. She walked in unbidden and unannounced.

It was ten o'clock. The sun shown softly through the

languid purple haze that brooded upon the valley. Crickets and grasshoppers crackled through the grasses and ferns. The noble mountains glimmered mistily in the distance.

Mrs. Palmer was sewing a patch on a table-cloth. Emarine was polishing silverware. "Oh!" she said, with a start. "You, is 't?"

"Yes," said Mrs. Endey, sitting down, "me. I come to spen' the day."

"I didn't hear yuh knock," said Mrs. Palmer, dryly. She was tall and stoop-shouldered. She had a thin, sour face and white hair. One knew, only to look at her, that life had given her all its bitters and but few of its sweets.

"I reckon not," said Mrs. Endey, "seein' I didn't knock. I don't knock at my own daughter's door. Well, forever! Do you patch table-cloths, Mis' Parmer? I never hear tell! I have see darnt ones, but I never see a patched one." She laughed aggravatingly.

"Oh, that's nothin'," said Emarine, over her shoulder, "we have 'em made out o' flour sacks here, fer breakfas'."

Then Mrs. Palmer laughed—a thin, bitter laugh. Her face was crimson. "Yaas," she said, "I use patched table-cloths, an' table-cloths made out o' flour sacks; but I never did wear underclo's made out o' unbleached muslin in *my* life."

Then there was a silence. Emarine gave her mother a look, as much as to say—"What do you think of that?" Mrs. Endey smiled. "Thank mercy!" she said. "Dog-days 'll soon be over. The smoke's liftin' a leetle. I guess you an' Orville 'll git your house painted afore the fall rain comes on, Emarine? It needs it turrable bad."

"They ain't got the paintin' of it," said Mrs. Palmer, cutting a thread with her teeth. "It don't happen to be their house."

"Well, it's all the same. It 'll git painted if Emarine wants it sh'u'd. Oh, Emarine! Where'd you git them funny teaspoons at?"

"They're Orville's mother's." Emarine gave a mirthful titter.

"I want to know! Ain't them funny? Thin's no name fer 'm. You'd ought to see the ones my mother left me, Mis' Parmer—thick, my! One 'u'd make the whole dozen o' you'rn. I'll have 'em out an' ask you over to tea."

"I've heerd about 'em," said Mrs. Palmer, with the placidity of a momentary triumph. "The people your mother worked out fer give 'em to her, didn't they? My mother got her'n from her gran'mother. She never worked out. She never lived in much style, but she al'ays had a plenty."

"*My-O!*" said Mrs. Endey, scornfully.

"I guess I'd best git the dinner on," said Emarine. She pushed the silver to one side with a clatter. She brought some green corn from the porch and commenced tearing off the pale emerald husks.

"D'you want I sh'u'd help shuck it?" said her mother.

"No; I'm ust to doin' 't alone."

A silence fell upon all three. The fire made a cheerful noise; the kettle steamed sociably; some soup-meat, boiling, gave out a savory odor. Mrs. Endey leaned back comfortably in her rocking-chair. There was a challenge in the very fold of her hands in her lap.

Mrs. Palmer sat erect, stiff and thin. The side of her face was toward Mrs. Endey. She never moved the fraction of an inch, but watched her hostilely out of the corner of her eye, like a hen on the defensive.

It was Mrs. Endey who finally renewed hostilities. "Emarine," she said, sternly, "what are you a-doin'? Shortenin' your biscuits with *lard?*"

"Yes."

Mrs. Endey sniffed contemptuously. "They won't be fit to eat! You feathered your nest, didn't you? Fer mercy's sake! Can't you buy butter to shorten your biscuits with? You'll be makin' patata soup next!"

Then Mrs. Palmer stood up. There was a red spot on each cheek.

"Mis' Endey," she said, "if yuh don't like the 'comadations in this house, won't you be so good 's to go where they're better? I must say I never wear underclo's made out o' unbleached muslin in *my* life! The hull town's see 'em on your clo's line, an' tee-hee about it behind your back. I notice your daughter was mighty ready to git in here an' shorten biscuits with lard, an' use patched table-cloths, an'—"

"*Oh, mother!*"

It was her son's voice. He stood in the door. His face was white and anxious. He looked at the two women; then his eyes turned with a terrified entreaty to Emarine's face. It was hard as flint.

"It's time you come," she said, briefly. "Your mother just ordered my mother out o' doors. Whose house is this?"

He was silent.

"Say, Orville Parmer! whose house is this?"

"Oh, Emarine!"

"Don't you 'oh, Emarine' me! You answer up!"

"Oh, Emarine, don't let's quar'l. We've only b'en married a month. Let them quar'l, if they want—"

"You answer up. Whose house is this?"

"It's mine," he said in his throat.

"You'rn! Your mother calls it her'n."

"Well, it is," he said, with a desperation that rendered the situation tragic. "Oh, Emarine, what's mine 's her'n. Father left it to me, but o' course he knew it 'u'd be her'n, too. She likes to call it her'n."

"Well, she can't turn my mother out o' doors. I'm your wife an' this is my house, if it's you'rn. I guess it ain't hardly big enough fer your mother an' me, too. I reckon one o' us had best git out. I don't care much which, only I don't knuckle-down to nobody. I won't be set upon by nobody."

"Oh, Emarine!" There was terror in his face and voice. He huddled into a chair and covered his eyes with both hands. Mrs. Palmer, also, sat down, as if her limbs had suddenly refused to support her. Mrs. Endey ceased rocking and sat with folded hands, grimly awaiting developments.

Emarine stood with the backs of her hands on her hips. She had washed the flour off after putting the biscuits in the oven, and the palms were pink and full of soft curves like rose leaves; her thumbs were turned out at right angles. Her cheeks were crimson, and her eyes were like diamonds.

"One o' us 'll have to git out," she said again. "It's fer you to say which 'n, Orville Parmer. I'd just as soon. I won't upbraid you, 'f you say me."

"Well, I won't upbraid choo, if yuh say me," spoke up his mother. Her face was gray. Her chin quivered, but her voice was firm. "Yuh speak up, Orville."

Orville groaned—"Oh, mother! Oh, Emarine!" His head sunk lower; his breast swelled with great sobs—the dry, tearing sobs that in a man are so terrible. "To think that you two women sh'u'd both love me, an' then torcher me this way! Oh, God, what can I do er say?"

Suddenly Emarine uttered a cry, and ran to him. She tore his hands from his face and cast herself upon his breast, and with her delicate arms locked tight about his throat, set her warm, throbbing lips upon his eyes, his brow, his mouth, in deep, compelling kisses. "I'm your wife! I'm your wife! I'm your wife!" she panted. "You promised ev'rything to get me to marry you! Can you turn me out now, an' make me a laughin'-stawk fer the town? Can you give *me* up? You love me, an' I love you! Let me show you how I love you—"

She felt his arms close around her convulsively.

Then his mother arose and came to them, and laid her wrinkled, shaking hand on his shoulder. "My son," she said, "let *me* show yuh how *I* love yuh. I'm your mother. I've worked fer yuh, an' done fer yuh all your life, but the time's come fer me to take a back seat. It's be'n hard—it's be'n offul hard—an' I guess I've be'n mean an' hateful to Emarine—but it's be'n hard. Yuh keep Emarine, an' I'll go. Yuh want her an' I want choo to be happy. Don't choo worry about me—I'll git along all right. Yuh won't have to decide—I'll go of myself. That's the way *mothers* love, my son!"

She walked steadily out of the kitchen; and though her head was shaking, it was carried high.

Part III

It was the day before Christmas—an Oregon Christmas. It had rained mistily at dawn; but at ten o'clock the clouds had parted and moved away reluctantly. There was a blue and dazzling sky overhead. The rain-drops still sparkled on the windows and on the green grass, and the last roses and chrysanthemums hung their beautiful heads heavily beneath them; but there was to be no more rain. Oregon City's mighty barometer—the Falls of the Willamette—was declaring to her people by her softened roar that the morrow was to be fair.

Mrs. Orville Palmer was in the large kitchen making preparations for the Christmas dinner. She was a picture of dainty loveliness in a lavender gingham dress, made with a full skirt and a shirred waist and big leg-o'-mutton sleeves. A white apron was tied neatly around her waist.

Her husband came in, and paused to put his arm around her and kiss her. She was stirring something on the stove, holding her dress aside with one hand.

"It's goin' to be a fine Christmas, Emarine," he said, and

sighed unconsciously. There was a wistful and careworn look on his face.

"Beautiful!" said Emarine, vivaciously. "Goin' down-town, Orville?"

"Yes. Want anything?"

"Why, the cranberries ain't come yet. I'm so uneasy about 'em. They'd ought to 'a' b'en stooed long ago. I like 'em cooked down an' strained to a jell. I don't see what ails them groc'rymen! Sh'u'd think they c'u'd get around some time before doomsday! Then, I want—here, you'd best set it down." She took a pencil and a slip of paper from a shelf over the table and gave them to him. "Now, let me see." She commenced stirring again, with two little wrinkles between her brows. "A ha'f a pound o' citron; a ha'f a pound o' candied peel; two pounds o' cur'nts; two pounds o' raisins—git 'em stunned, Orville; a pound o' sooet—make 'em give you some that ain't all strings! A box o' Norther' Spy apples; a ha'f a dozen lemons; four-bits worth o' walnuts or a'monds, whichever's freshest; a pint o' Puget Sound oysters fer the dressin', an' a bunch o' cel'ry. You stop by an' see about the turkey, Orville; an' I wish you'd run in 's you go by mother's an' tell her to come up as soon as she can. She'd ought to be here now."

Her husband smiled as he finished the list. "You're a wonderful housekeeper, Emarine," he said.

Then his face grew grave. "Got a present fer your mother yet, Emarine?"

"Oh, yes, long ago. I got 'er a black shawl down t' Charman's. She's b'en wantin' one."

He shuffled his feet about a little. "Unh-hunh. Yuh—that is—I reckon yuh ain't picked out any present fer—fer my mother, have yuh, Emarine?"

"No," she replied, with cold distinctness. "I ain't."

There was a silence. Emarine stirred briskly. The lines grew deeper between her brows. Two red spots came into her cheeks. "I hope the rain ain't spoilt the chrysyanthums," she said then, with an air of ridding herself of a disagreeable subject.

Orville made no answer. He moved his feet again uneasily. Presently he said: "I expect my mother needs a black shawl, too. Seemed to me her'n looked kind o' rusty at church Sunday. Notice it, Emarine?"

"No," said Emarine.

"Seemed to me she was gittin' to look offul old. Emarine"—his voice broke; he came a step nearer—"it'll be the first Christmas dinner I ever eat without my mother."

She drew back and looked at him. He knew the look that flashed into her eyes, and shrank from it.

"You don't have to eat this 'n' without 'er, Orville Parmer! You go an' eat your dinner with your mother, 'f you want! I can get along alone. Are you goin' to order them things? If you ain't, just say so, an' I'll go an' do 't myself!"

He put on his hat and went without a word.

Mrs. Palmer took the saucepan from the stove and set it on the hearth. Then she sat down and leaned her cheek in the palm of her hand, and looked steadily out of the window. Her eyelids trembled closer together. Her eyes held a far-sighted look. She saw a picture; but it was not the picture of the blue reaches of sky, and the green valley cleft by its silver-blue river. She saw a kitchen, shabby, compared to her own, scantily furnished, and in it an old, white-haired woman sitting down to eat her Christmas dinner alone.

After a while she arose with an impatient sigh. "Well, I can't help it!" she exclaimed. "If I knuckled-down to her this time, I'd have to do 't ag'in. She might just as well get ust to 't, first as last. I wish she hadn't got to lookin' so old an' pitiful, though, a-settin' there in front o' us in church Sunday after Sunday. The cords stand out in her neck like well-rope, an' her chin keeps a-quiv'rin' so! I can see Orville a-watch-in' her—"

The door opened suddenly and her mother entered. She was bristling with curiosity. "Say, Emarine!" She lowered her voice, although there was no one to hear. "Where d' you s'pose the undertaker's a-goin' up by here? Have you hear of anybody—"

"No," said Emarine. "Did Orville stop by an' tell you to hurry up?"

"Yes. What's the matter of him? Is he sick?"

"Not as I know of. Why?"

"He looks so. Oh, I wonder if it's one o' the Peterson children where the undertaker's a-goin'! They've all got the quinsy sore throat."

"How does he look? I don't see 's he looks so turrable."

"Why, Emarine Parmer! Ev'rybody in town says he looks *so!* I only hope they don't know what ails him!"

"What *does* ail him?" cried out Emarine, fiercely. "What are you hintin' at?"

"Well, if you don't know what ails him, you'd ort to; so I'll tell you. He's dyin' by inches ever sence you turned his mother out o' doors."

Emarine turned white. Sheet lightning played in her eyes.

"Oh, you'd ought to talk about my turnin' her out!" she burst out, furiously. "After you a-settin' here a-quar'l'n' with her in this very kitchen, an' eggin' me on! Wa'n't she goin' to turn you out o' your own daughter's home? Wa'n't that what I turned her out fer? I didn't turn her out, anyhow! I only told Orville this house wa'n't big enough fer his mother an' me, an' that neither o' us 'ud knuckle-down, so he'd best take his choice. You'd ought to talk!"

"Well, if I egged you on, I'm sorry fer 't," said Mrs. Endey, solemnly. "Ever sence that fit o' sickness I had a month ago, I've feel kind o' old an' no-account myself, as if I'd like to let all holts go, an' just rest. I don't spunk up like I ust to. No, he didn't go to Peterson's—he's gawn right on. My land! I wonder 'f it ain't old gran'ma Eliot; she had a bad spell—no, he didn't turn that corner. I can't think where he's goin' to!"

She sat down with a sigh of defeat.

A smile glimmered palely across Emarine's face and was gone. "Maybe if you'd go up in the antic you could see better," she suggested, dryly.

"Oh, Emarine, here comes old gran'ma Eliot herself! Run an' open the door fer 'er. She's limpin' worse 'n usual."

Emarine flew to the door. Grandma Eliot was one of the few people she loved. She was large and motherly. She wore a black dress and shawl and a funny bonnet, with a frill of white lace around her brow.

Emarine's face softened when she kissed her. "I'm so glad to see you," she said, and her voice was tender.

Even Mrs. Endey's face underwent a change. Usually it wore a look of doubt, if not of positive suspicion, but now it fairly beamed. She shook hands cordially with the guest and led her to a comfortable chair.

"I know your rheumatiz is worse," she said, cheerfully, "because you're limpin' so. Oh, did you see the undertaker go up by here? We can't think where he's goin' to. D' you happen to know?"

"No, I don't; an' I don't want to, neither." Mrs. Eliot laughed comfortably. "Mis' Endey, you don't ketch me foolin' with undertakers till I have to." She sat down and removed her black cotton gloves. "I'm gettin' to that age when I don't care much where undertakers go to so long 's they let *me* alone. Fixin' fer Christmas dinner, Emarine dear?"

"Yes, ma'am," said Emarine in her very gentlest tone. Her mother had never said "dear" to her, and the sound of it on this old lady's lips was sweet. "Won't you come an' take dinner with us?"

The old lady laughed merrily. "Oh, dearie me, dearie me! You don't guess my son's folks could spare me now, do you? I spend ev'ry Christmas there. They most carry me on two chips. My son's wife, Sidonie, she nearly runs her feet off waitin' on me. She can't do enough fer me. My, Mrs. Endey, you don't know what a comfort a daughter-in-law is when you get old an' feeble!"

Emarine's face turned red. She went to the table and stood with her back to the older woman; but her mother's sharp eyes observed that her ears grew scarlet.

"An' I never will," said Mrs. Endey, grimly.

"You've got a son-in-law, though, who's worth a whole townful of most son-in-laws. He was such a good son, too; jest worshipped his mother; couldn't bear her out o' his sight. He humored her high an' low. That's jest the way Sidonie does with me. I'm gettin' cranky 's I get older, an' sometimes I'm reel cross an' sassy to her; but she jest laffs at me, an' then comes an' kisses me, an' I'm all right ag'in. It's a blessin' right from God to have a daughter-in-law like that."

The knife in Emarine's hand slipped, and she uttered a little cry.

"Hurt you?" demanded her mother, sternly.

Emarine was silent, and did not turn.

"Cut you, Emarine? Why don't you answer me? Aigh?"

"A little," said Emarine. She went into the pantry, and presently returned with a narrow strip of muslin which she wound around her finger.

"Well, I never see! You never will learn any gumption! Why don't you look what you're about? Now, go around Christmas with your finger all tied up!"

"Oh, that'll be all right by to-morrow," said Mrs. Eliot, cheerfully. "Won't it, Emarine? Never cry over spilt milk, Mrs. Endey; it makes a body get wrinkles too fast. O' course Orville's mother's comin' to take dinner with you, Emarine."

"Dear me!" exclaimed Emarine, in a sudden flutter. "I don't see why them cranberries don't come! I told Orville to hurry 'em up. I'd best make the floatin' island while I wait."

"I stopped at Orville's mother's as I came along."

"How?" Emarine turned in a startled way from the table.

"I say, I stopped at Orville's mother's as I come along, Emarine."

"Oh!"

"She well?" asked Mrs. Endey.

"No, she ain't; shakin' like she had the Saint Vitus dance. She's failed harrable lately. She'd b'en cryin'; her eyes was all swelled up."

There was quite a silence. Then Mrs. Endey said—"What she b'en cryin' about?"

"Why when I asked her she jest laffed kind o' pitiful, an' said: 'Oh, only my tomfoolishness, o' course.' Said she always got to thinkin' about other Christmases. But I cheered her up. I told her what a good time I always had at my son's, and how Sidonie jest couldn't do enough fer me. An' I told her to think what a nice time she'd have here 't Emarine's to-morrow."

Mrs. Endey smiled. "What she say to that?"

"She didn't say much. I could see she was thankful, though, she had a son's to go to. She said she pitied all poor wretches that had to set out their Christmas alone. Poor old lady! she ain't got much spunk left. She's all broke down. But I cheered her up some. Sech a *wishful* look took holt o' her when I pictchered her dinner over here at Emarine's. I can't seem to forget it. Goodness! I must go. I'm on my way to Sidonie's, an' she'll be comin' after me if I ain't on time."

When Mrs. Eliot had gone limping down the path, Mrs. Endey said: "You got your front room red up, Emarine?"

"No; I ain't had time to red up anything."

"Well, I'll do it. Where's your duster at?"

"Behind the org'n. You can get out the wax cross again. Mis' Dillon was here with all her childern, an' I had to hide up ev'rything. I never see childern like her' n. She lets' em handle things so!"

Mrs. Endey went into the "front room" and began to dust the organ. She was something of a diplomat, and she wished to be alone for a few minutes. "You have to manage Emarine by contrairies," she reflected. It did not occur to her that this was a family trait. "I'm offul sorry I ever egged her on to turnin' Orville's mother out o' doors, but who'd 'a' thought it 'u'd break her down so? She ain't told a soul either. I reckoned she'd talk somethin' offul about us, but she ain't told a soul. She's kep' a stiff upper lip an' told folks she al'ays expected to live alone when Orville got married. Emarine's all worked up. I believe the Lord hisself must 'a' sent gran'ma Eliot here to talk like an angel unawares. I bet she'd go an' ask Mis' Parmer over here to dinner if she wa'n't afraid I'd laff at her fer knucklin'-down. I'll have to aggravate her."

She finished dusting, and returned to the kitchen. "I wonder what gran'ma Eliot 'u'd say if she knew you'd turned Orville's mother out, Emarine?"

There was no reply. Emarine was at the table mixing the plum pudding. Her back was to her mother.

"I didn't mean what I said about bein' sorry I egged you on, Emarine. I'm glad you turned her out. She'd *ort* to be turned out."

Emarine put a handful of floured raisins into the mixture and stirred it all together briskly.

"Gran'ma Eliot can go talkin' about her daughter-in-law Sidonie all she wants, Emarine. You keep a stiff upper lip."

"I can 'tend to my own affairs," said Emarine, fiercely.

"Well, don't flare up so. Here comes Orville. Land, but he does look peakid!"

...

After supper, when her mother had gone home for the night, Emarine put on her hat and shawl.

Her husband was sitting by the fireplace, looking thoughtfully at the bed of coals.

"I'm goin' out," she said, briefly. "You keep the fire up."

"Why, Emarine, it's dark. Don't choo want I sh'u'd go along?"

"No; you keep the fire up."

He looked at her anxiously, but he knew from the way she set her heels down that remonstrance would be useless.

"Don't stay long," he said, in a tone of habitual tenderness. He loved her passionately, in spite of the lasting hurt she had given him when she parted him from his mother. It was a hurt that had sunk deeper than even he realized. It lay heavy on his heart day and night. It took the blue out of the sky, and the green out of the grass, and the gold out of the sunlight; it took the exaltation and the rapture out of his tenderest moments of love.

He never reproached her, he never really blamed her; certainly he never pitied himself. But he carried a heavy heart around with him, and his few smiles were joyless things.

For the trouble he blamed only himself. He had promised Emarine solemnly before he married her that if there were any "knuckling-down" to be done, his mother should be the one to do it. He had made the promise deliberately, and he could no more have broken it than he could have changed the color of his eyes. When bitter feeling arises between two relatives by marriage, it is the one who stands between them—the one who is bound by the tenderest ties to both—who has the real suffering to bear, who is torn and tortured until life holds nothing worth the having.

Orville Palmer was the one who stood between. He had built his own cross, and he took it up and bore it without a word.

Emarine hurried through the early winter dark until she came to the small and poor house where her husband's mother lived. It was off the main-traveled street.

There was a dim light in the kitchen; the curtain had not been drawn. Emarine paused and looked in. The sash was lifted six inches, for the night was warm, and the sound of voices came to her at once. Mrs. Palmer had company.

"It's Miss Presley," said Emarine, resentfully, under her breath. "Old gossip!"

"—goin' to have a fine dinner, I hear," Miss Presley was saying. "Turkey with oyster dressin', an' cranberries, an' mince an' pun'kin pie, an' reel plum puddin' with brandy poured over 't an' set afire, an' wine dip, an' nuts, an' raisins, an' wine itself to wind up on. Emarine's a fine cook. She knows how to get up a dinner that makes your mouth water to think about. You goin' to have a spread, Mis' Parmer?"

"Not much of a one," said Orville's mother. "I expected to, but I c'udn't get them fall patatas sold off. I'll have to keep 'em till spring to git any kind o' price. I don't care much about Christmas, though"—her chin was trembling, but she lifted it high. "It's silly for anybody but childern to build so much on Christmas."

Emarine opened the door and walked in. Mrs. Palmer arose slowly, grasping the back of her chair. "Orville's dead?" she said, solemnly.

Emarine laughed, but there was the tenderness of near tears in her voice. "Oh, my, no!" she said, sitting down. "I run over to ask you to come to Christmas dinner. I was too busy all day to come sooner. I'm goin' to have a great dinner, an' I've cooked ev'ry single thing of it myself! I want to show you what a fine Christmas dinner your daughter-'n-law can get up. Dinner's at two, an' I want you to come at eleven. Will you?"

Mrs. Palmer had sat down, weakly. Trembling was not the word to describe the feeling that had taken possession of her. She was shivering. She wanted to fall down on her knees and put her arms around her son's wife, and sob out all her loneliness and heartache. But life is a stage; and Miss Presley was an audience not to be ignored. So Mrs. Palmer said: "Well, I'll be reel glad to come, Emarine. It's offul kind o' yuh to think of 't. It 'ud 'a' be'n lonesome eatin' here all by myself, I expect."

Emarine stood up. Her heart was like a thistle-down. Her eyes were shining. "All right," she said; "an' I want that you sh'u'd come just at eleven. I must run right back now. Good-night."

"Well, I declare!" said Miss Presley. "That girl gits prettier ev'ry day o' her life. Why, she just looked full o' *glame* to-night!"

...

Orville was not at home when his mother arrived in her rusty best dress and shawl. Mrs. Endey saw her coming. She gasped out, "Why, good grieve! Here's Mis' Parmer, Emarine!"

"Yes, I know," said Emarine, calmly. "I ast her to dinner."

She opened the door, and shook hands with her mother-in-law, giving her mother a look of defiance that almost upset that lady's gravity.

"You set right down, Mother Parmer, an' let me take your things. Orville don't know you're comin', an' I just want to see his face when he comes in. Here's a new black shawl fer your Christmas. I got mother one just like it. See what nice long fringe it's got. Oh, my, don't go to cryin'! Here comes Orville."

She stepped aside quickly. When her husband entered his eyes fell instantly on his mother, weeping childishly over the new shawl. She was in the old splint rocking-chair with the high back. "*Mother!*" he cried; then he gave a frightened, tortured glance at his wife. Emarine smiled at him, but it was through tears.

"Emarine ast me, Orville—she ast me to dinner o' herself! An' she give me this shawl. I'm—cryin'—fer—joy—"

"I ast her to dinner," said Emarine," but she ain't ever goin' back again. She's goin' to *stay*. I expect we've both had enough of a lesson to do us."

Orville did not speak. He fell on his knees and laid his head, like a boy, in his mother's lap, and reached one strong but trembling arm up to his wife's waist, drawing her down to him.

Mrs. Endey got up and went to rattling things around on the table vigorously. "Well, I never see sech a pack o' loonatics!" she exclaimed. "Go an' burn all your Christmas dinner up, if I don't look after it! Turncoats! I expect they'll both be fallin' over theirselves to knuckle-down to each other from now on! I never see!"

But there was something in her eyes, too, that made them beautiful.

"A Point of Knuckling-Down" was published in *McClure's Magazine* in December 1895. It was reprinted in Higginson's collections *The Flower That Grew in the Sand and Other Stories* (1896) and *From the Land of the Snow-Pearls: Tales from Puget Sound* (1897), and in newspapers and magazines around the United States. "A Point of Knuckling-Down" is one of Higginson's longest and most developed stories. Divided into three parts, the story focuses on the extended power struggle between a mother-in-law, Mrs. Palmer, and her newly married son's wife, Emarine. The two strong-willed women compete for domestic control throughout the story; neither woman is willing to be the one who 'knuckles down' to the other. Mrs. Palmer's son, Emarine's mother, and various neighbors become involved in an attempt to help resolve the stubborn dispute. After months of conflict, the situation between the two determined women is finally resolved, in a way that may surprise readers.

"The Blow-Out at Jenkins's Grocery"
• 1896 •

THE HANDS OF THE BIG, round clock in Mr. Jenkins's grocery store pointed to eleven. Mr. Jenkins was tying a string around a paper bag containing a dollar's worth of sugar. He held one end of the string between his teeth. His three clerks were going around the store with little stiff prances of deference to the customers they were serving. It was the night before Christmas. They were all so worn out that their attempts at smiles were only painful contortions.

Mr. Jenkins looked at the clock. Then his eyes went in a hurried glance of pity to a woman sitting on a high stool close to the window. Her feet were drawn up on the top rung, and her thin shoulders stooped over her chest. She had sunken cheeks and hollow eyes; her cheek-bones stood out sharply.

For two hours she had sat there almost motionless. Three times she had lifted her head and fixed a strained gaze upon Mr. Jenkins and asked, "D'yuh want to shet up?" Each time, receiving an answer in the negative, she had sunk back into the same attitude of brute-like waiting.

It was a wild night. The rain drove its long, slanting lances down the window-panes. The wind howled around corners, banged loose shutters, creaked swinging sign-boards to and fro, and vexed the telephone wires to shrill, continuous screaming. Fierce gusts swept in when the door was opened.

Christmas shoppers came and went. The woman saw nothing inside the store. Her eyes were set on the doors of a brightly lighted saloon across the street.

It was a small, new "boom" town on Puget Sound. There

was a saloon on every corner, and a brass band in every saloon. The "establishment" opposite was having its "opening" that night. "At home" cards in square envelopes had been sent out to desirable patrons during the previous week. That day, during an hour's sunshine, a yellow chariot, drawn by six cream-colored horses with snow-white manes and tails, had gone slowly through the streets, bearing the members of the band clad in white and gold. It was followed by three open carriages, gay with the actresses who were to dance and sing that night on the stage in the rear of the saloon. All had yellow hair and were dressed in yellow with white silk sashes, and white ostrich plumes falling to their shoulders. It was a gorgeous procession, and it "drew."

The woman lived out in the Grand View addition. The addition consisted mainly of cabins built of "shakes" and charred stumps. The grand view was to come some ten or twenty years later on, when the forests surrounding the addition had taken their departure. It was a full mile from the store.

She had walked in with her husband through the rain and slush after putting six small children to bed. They were very poor. Her husband was shiftless. It was whispered of them by their neighbors that they couldn't get credit for "two bits" except at the saloons.

A relative had sent the woman ten dollars for a Christmas gift. She had gone wild with joy. Ten dollars! It was wealth. For once the children should have a real Christmas—a good dinner, toys, candy! Of all things, there should be a wax doll for the little girl who had cried for one every Christmas, and never even had one in her arms. Just for this one time they should be happy—like other children; and she should be happy in their happiness—like other mothers. What did it matter that she had only two calico dresses and one pair of shoes, half-soled at that, and capped across the toes?

"The Blow-Out at Jenkins's Grocery"

Her husband had entered into her childish joy. He was kind and affectionate—when he was sober. That was why she had never had the heart to leave him. He was one of those men who are always needing, pleading for—and, alas! receiving—forgiveness; one of those men whom their women love passionately and cling to forever.

He promised her solemnly that he would not drink a drop that Christmas—so solemnly that she believed him. He had helped her to wash the dishes and put the children to bed. And he had kissed her.

Her face had been radiant when they came into Mr. Jenkins's store. That poor, gray face with its sunken cheeks and eyes! They bought a turkey—and with what anxious care she had selected, it, testing its tenderness, balancing it on her bony hands, examining the scales with keen, narrowed eyes when it was weighed; and a quart of cranberries, a can of mince meat and a can of plum pudding, a head of celery, a pint of Olympia oysters, candy, nuts—and then the toys! She trembled with eagerness. Her husband stood watching her, smiling good-humoredly, his hands in his pockets. Mr. Jenkins indulged in some serious speculation as to where the money was coming from to pay for all this "blow-out." He set his lips together and resolved that the "blow-out" should not leave the store, under any amount of promises, until the cash paying for it was in his cash-drawer.

Suddenly the band began to play across the street. The man threw up his head like an old war-horse at the sound of a bugle note. A fire came into his eyes; into his face a flush of excitement. He walked down to the window and stood looking out, jingling some keys in his pocket. He breathed quickly.

After a few moments he went back to his wife. Mr. Jenkins had stepped away to speak to another customer.

"Say, Molly, old girl," he said affectionately, without looking at her, "yuh can spare me enough out o' that tenner to git a plug o' tobaccer for Christmas, can't yuh?"

"W'y—I guess so." said she slowly. The first cloud fell on her happy face.

"Well, jest let me have it, an' I'll run out an' be back before yuh're ready to pay for these here things. I'll only git two bits' worth." She turned very pale.

"Can't yuh git it here, Mart?"

"No," he said in a whisper; "his'n ain't fit to chew. I'll be right back, Molly—honest."

She stood motionless, her eyes cast down, thinking. If she refused, he would be angry and remain away from home all the next day to pay her for the insult. If she gave it to him—well, she would have to take the chances. But oh, her hand shook as she drew the small gold piece from her shabby purse and reached it to him. His big, warm hand closed over it.

She looked up at him. Her eyes spoke the passionate prayer that her lips could not utter.

"Don't stay long, Mart," she whispered, not daring to say more.

"I won't, Molly," he whispered back. "I'll hurry up. Git anything yuh want."

She finished her poor shopping. Mr. Jenkins wrapped everything up neatly. Then he rubbed his hands together and looked at her, and said: "Well, there now, Mis' Dupen."

"I—jest lay 'em all together there on the counter," she said hesitatingly. "I'll have to wait till Mart comes back before I can pay yuh."

"I see him go into the s'loon over there," piped out the errand boy shrilly.

At the end of half an hour she climbed upon the high stool and fixed her eyes upon the saloon opposite and sat there.

She saw nothing but the glare of those windows and the

light streaming out when the doors opened. She heard nothing but the torturing blare of the music. After awhile something commenced beating painfully in her throat and temples. Her limbs grew stiff—she was scarcely conscious that they ached. Once she shuddered strongly, as dogs do when they lie in the cold, waiting.

At twelve o'clock Mr. Jenkins touched her kindly on the arm. She looked up with a start. Her face was gray and old; her eyes were almost wild in their strained despair.

"I guess I'll have to shet up now, Mis' Dupen," he said apologetically. "I'm sorry—"

She got down from the stool at once. "I can't take them things," she said, almost whispering. "I hate to of put yuh to all that trouble of doin' 'em up. I thought—but I can't take 'em. I hope yuh won't mind—very much." Her bony fingers twisted together under her thin shawl.

"Oh, that's all right," said Mr. Jenkins in an embarrassed way. She moved stiffly to the door. He put out the lights and followed her. He felt mean, somehow. For one second he hesitated, then he locked the door, and gave it a shake to make sure that it was all right.

"Well," he said, "good-night. I wish you a mer—"

"Good-night," said the woman. She was turning away when the doors of the saloon opened for two or three men to enter. The music, which had ceased for a few minutes, struck up another air—a familiar air.

She burst suddenly into wild and terrible laughter. "Oh, my Lord," she cried out, "they're a-playin' 'Home, Sweet Home!' *In there!* Oh, my Lord! *Wouldn't that kill yuh!*"

"The Blow-Out at Jenkins's Grocery" was published in *The Black Cat* in December 1896. It was reprinted in *From The Land of the Snow-Pearls: Tales From Puget Sound* (1897).

"The Blow-Out at Jenkins's Grocery" takes place in a small town on Puget Sound on a stormy Christmas Eve. Molly Dupen is married to a man whose idleness and drinking has impoverished his large family. On this day, however, Molly has received in the mail an unexpected and much-needed holiday gift of money from a distant relative. As she eagerly shops in Jenkins's grocery store for Christmas dinner ingredients, toys, and candy for her six young children, her husband yearns to join the noisy revelry coming from the saloon across the street. "The Blow-Out at Jenkins's Grocery" focuses on issues of marriage, motherhood, and why people make the often flawed choices that they do.

"The Stubbornness of Uriah Slater"
• 1899 •

"What did I tell you?" cried Mrs. Snodgrass, with a little crow of triumph following along after her words. "He's gone an' hired the second-best kerriage instid of the first-best for his own weddin'. What did I tell you? Let *me* alone! It don't take me long to size up a man that only hired one kerriage, outside of the mourners an' pull-bearers, at his father's funeral." She turned from the window to cast a withering glance at Mrs. Simonton, who stood behind her with a routed air. " 'Oh, he'll get the best for his own weddin',' says you." She imitated Mrs. Simonton's tone. " 'He'll get the one that's closed instid of the canopy-top, even if it is a dollar more,' says you. What you got to say now?"

Mrs. Simonton had not a word to say. The bridal carriage was now passing the gate. The canopy was bobbing and bowing from side to side, as first one wheel and then another went into a rut. The bridegroom sat up with a straight back and a red, conscious face. The bride held her face a little from him with a modest air.

The two women in the window bent instantly over a pot of blooming hydrangeas, but stared still, with their chins held in, in a surreptitious way that made their eyebrows glimmer like little flounces of lace in their own vision. The bride gave them a brief glance—one that unconsciously appealed to them to spare her. But they were as unconscious of its meaning as she.

"She's feathered her nest with mighty poor feathers," said Mrs. Snodgrass, lifting her head and staring boldly after the swaying carriage when it had passed.

"He's got his house all paid for," said Mrs. Simonton, timidly.

Mrs. Snodgrass threw up her head with a scornful smile.

"An' some money in the bank besides."

"Yes, I've heard that story time an' again, an' every time I've heard it I thinks, says I: 'Well! I wouldn't have my Isaphene marry a man as stubborn's he is for two houses all paid for an' money in three banks.' You'll see. She won't get a thing her own way."

"W'y—is he so turrable stubborn?"

"Is he!"

"I heard she wanted a row of crissyanthums all along the front fence, an' he went right off an' got 'em. That don't look so turrable stubborn. Her mother's a-braggin' about it."

"You wait." Mrs. Snodgrass smiled loftily. "It takes a little while for stubborn to out. Mebbe he wanted the crissyanthums hisself. Mebbe he asked her what kind o' flowers she wanted along the front fence. I'd brag about a little thing like that!"

"He ain't got a bad habit to his name," said Mrs. Simonton. Two red spots burned in her hollow cheeks. "Not a one. He don't drink—he don't *tech* drink—he don't gamble, an' he don't set around downtown half the night playin' cards for the cigars. I've hear say that it's even agen his principles to put a nickel in the slot—"

"Oh my!" interrupted Mrs. Snodgrass, with an exasperating laugh. "Where's he keep his wings? I never see 'em. Where's he keep 'em at? I drether a man 'ud have a habit than to be a mule. I drether a man 'ud set downtown an' play cards till daylight than to go an' buy a sorrel horse because I asked for a dapple one, or a white Leghorn rooster because I asked for a *Braymin*." She gave a little start, and bent her head over the hydrangea again. "Here come all the people that's been to the church," she said, digging imaginary worms out of the earth with a hair-pin. "Who's them three women a-walkin' along together ahead? Hunh—*three umberells!* A ghost couldn't get past 'em, let alone flesh an' blood. As if September sun 'ud hurt their complexions!"

"I'll have to go," said Mrs. Simonton, getting up reluctantly when the last wedding-guest had gone by, holding her lavender gown up high on both sides. "The childern 'll be gettin' home from school."

"Well, come again," said Mrs. Snodgrass, cordially. She went to the door and waited until her departing guest had reached the corner of the house; then she stepped out on the porch, and slanting one hand up over her eyes, called out, in a tone of repressed triumph: "You just wait till along about— well, let's say April—an' see if there ain't a divorced *mule* in this neighborhood... Look out! you'll tear your dress! It's caught in a quivass of the walk."

That winter was a severe one on Puget Sound. Snow dusted itself twice over the green lawns, and once the thermometers registered twenty degrees above zero! Everyone went around shivering, and declaring that the climate was changing since the advent of the railroads. Ladies locked themselves indoors, and looked out the windows at the strange white world with wide, anxious eyes. They fed the birds generously, and hoped to mercy the sea-gulls would not starve. One old pioneer said gloomily that if it kept on, the first thing a body knew the end of the bay would freeze over, and then you might as well live somewhere in the East! His tone meant that he could not imagine any situation more disheartening than that.

There was a slight snowfall the last week in February. But on the first of March a chinook wind came overnight and blew its soft velvety breath over land and sea, and sent its wild sweet laughter in at doors and windows. In the morning there was a green world again sloping from the glimmering white lines of the Olympics, the Cascades, and the Selkirks down to the blue water. The sea-gulls circled through the yellow sunlight, screaming; or drove one another gravely from piling to piling along the shore; or drifted out to the ocean again, rising and falling upon the satiny waves. The pussy-willows trembled like silver clouds against the green background of the hill.

Mrs. Slater, the bride of six months, looked out the kitchen window as she arose from the breakfast table. They ate breakfast in the big cozy kitchen because Mr. Slater preferred it there. She was a pretty young woman with a sweet face. Her figure was round and slender. She wore a neat house dress made with a full skirt and a yoke-waist. Her apron and collar were white and fresh; her brown hair was arranged smoothly, with only a few unmanageable "lovelocks" about her brow and neck. Her apron was tied with long wide strings with deep hems on the ends. The bows were pulled out carefully. In her cheeks were both dimples and roses.

"Oh, Uriah," she cried out, joyfully! "See how green the hill is! It's spring at last. I'm so glad. I'm going out to look for a four-leaf clover."

"I wouldn't be so foolish," said Uriah, pushing his chair back against the wall with a great noise.

"What is it, Uriah?"

"I say I wouldn't be so foolish. Orilla, you do act so foolish!"

She turned and looked at him. A little red came into her face.

"Why, Uriah Slater! I wouldn't call my wife foolish. Why, you used to look for four-leaf clovers with me. You used to get down on your knees in the yard at mother's an' look an' *look*."

"Well, what if I did?" said Mr. Slater, reddening. "I wa'n't married then. It didn't seem so foolish then. You don't expect me to go on lookin' for four-leaf clovers the rest of my natural life, do you?"

He stood up tall and stiff in his working-clothes. He was a good-looking man. He had dark hair and a dark mustache. His eyes were gray. The back of his neck was straight and full. In his wife's eyes he was so handsome—so perfect physically—that she had always scented a possible rival in every woman she met. He was, in truth, the kind of man that is most admired by women—being at once attractive and indifferent.

The old ladies of the town had asserted with one mind that it was perfectly scandalous the way the girls had all run after him before his marriage. His own mother had laughed about it with poorly repressed triumph.

"Oh no," she would say, humorously, to her confidential friends, "I'm never lonesome. Women with sons never get lonesome, even if they are widows. Melinda Woolard, she brings her embroidery over regular, an' sets an' works buttercups an' wild roses till you can't rest. Mirandy White, she brings fine sewing, an' hems an' tucks an' ruffles all day. Sofia Kildall, she brings E. P. Roe's novels, an' reads out loud till I declare to goodness I want to go outdoors an' *shriek*. An' all Uriah ever says is: 'What on earth makes them fool girls run here so? Don't they suppose I know enough to ask 'em if I wanted 'em?' You just wait till he gets his eye on the right one, though," Uriah's mother would conclude, nodding her head knowingly, "an' then you'll see. He'll run after her fast enough. He'll run errands for her, an' carry flowers to her, an' take her around on two chips. His father acted just like that after me," she said, proudly. "I declare I couldn't express a wish but I got it." Then she sighed, and added, "Until we'd been married quite a spell, anyhow."

Uriah's mother's prophecy had been fulfilled. Uriah had fallen in love with Orilla Baldy, and never did lover sue more humbly and untiringly than he. He bought a new horse and "buggy," and took her driving every Sunday afternoon. Three times a week, no matter how tired he might be, he shaved and dressed up in his best suit, and walked boldly past all the neighbors with his chin up to spend the evening with Orilla in her little parlor furnished with red plush. He always had candy in his pocket; and frequently he carried a big bouquet of honeysuckles or ragged-robins openly where the whole world might see if it desired. Isaphene Snodgrass, who had cultivated his mother more assiduously than any of the others, always did see.

Orilla was a happy girl in those courtship days—happy in her shy enchanting way. To be courted in so devoted a fashion by the most desirable young man in the whole county was surely bliss enough; but added to this was the satisfaction that every girl of her acquaintance had tried to win him and had been scorned. Her nature was so sweet that the triumph she felt was a very gentle and almost deprecatory one. Still, it was a triumph.

It was long before she would consent, however, to an early marriage. Pleadings and persuasions were of no avail. Perhaps Orilla was a wise young woman when she voluntarily prolonged her much-envied courtship. But one evening in August, after an hour of more urgent pleading than usual, Mr. Uriah Slater suddenly arose from the red plush sofa and went looking around for his hat.

"Well, all is," he said, calmly and distinctly, "I'm all ready to get married. The house is all ready to furnish up, an' I've got money to do it. It suits me to get married in September. If you had any good reason not to, it 'ud be different. But you ain't. I don't propose to dangle an' dangle after you if you don't want to marry me. If you don't, just say so right out. If you do, it'll have to be in September."

Terrified at the thought of losing him, Orilla fled like a dove to his breast. She sobbed out that he was unkind, cruel... to speak to her so sternly... She had meant all the time to be married in September.

"Then why didn't you say so?" said Mr. Uriah Slater. And how could a maiden reply to such a question?

Mr. Slater put his hat down again upon a chair, and the wedding was all planned and the day named before he went home. Orilla's mother was consulted, and gave her consent without hesitation. There never had been any coyness concerning the matter on her part. When Uriah had first revealed his admiration of Orilla, Mrs. Baldy had confided proudly to her sister that she wouldn't confess it to another living soul, but that she meant to help things along all she could without giving rise to talk, for she did know a good match when she saw it.

The next time Uriah came he brought a ring—a flat circle of gold set with a very pretty amethyst. If ever an innocent heart thrilled with perfect happiness, Orilla's did then. They had been engaged all summer, yet not a word had been said concerning a ring. She had seen her mother glance at her hand every evening after he had gone home. She had seen every girl in town glance at her hand time and again. Once Isaphene Snodgrass had cried out, right in company: "Where's your ring? You don't seem to be getting a ring very fast," and all the other girls had laughed. It had rankled. Orilla hated herself for caring about a ring, but she did care. It had even caused her mother humiliation. Her sister, with the characteristic frankness of blood relations—and relations by marriage—had openly suspected that he must be a little "close." Mrs. Baldy had a qualm whenever she remembered the ring that did not come.

When it did make its shining appearance she could have embraced Uriah Slater. "It must of cost a lot of money," she said next day.

"It's so beautiful," said dear Orilla, holding it to her lips, "that I don't mind having waited so long," and she was always forgetting her gloves.

The second indication that Uriah gave of stubbornness in his disposition was on the wedding-day—of all days on earth!

Two days before, Mrs. Baldy's sister had come hurrying over, breathless, "right out of the middle of a cake!"

"I thought I'd come right over an' tell you," she said. "Mis' Snodgrass was in, a-talking, an' she says she bets he hires the canopy-top. She says he only hired one kerriage, outside o' the mourners an' pall-bearers, at his father's fun'ral. She says his mother besought him an' besought him. She finally told Mis' Snodgrass that the more you besought him the stubborner he got. I thought I'd come right over an' tell you."

That same evening Mrs. Baldy said, clearing her throat carelessly: "Oh, be sure they don't send you the canopy-top, Uriah. It might rain, an' Orilla would get her white dress ruined. It don't look nice, either, a-bobbing from side to side like a cork. The closed kerriage is the one for weddings."

Uriah looked at her, and looked away again. "You got your cake all made, Orilla?" he said.

When the canopy-top came to the door on the wedding-day Mrs. Baldy was speechless for a moment. Then she cried out: "Why, Uriah Slater! Look-a-here what they've sent!"

"I know," said Uriah, unmoved. "I told 'em to. It's the one I wanted, an' it ain't going to rain." Then he turned and looked her full in the face. "It's a dollar cheaper," he said.

Mrs. Baldy choked, and Orilla felt tears of humiliation coming to her eyes.

But if Mr. Slater had given but few indications of stubbornness before marriage, he made handsome amends by giving what his mother-in-law would have called "a plenty" of them during the six months that followed. Devotedly as she loved him, Orilla trembled at the change which the hey-presto of a marriage ceremony had wrought in him. The adorer had become the adored, the beseecher the besought. His tender attentions ceased as if by magic. He settled down at once to the occupation of his lifetime, which had necessarily been interrupted during his courtship—that of making Mr. Uriah Slater comfortable.

His meals were to be on time. The dishes he specially favored were to be cooked. Expenses were to be kept down. His chair and his slippers were to be in their assigned places when he came home.

Orilla obeyed all his wishes as joyfully as a bird. It was her happiness to make him comfortable, to wait upon him, and humor his whims. But before his plain, calm, seemingly premeditated obstinacy she was helpless.

If she desired Mocha coffee, he bought Java; if uncolored tea, he bought green; if white Castile soap, he bought mottled.

"Oh, Uriah," she cried, one day, "what made you buy mottled? I told you white."

"Mottled's best," he replied, briefly.

"But, Uriah, not for flannels. I wanted it to wash flannels with."

"Mottled's the best," said Uriah, calmly. "It lathers more."

On another occasion she asked him to buy a gingham dress for her. "Get pink, Uriah," she said, clasping her hands over his arms and laying her soft cheek against his shoulder. "Pink looks nice on me."

"You've got one pink one already," he replied, staring straight ahead of him.

"I'd like another, Uriah. I'd rather have that than anything else. It looks better on me than any other color."

"Pink ain't the only color on earth. I don't see any use in havin' 'em all pink. I see a yellow gingham in at Slattery's—"

"Oh, Uriah, I can't wear yellow. I could wear pale blue or

green, if you don't like pink—but I'd rather have pink myself. But I *can't* wear yellow—an' I *won't*," she ended, laughing merrily up into his face and kissing him.

That settled it. Uriah brought home a gingham of a fierce orange-color, with a black stripe cleaving its awfulness.

And so, gradually, the tremble came to Orilla's heart. It was the spring coming on, she told herself sternly, when a little faintness seized her after a "difference of opinion," as she came to call it, with Uriah. It was silly of her to care because Uriah did not always think as she did. How could she have expected that? Did he not love her? What if he never did kiss her now unless she put up her lips first, thereby reminding him? Had he not chosen her boldly and ardently, from among all the girls in town? Was not that sufficient bliss for any woman, without moping around hysterically because he forgot to kiss her when he went to work, or preferred orange gingham to pink?

One evening at the supper table, after a brief estrangement, she stretched out a gentle hand and laid it on his in reconciliation. "Do you love me, Uriah?" she whispered, her tender eyes full of repentant tears—repentant because he had abused her and she had timidly resented it! "Oh, of course," he replied, impatiently, with his mouth full, not looking at her. "Pass the butter—can't you?"

Orilla learned so rapidly in those days that she was able to pass from the primer of marriage into the fifth reader, skipping the first, second, third, and fourth.

But on that first day of March a thrill of the old happiness was in her heart. Those pulses are sluggish indeed that cannot be quickened by the velvet-voiced bugle of the chinook wind when it goes singing and calling over hill and sea.

"Well, never mind, Uriah," she said, good-naturedly; "I'll find four-leaf clovers for both of us. I don't mind being foolish in such a nice way. And, besides"—she leaned her cheek against his shoulder and looked roguishly up into his face—"you like foolish people, Uriah, don't you?"

"Unh—hunh!" said Uriah, smiling in spite of himself.

"Then it's all settled. Oh, Uriah, the ground is soft now, and we must have the well dug. It's just the time."

Uriah's face clouded over again. "Orilla, you do beat all! I ain't hear anything but well—*well*—all winter. Don't you s'pose I know enough to get the well dug when I'm ready? You keep at me the whole during time. It gets to be awful monotonous."

Tears stung their way up into Orilla's eyes.

"You don't know how unhandy it is to get water from the spring, Uriah. You're real good to carry it twice a day, but I have to carry it a dozen times, or do without. Sometimes when I go out all het up so, I'm afraid I'll get pneumony of the lungs."

"My soul! you do take duck-fits about nothing," said Uriah. "I've had a man engaged for a week to dig that well. He's coming to-morrow. Just as if I didn't know when's the time to dig a well! Keep at me the whole during time!"

"Don't be cross, Uriah. You don't know how unhandy it is to get along without a well. Come out in the yard," she added, timidly, "and I'll show you right where I want it."

Uriah bristled up and reddened. "It's going to be right alongside of the front gate," he said.

Orilla burst out laughing merrily. It wasn't a very funny joke, she thought, but if Uriah wished to be humorous, even in a poor way, she would try to appreciate his humor.

Uriah looked at her. His face grew redder. The back of his neck flamed suddenly up to his hair. "I don't see anything funny."

"How, Uriah?"

"I say I don't see anything funny. What makes you laugh so?"

"Why, just at the idea of a well alongside the front gate!"

"What is there so terrible funny in that?" hissed out Uriah.

"That's the place for it, and that's where it's going to be."

Orilla looked up at him in a quick, startled way. Her face paled. "You're not in earnest? Uriah Slater, you say you're not in earnest!"

"I never was more in earnest in my life. That well is going to be dug right alongside of the front gate, or it ain't going to be dug at all."

There was a silence. The kettle steamed vigorously on the stove, its lid lifting and falling musically. Orilla stood looking out the window with wide eyes. Her face was like marble, save where two round crimson spots burned in her cheeks. Presently she turned and fronted her husband.

"Uriah," she said, "I don't want a well by the front gate." Her voice was calm and gentle. Her eyes looked steadily and dauntlessly into his. "I thought you were only in fun. I never thought you could be in earnest. I do the house-work and the washing, and I want the well where it'll be handiest for me." She put her hand pleadingly on his arm. "Come out in the yard with me, Uriah, an' I'll show you right where I want it. You can't help seeing it's just the place for it."

He shook her off fiercely.

"I'm going to work," he growled, looking at the clock. "I ain't got time for any more foolishness."

"It ain't foolishness, Uriah. I want it settled where the well is to be—"

"It's all settled. Didn't I tell you it was? Didn't I—"

"That don't settle it, Uriah. I'm your wife, and I've got a right to say—"

He strode to the door and went out, slamming it behind him. She ran after him, and stood on the porch as he went down the steps. The red spots burned deeper in her cheeks. The wind blew her dress in light folds about her, and lifted the lovelocks from her brow and neck. There was a kind of terror in her eyes.

"Uriah," she called out, "I don't want a well alongside of my front gate, and I won't have it there! Look-a-here, Uriah—"

He went right on without turning, as fast as he could go. He walked stiffly, holding his head high and the back of his neck straight and full.

"Uriah Slater!" she called once more. "You look-a-here!"

But he went on, and did not look or turn.

...

When Uriah came home that evening Orilla received him as if no unpleasantness had occurred. "Oh!" she said, kindly, when he came in; "you, is it?" And she went to him and kissed his unresponsive mouth.

The supper was better than usual, and it was always good. There was a deliciously broiled steak, covered with mushrooms, which Orilla had gathered in the fields. They were stewed and thickened and browned, then poured over the steak in its simple blue platter. The potatoes had been steamed, and shredded through a colander, and were drifted round and round in large snowy flakes in an oval plate. There was a dish of tomatoes, and there were light golden biscuits that would fall apart when touched into crisp delicate halves. A bread pudding was browning slowly on the oven grate, and would presently make its appearance with little cones of velvety hard sauce upon it, the whole lightly dusted with nutmeg. But most tempting of all, perhaps, was the glass dish of perfectly brandied peaches, which this small scheming lady had taken from her hoarded store and set close to Uriah's plate. But her gentle designs were fruitless. Uriah ate heartily, but he did not talk. Orilla chatted pleasantly, not resenting his silence. Occasionally, however, she gave him a brief frightened look. Once or twice, remembering a resolution she had made that day after deep and careful thought, she shivered suddenly and helplessly.

In the morning, as they arose from the breakfast table, some one came to the door. Uriah opened it. "Oh!" he said; "you come to dig the well, did you? I'll come right out an' show you where."

He went into another room to get his hat. Orilla pushed the door shut, and stood against it. As he came back she faced him, gray and stony as death.

"Uriah," she said, gently. She put her arms up—they were shaking—around his neck. "You'll put the well where I want it, won't you? If you love me, Uriah, say yes."

Uriah's face grew purple. "Lemme by!" he hissed. "I'll put it right where I said I would!"

"Uriah"—her lips were shaking too now, and her voice was nothing like her own—"I beg you, I beseech you, to give up to me in this. I've been giving up to you ever since we got married. You give up to me this time—"

"Lemme by!" said Uriah.

"You give up to me this time, Uriah. If you don't—"

"Lemme by!"

"If you don't—" She shuddered hard. Her lips went on moving, but no sound came from them. Her arms fell down at her sides. Uriah pushed her aside and went out. She stood where he had left her. Her white lips still moved, and still no sound came from them.

When Uriah came home that evening the well was partly dug beside the front gate. He grinned, and went into the house. It was cool and dark. On the table was a letter, which read:

> "DEAR URIAH, I've gone home. I can't ever live with you again. It'll break my heart. I'll love you just the same till the last day of my life. But I can't ever live with you again. ORILLA."

"Talk's cheap," grinned Uriah. "I'll give her three days. The well 'll be giving water by that time."

But days passed, and Orilla did not return. At first Uriah was amused; then he became angry; then furious; finally his anger gave place to terror. The well was finished, but not a drop of water had he drawn from it. He could not pass it without a shudder.

It was a full month before he could make up his mind to go after Orilla and bring her home. When he did go, it was without a misgiving.

Orilla was alone. It was a soft April evening. The doors and the windows were open, but there was a fire in the big fireplace. Before it Orilla sat in a low chair. Her hands lay listlessly in her lap. She did not see Uriah until he was in the room.

"Oh, Uriah," she said, "is it you?" She arose politely and drew a chair to the fire. "Mother's at prayer-meeting. You sit down."

"I didn't come to see your mother." He stood awkwardly before her. "I come to see you, Orilla. Oh, Orilla"—his voice shook, as in the old days when he had been the humble wooer—"I've come to ask you to forgive me, an'—an'—take you home!"

"Oh, I forgive you," said Orilla. She had a white, tired look. "But I can't ever go back."

It had never occurred to him that she would refuse. "She just wants to make me knuckle-down," he had thought, judging her by his own small soul. "She wants to scare me into it."

But now a sudden terror clutched his heart. He pleaded earnestly and desperately. "Orilla, I own up I was wrong. I'm stubborn. I was born stubborn. But you're the only woman I ever loved, an' I want you. *Dang* the well! You can have your own way. I'll fill it up with gravel! I'll dig one wherever you want it! I'll—I'll"—he hesitated, wondering, even in that critical moment, if any further concession was necessary; some-

thing in her face made him feel that it was, and he went on—
"*I'll put a pump in, too!*"

"No, Uriah," said Orilla, slowly. "I'll never go back. You needn't to say any more. I love you. I've suffered, and I'll keep on suffering. But I can stand this kind of suffering better'n I could stand a lifetime of being nagged at and hissed at and contraried every time you happened to feel stubborn. Six months of it's a plenty for me. You needn't to worry about me. I'll get along. It ain't the well. It's—it's—what it means when you look ahead to a whole lifetime of it... You needn't to say any more. You might as well talk to a stone wall. I ain't a woman to change, and I'll always love you. But I'll never live with you again. We can be just as good friends, though... You sit down, Uriah. The evening's coolish, ain't it?"

She took up the tongs with a firm hand and stirred the fire. The sparks went up the chimney in a scarlet stream.

"THE STUBBORNNESS OF URIAH SLATER" was published in *Harper's Bazaar* in 1899.

In "The Stubbornness of Uriah Slater," newlyweds Orilla and Uriah Slater begin their married life together in a small town on Puget Sound. Though Uriah had been an ardent suitor before they married, he now reveals himself as both obstinate and contrary. Uriah firmly adheres to his own judgment in all matters large and small, including details of housekeeping and other domestic issues. Whatever opinion Orilla expresses, Uriah deliberately chooses the opposite and refuses to discuss it. In "The Stubbornness of Uriah Slater," Higginson explores how the expectations of married life may differ from the reality of that life and how women and men adjust or fail to adjust to their new roles.

"M'liss's Child"
• 1905 •

"I just thought maybe you would," said Mrs. Herb, with a little scared catch in her voice at her own audacity. There was a dashed look across her eyes.

"You wasted just that much of your thoughts," said Mrs. Purple calmly. Her lips were set in a straight, uncompromising line. She sat stiff and erect in her chair, like a gaunt stone rising out of the sea. It was a rocking-chair, but there was no rock to it when she sat in it. She held that rocking was for women with no backbone to them; like Mrs. Herb, for instance, who was now rocking to and fro almost wildly.

"Seeing you was the deacon's wife," added Mrs. Herb, faintly.

"Seeing I'm the deacon's wife," returned Mrs. Purple firmly, "is precisely why I don't uphold sin."

She arose, and, drawing a strong linen handkerchief from her belt, made little flicks and dabs at some imaginary dust on the lamp. Then she lifted her voice.

"Maybelle! Oh, Maybelle!"

A young girl came into the room, and her mother's face softened at sight of her. She was just blooming into a beautiful womanhood. She was all soft curves and dimples. Her color was like a wild rose blending into cream. Her dark curls were tied together with a rose ribbon at the nape of her neck. Her eyes were large and softly dark, like a gazelle's.

"Did you call, mother?"

"Yes, I called. Mis' Herb's here. My land! don't you see her?"

Maybelle blushed. "How-do-you-do, Mrs. Herb?"

"How-do-you-do, Maybelle? My! You look as sweet as peaches and cream. They can't a one of 'em give you come-uppin's, can they?"

"I guess they can't," bragged Mrs. Purple, seating herself and folding her hands across her waist complacently. "They can't a one of 'em hold a candle to Maybelle, if I do say it myself," she added proudly.

"Oh, mother!"

Maybelle sat down and her eyelids fell over her eyes; her face burned crimson.

"Well, they can't! An' the best of it is"—Mrs. Purple turned to Mrs. Herb again—"she's as good as she is pretty. She ain't got a fault an' she never done a wrong thing in her life. Smell that mignonette?" she added, suddenly turning toward the open window. "Congressman Smith, he sent me the seed from Washington. Fine—my-*O!* You can smell it to the cow-butter store in the next block. He sent nasturtiums, an' sweet williams, an' sweet peas, an' sunflowers. He's awful clever. I never see his beat!" She turned from the window. The beam dwindled out of her eyes. "An' then, me with a girl like Maybelle an' a son like Herbert, you set there an' want I should uphold a girl that acts up the way that M'liss Dement does!"

Mrs. Herb put back her thin shoulders and drew herself up.

"She don't act up so now," she said apologetically.

"Well, she did once," Mrs. Purple said, drumming the table with her fingers. "I don't know what she does or what she don't do now. But I do know that I'll fight her comin' into the church, tooth an' toe nail. I never see the sense myself of livin' decent an' doin' decent—an' then havin' people that's cut up all kind of capers set up on a level with you… Well, will you look at there? Will you just look at there?"

She pointed with a bony finger out of the window. A young woman was coming down the street. She was tall and of splendid figure. A wealth of blond hair was twisted around her head. She carried herself with a proud and swinging stride. She wore a black dress, made with a long train. This she was holding up with both hands. Suddenly she observed the three faces in the window. Instantly her head went up. As she turned across the street, defiantly facing them, she flung her train to its full length with a grand flourish and swept across, the dust trailing in a great cloud behind her.

"It's that M'liss Dement!" announced Mrs. Purple, drawing in her breath. "The impudent heifer! Seems to me you said she wa'n't actin'-up any more. I'd like to know what you call that."

As the three women stood grouped close to the window, peering with narrowed eyes, the girl took another look at them. Her handsome brown eyes fairly blazed out a red fire. There was a water hydrant on the corner, and as she approached it she flung one foot with a flourish to the very top of it, and calmly tied her shoe in the faces of her scandalized observers. She tied it slowly, untied it, and tied it again, displaying a generous length of well-filled hose. Finally she pushed the ends of the laces down into her shoe, and, setting her foot upon the sidewalk with an audacious fling, she sailed on by, her train sweeping the dust behind her.

Mrs. Purple drew back from the window and sat down, drawing in her breath hard through close-set lips.

"Maybelle," she said sternly, "listen here. I don't ever want to hear tell of your so much as speakin' to that M'liss Dement again."

Maybelle did not reply. Her face was pale and scared-looking.

"You hear?" demanded her mother.

"Yes, ma'am."

"Well, see you mind. I don't care if she does live in the same block. I don't care if you did play with her all your life. Mis' Herb is goin' to stay to tea. You can be buildin' a fire 'n the kitchen stove. Stir up a warm sponge cake an' make some rhubarb-sauce. You like rhubarb sauce, don't you, Mis' Herb?" she added, with a polite afterthought. "An' then fry the chicken an' cream the potatoes—an' I guess you'd better step spry. Mis' Herb an' I are goin' to a mothers' meetin' after tea."

...

At eight o'clock that evening the mothers of the church were sitting solemnly around the sides of the church parlor. Mrs. Purple was the most important woman in the town, and she held herself with a great air. She sat erect. Her hands were folded in her lap; her chin was high and was set in determined folds. She was the only woman present in a silk dress and kid gloves. The handkerchief tucked in her belt was bordered with real lace, too.

When the last "mother" had entered and sunk hastily into her chair, there was an ominous silence. Invisible lightning seemed to be darting around the room, sending little shocks, half pleasant and half terrible, from one solemn-faced woman to another.

Presently, in a shadowy corner, Mrs. Eaton arose. Her face was pale and her voice shook as she began speaking.

"Sisters," said she, "we've met here to-night to talk over in a friendly spirit takin' M'liss Dement into the church. There's some of us for it an' some of us agen it. I'm for it myself. I think she's sorry for all she's done an' wants to do better. She thinks the church'll help her, an' I think the church had ought to help her."

She sat down and Mrs. Purple stood up.

"All is," she began in a deep voice, "I just want to know if the church is for God-fearin', decent people—or is it for riffraff?"

She sat down, breathing heavily. There was silence, save for much clearing of throats. It was almost like a bronchial epidemic. Then Mrs. Eaton spoke without rising.

"I think the church is for everybody that does right," she said, and her voice was steadier, "an' for everybody that wants to get started to doin' right."

"I don't agree with you," said Mrs. Purple in a cold way that had its effect. "I don't want to see any church I belong to desecrated with riffraff. If that M'liss Dement isn't riffraff, I don't know riffraff when I see it."

A new "mother" stood up. She had never spoken in meeting, and now at the sound of her own voice the blood rushed away from her face, her knees trembled, and she swayed to and fro like a lily in a storm.

"May I ask," she said, in a thin, piping voice, "what her particular sin was?"

She gave a final sway and sank limply into her chair.

The funny Mrs. Deacon Lark—of whom it was said that she would like as not laugh at her mother's funeral, she laughed so at nothing—tittered right out in meeting.

"I've heard tell of original sin," she spoke up, "but I never did hear tell of particular sin. Now I'm particular about my housework and my clothes, and so the next time I have a sin I'm going to have a particular sin. I'm not sure but I'll have an especial sin."

Several mothers smiled but one glance at Mrs. Purple's face froze the smiles on their lips.

"This is no picnic," she said sternly, and every hair on her chin seemed to stand out straight.

"No, it's more like a funeral!" tittered back the irrepressible Mrs. Lark. "But it isn't *my* funeral. 'Tis poor M'liss Dement's. When I have a funeral I'll have a particular one."

No one answered the new mother's question aloud, but her

nearest neighbor whispered to her and both women flushed scarlet.

Mrs. Eaton arose again. She held fast with both hands to the back of a chair, but there was more determination in her manner.

"Maybe some of you don't know," she said, "what a hard life M'liss Dement has had. So I'll tell you. She's never had any chance. Her mother was a good but coarse woman. She swore every other word she spoke. She swore just like a horse eats hay—without knowin' she did it. Nobody associated with her. M'liss's father is just a low, drunken bum. Since Mrs. Dement died an' M'liss has been growin' up, nobody has let their daughters or sons associate with her, although"—she looked full at Mrs. Purple—"they used to let 'em play with her when they was all little together. M'liss got to talkin' rough like her mother, an' after her mother died she took to bleachin' her hair an' paintin' her face, an' havin' young men sittin' on the steps with her late at night. Now it seems to me that us mothers neglected our duties there and then. We might have talked to her, an' been kind to her, an' argyfied her out of it, instead of settin' ourselves up on Liberty statues. Some of us hold our chins so high we just about think we're Lord A'mighty hisself."

Mrs. Purple's chin went an inch higher.

"Some of us have a right to hold our chins high," she announced in a deep bass. "People who live right an' do right ain't no call to duck their chins down in front."

"Holding your chin high gives you more than one chin," piped up Mrs. Lark.

Mrs. Purple gave her a look.

"You can rub your extra chins away, though," persisted Mrs. Lark, returning the look undaunted, "if you do this."

She made swift passes under her chin with the palm of her hand to the right and to the left.

"I remember," continued Mrs. Eaton, not noticing the interruption, "one night, a year or so ago, Mrs. Purple's son Herbert was standing at the gate talking to M'liss 'long about dusk, and, my land! Mrs. Purple come running out an' called him as if he was stealing. I think, says I, well, poor M'liss *has* to take up with the low-down because the decent ain't allowed to so much as pass the time o' day with her."

Mrs. Purple stood up and the very atmosphere seemed to tremble. "Them that have no young men sons," she said in her deepest voice, "can talk. Them that have young men sons like my young man son'll take care of 'em. Herbert never done a wrong act in his life. He never drank a drop, nor played a card, nor smoked a cigar, nor run around with onery girls. He's as near perfect as God makes 'em; an' I don't propose to have no M'liss Dement in the church, like a snake in the grass, pretendin' to repent-up her sins an' do better—just so's she'll get a chance at our sons! Herbert's away in college, studyin' to be a minister; but he's comin' home soon, an' while I ain't afraid of his noticin' M'liss Dement *now*, with all the disgrace she's piled on herself, still I don't want such persons in my church with a young man son around." Mrs. Purple was growing more excited; her face was a dull crimson and she was breathing heavily. "If M'liss Dement wants to come into this church, let her confess up. Let her tell us the name of the father of her child! That's what we want to know."

"Oh, my!" cried Mrs. Lark, throwing her hand over her face and peering through her fingers in a shocked way. "See me blush!"

Mrs. Eaton cleared her throat.

"Well, now," said she deliberately, "the finest thing I know about M'liss is just that—that she won't tell. There's something fine in a girl that takes a thing like that all on herself, and won't tell on the man."

"I'd like to give the man a skimmity-ride!" cried Mrs. Lark. "I'd go along and whip the donkey to make it go on a trot."

"No girl ever went through such disgrace as M'liss has been through," went on Mrs. Eaton. "All we could find out was that she had a child. We couldn't get a word out of her. She cried day and night, till some of us felt sorry for her and turned over every stun to get her to tell who the man was. We told her we'd make him marry her, an' then we'd overlook it—"

"I'll tell you what!" cried Mrs. Lark. "Let's appoint a committee of three to go and ask her once more. We'll give her one more chance. It'll work just like heads an' tails. If she tells, she's in, if she won't tell, she's out. I'll suggest Mrs. Purple and Mrs. Eaton and"—she spread her hand modestly over her heart—"*me*. We'll be a committee to make fur fly."

There was a general murmur of approval, and a stirring of relief among the mothers. "I'm willing," said Mrs. Eaton.

There was quite a silence. Then Mrs. Purple said: "Well, I'm willing, too. But first I feel it my duty to tell you all that I see M'liss Dement do a sinful thing this very day. Mis' Herb, she see it, too, with her own eyes, an' my innocent Maybelle, as chaste as the snow, she see it, too. It proves that M'liss Dement ain't repented-up very fast."

"What did you see her do?" cried the new mother, unable to restrain her emotions longer.

"I see her kick clear over the hydrant on the corner by my house!"

There was another silence—a longer one. Then Mrs. Lark burst into a wild peal of laughter.

"I'd like to see her do it! I'm a high kicker myself. I can kick the electric-light bulb in our sitting room every time I try. I kicked a stick of wood off the deacon's shoulder one day. I slipped and fell and hit my head on the door knob. It took three doctors to bring me to—"

"It's all settled then," said Mrs. Purple, firmly interrupting.

"You ladies can call at my house at two to-morrow afternoon. But I'll say right here an' now, that when that M'liss Dement comes into this church, I an' my pocketbook go out."

At that the face of the minister's wife, who had taken no part in the discussion, grew long.

Mrs. Lark looked back over her shoulder at Mrs. Purple. "You'd ought to be a railroad company!" she said flippantly. "My, oh, *me!* I like human nature! I tell you, I could have human nature for breakfast, dinner, and supper, and never get enough of it."

...

M'liss Dement lived in a little four-room house in an old orchard. There was a general air of neglect and shiftlessness about the whole place. The paint was all peeling off the house, showing different colors underneath. The fence was so rotten that it seemed to go around the orchard in undulations. The leaves of the trees were curled tightly and eaten by aphides. The grass had never been cut. It grew tall and rank on both sides of the narrow, crooked path leading to the front door.

"I expect it'll take all of us to get this gate open," complained Mrs. Purple. "It sags so."

"The hinge is broken in two," said Mrs. Lark, who was unusually quiet.

"I never saw a place go all to rack so," said Mrs. Purple.

"Well, what can you expect?" asked Mrs. Eaton. "M'liss can't keep it up. Her father's drunk all the time, an' she can't hire it done. I guess she has enough to do without fixin' hinges."

"Humph!" said Mrs. Purple. After a moment she added: "I'd think she could fix a hinge on a gate."

"Well, maybe she could, if she don't have too much else to do. Maybe she don't have the heart to fix up things. I've noticed that when folks get down an' other folks stand all over 'em with both feet to keep 'em down, they ain't got much heart to slave an' fix up things. I've noticed—"

She stopped abruptly. The three women stood still. They had turned a bend in the path, and there under an old apple tree sat M'liss, deep in the grass. She wore a gingham dress, open at the neck. Her blond hair had been recently washed and shone like gold in the sun. In her arms was a child about a year old. He was trying to catch the tossing locks of her hair, and shrieked with delight when he succeeded.

Mrs. Purple could scarcely breathe for amazement.

The look of love and tenderness on the girl's face was a revelation. The child reached up and patted her cheek; she stooped quickly and burst into tears as she pressed him to her and kissed him passionately.

The next moment, straight through her tears, she saw the three women.

She stood up slowly. The child saw them and toddled to them through the tangled grass. They saw that he was very beautiful. He had large dark eyes and dark curls. He looked sweet and well cared for. He was making straight for Mrs. Purple, clutching a dandelion in his hand.

M'liss stood like a statue; her arms hung down at her sides. Her face had grown very white, but her eyes were steady.

"What do you want?" she asked, looking straight at Mrs. Purple. But for once Mrs. Purple did not reply. Mrs. Eaton took two or three steps forward.

"Why, M'liss—" she began kindly, but the girl lifted her hand impatiently.

"I asked Mrs. Purple what she wants here, and she's got to answer or go."

The child began pulling at Mrs. Purple's dress, offering her the flower. "Dan'yine—dan'yine," he kept saying, but she paid no attention.

"Well, M'liss Dement," she said slowly and sternly, "we're a committee of mothers come to ask you once more to tell who's the father of your child."

A scarlet stain went across the girl's face, as though it had followed the blow of a hand. The tears seemed to still stand, frozen in her eyes.

"What's that to you?" she demanded defiantly. "I'm its mother. I've never denied it. I've never hid it or cast it off on somebody else. I take good care of it, and own it right out to the whole world. What's it to you who its father is?"

"You've been wantin' to come into the church," said Mrs. Purple in a cold way. "We had a mothers' meetin' about it. I'm agen takin' you in unless you tell who its father is. That's what it is to us. You tell, an' maybe we'll take you in; you don't tell, an' you can stay out."

There was a long silence; then the girl spoke slowly but passionately.

"Lord God Almighty," she said, and it didn't sound like an oath, even to Mrs. Purple; it sounded more like a prayer. "If the church is made up of people like this, I'll stay out. Now, you listen here. I've got some things to say, and then you can go; and if you ever come here again on such an errand I'll turn the dog loose. Now listen here. You all know just how much chance I've had alongside of other girls. You let your daughters play with me while we were little, but as we grew up you weaned them away from me, one by one, and I felt more and more alone. After my mother died I got desperate—here alone day after day, father drunk. I went to acting wild and impudent, as if I didn't care"—she burst out suddenly into a kind of terrible laughter—"flinging my foot up on top of hydrants and that kind of thing, just to dar' you and tantalize you and egg you on, but"—her face grew as suddenly serious—"it never did me any good. I was always ashamed and sorry; but I couldn't come to you and say I was sorry, like other girls can. You'd only have sneered at me and asked me where I got my baby at and who its father was. So all I could do, after I showed up smart-Ellic like, was to come home and go to bed and hold the baby in my arms and cry all night—and envy my poor mother up there on the hill. You *good* women"—her tone was fierce with bitter scorn—"you never think that girls like me have any feelings or any remorse. You think we go to the bad with our eyes open, knowing what we're going into and not caring. You don't know how easy it is to go in, step by step, never realizing till it's too late. We don't have love and tenderness, like—well, like Maybelle, say"—her voice broke—"and when some man, that oughtn't to, speaks kind and gentle to us and acts as if he cared for us, we're so starved for that kind of thing that it just seems like heaven, and then the next thing we know it's too late. We're bad, without ever meaning to be bad, and you good women, you set your feet on us and you won't ever give us another chance to get up and be somebody again."

There was a silence; then Mrs. Purple said, in a tone that surprised even herself: "We're givin' you a chance now."

"Yes," said M'liss, wearily, "but what kind of a chance? You come here and act as if you was handling a boa constrictor with a pair of tongs. You make me feel like a devil in the bottomless pit, instead of a human being with a soul that might be saved by kindness. If my mother was alive, or even if my father was ever sober, I might stand it; but for a year it's been—well, it's been"—a cold perspiration started out on her face and she wiped it off with her sleeve—"just hell. Just that. Awake or asleep, day or night, just that. For a year I ain't thought of a thing except what to do for the child, and how to bear the shame. Night after night I've prayed to God to make me kind and gentle, and then the minute I'd see anybody look at me

"M'liss's Child"

cold and sneery, and draw their skirts up when they passed me, that minute I'd fly all to pieces and seem to go crazy. I'd fling up my head and go strutting, and maybe I'd burst out whistling 'Yankee Doodle' right in their faces. That day I saw you all peering out the window"—she looked at Mrs. Purple—"I'd have gone shrieking crazy if I couldn't have flung my foot to the top of that hydrant to shock you. It eased up my nerves. But I came home and cried myself sick. Father happened to be sober when I come in, and he said: 'Daught, I've bought some lylocks to take out to your mother's grave.' That finished me."... The child had found Mrs. Purple's hand and locked his chubby fingers around one of hers ... "Hunh! Tch, tch," she muttered, looking down at him grimly. He crowed with delight and good fellowship.

"But with all I was so wild and lawless," went on M'liss steadily, "I never done any real wrong but once. I never led any young man into wrong, and he didn't lead me into wrong. Thank God, I've never fell low enough, in all I've suffered for it, to blame him. He didn't mean to do wrong any more 'an I did."

"Then why don't he marry you?" asked Mrs. Purple, breathing deeply but silently.

A dull red went across the girl's face.

"Yes, why?" she said bitterly. "Because he belongs to a good family—a family with no drunkards or coarse oaths in it; with daughters that don't paint and bleach their hair, and fling their feet to the tops of water hydrants."

"You could stop all that," spoke up, for the first time, the strangely subdued Mrs. Lark.

"Yes," said M'liss, giving her a brief look, "but his family'd throw it in my teeth to the last day of my life. I guess I know."

There was a silence. No one contradicted her.

Suddenly she burst out wildly: "Oh, you *good* women! If you have any feelings I wonder where you keep 'em! Can't you put yourself in my place? Can't you see how terrible sweet sin can look before you get into it? And how awful afterward? Can't you guess what it is to go along the street and have people you've known all your life look the other way, or else stare you in the face so cold and hard that you nearly go mad with despair? To see men grin, or women run and peer out the windows at you with shocked faces? To have little children draw away and stare curiously at you, whispering among themselves, knowing you're different from other women? Can't you guess any of these things—and have more pity?"

She was sobbing now convulsively. Mrs. Eaton was weeping in sympathy, and there were tears in Mrs. Lark's eyes. As for Mrs. Purple—Mrs. Lark declared afterward that she "just stood there lookin' every which way for Sunday." But even Mrs. Eaton dared not approach the girl with any offer of tenderness; there was something lone and terrible in her grief that forbade it.

She controlled herself as suddenly as she had given way.

"It seemed as if I just couldn't go on like this any longer, as if there'd got to be a change one way or the other. In spite of all you think about me, I'm not naturally bad, and I just couldn't go down lower. I wanted to get a start the other way, for my own sake and the child's. So I thought if I'd join the church, you'd believe in me and help me up, and maybe learn to respect me by the time the child grows up. And what is the first thing the church does? It turns around and asks me to do the lowest thing I could do, before it'll take me in. As if it wasn't enough for my life to be ruined, without ruining the life of a young man, too!"

Mrs. Purple's face flushed darkly.

"It's not for the likes of you to criticise the church," she said sternly. "I guess, when all's said and done, the young man don't belong to such a terrible fine family. Terrible fine families don't raise sons that get girls into trouble and then desert 'em. They—"

M'liss put up her hand with a compelling gesture.

"I told you once he didn't get me into trouble. He wasn't to blame. And what's more, if it'll ease you any, seeing you're bursting with curiosity, I'll tell you this much: he doesn't know there is a child."

"My Lord!" said Mrs. Lark. Then there was a silence.

It was broken by M'liss.

"Now, I've told you everything there is to tell about myself. But I want to tell *you*"—she looked full into Mrs. Purple's eyes—"that, bad as I am, outcast that I am, I wouldn't change places with *you*, riding around in your carriage, holding your chin up and lording it over all creation! I'm glad you've come here. It's going to help me bear my life. It makes me see things different. I wouldn't swap my chance of heaven, church, or no church, for *yours!* I never harmed anybody but myself. Till this minute, I never judged anybody but myself. I never belonged to a church and then slandered that church by asking people to do lower, meaner things to get into it than they'd ever done in all their lives before. Having one woman like you in a church hurts the church more'n all your old pocketbook helps it. You needn't have me up in your mothers' meetings again—tearing me to pieces! I wouldn't *be* in your old church while you're in it! So there! You can put that in your old sanctimonious pipe and smoke it."

She caught the child up in her arms and went sweeping away, with the air of an outraged queen, through the long grass to the house.

...

It was a pleasant afternoon a month later. Mrs. Herb had run in to see Mrs. Purple. The two ladies were in the sitting room, darkened to keep the heat and the flies out. Mrs. Purple was working at Battenburg lace for a sideboard cover. She held it close to her face, wrinkling up her eyes as she worked.

"I don't see what keeps Maybelle so," she said. "She's taken to slyin' off in the orchard with a book every day lately. If I always had my drethers, though, I drether she'd spend her time that way than runnin' around. Some girls traipse so. She's a perfectly avaricious reader. Some girls are common an' associate with everybody. Maybelle's exclusive."

"She's certainly the nicest girl I know," said Mrs. Herb cordially. "Is the bishop comin' to dinner to-night?"

"Oh, yes," said Mrs. Purple loftily. "He always comes to our house to dinner. Congressman Smith, he comes, too, when he's in town. If he don't go nowhere else, Mr. Purple, he always brings him here."

Mrs. Herb wiped her glasses.

"I declare, my eyes are gettin' sore! There's a new eye oculist in town. I'm goin' to see him."

"I want to know," said Mrs. Purple, polite but uninterested. "Oh, here's Maybelle. W'y, you look as peakid! Where you been?"

Maybelle was indeed pale.

"Out in the orchard," she said faintly. She laid a book on the table and turned away.

"You shouldn't read so. Your eyes are all swelled up. You look as if you'd been cryin'. Is the dining room all red up?"

"Yes, ma'am."

"Well, then, you can make a tapiocy puddin'. Get the colloflower an' the sparrow-grass ready to put on. Your pa'll have a duck-fit if dinner ain't on time when the bishop's here."

"He's just that way, too," smiled Mrs. Herb. "I guess they all are, when it comes to that. He tews if breakfast's a minute late."

"That's the way. Oh, Maybelle! I had a letter from Herbert. He'll be home to-night or to-morrow mornin'. Is his room ready?"

"Yes, ma'am."

Maybelle's eyes burned a long searching look out of her pale face at her mother. Then she went out of the room.

Mrs. Herb was tatting. She fidgeted about in her chair. Twice she cleared her throat to speak, but each time her courage failed. She sat making swift, regular jabs into her left hand with her shuttle.

Suddenly she spoke; her voice seemed to leap right out of the middle of her throat.

"I suppose you know about M'liss?"

Mrs. Purple spoiled a stitch. Her brows drew into a scowl. "What about her?" she asked in a cold way.

"W'y, she's awful sick."

"Hunh."

"She's been sick a week."

"Hunh."

"They don't think now she'll live."

Mrs. Purple spoiled another stitch.

"Mis' Eaton goes in every forenoon, an' I go in every evenin'; an' her father's sobered up an' stays right with her. It's turned out to be appendiktis."

"Hunh."

"It's pitiful to see her. She will have the baby right on the bed, an' holds his hand against her lips all the time. The little fellow just worships her, an' won't be satisfied a minute away from her except to eat. She know's she's goin' to die, an' she just moans to God day an' night, to know what'll become of her baby."

Mrs. Herb knew she was on a dangerous subject. Since the committee of mothers had called on M'liss, no one had dared to mention her name to Mrs. Purple; so what her thoughts were on the subject no one knew.

She held her chin higher than ever, and swept into church with the haughty pride of a duchess, to sit with stiff, level shoulders through the sermon. She never sagged down to one side or the other like the frivolous Mrs. Lark, who was constantly resting her cheek on her hand. She was always a deacon's wife, the entertainer of Congressman Smith, and the first lady of the town.

She was the chief patroness of the Children's Home, the Normal School, the Library, the Hospital, and the Asylum for the Blind.

Mrs. Herb took heart from the silence. "I never was so sorry for anybody. 'What'll become of my boy?' she wails over an' over; she's getting fainter now. 'I don't care what becomes of me; but what'll become of my boy?' You know how a voice sounds when it gets death in it? Well, I can hear her all night long, moanin', 'What'll become of my boy?' If I didn't have so many children I'd take him myself."

"Nice stock," said Mrs. Purple sternly. Her face had a gray look.

"Well, it's bad on her side, but I guess the father must be of good fambly. I never saw a finer boy. Handsome—my-*O!* An' sweet disposition. Mis' Eaton has children an' a sick mother on her hands, or she'd take him."

Mrs. Herb was so frightened now at her own audacity that the shuttle was fairly flying under and over the thread.

"I hope Maybelle gets a good 'do', on that puddin'," said Mrs. Purple calmly. "If it's bad her pa'll be able to step on his own chin."

"Is that so? That fly-away Mis' Lark would of took him in a minute; but Lark, he set that big foot of his down. Mule!"

"Herbert graduated at the head of his class," announced Mrs. Purple. She never bent her proud and stubborn old head over her work. When she could not see, she held the work higher. She lifted it higher now.

"They're makin' a terrible fuss over him. The head professor, he says Herbert'll make his mark in the world. They talk about my holdin' my chin so high. I've good call to, I guess. Children like my children don't grow on trees, so's you can walk along an' pick 'em off. They come from generations of right-livin' people. There's never been any disgrace in my family—clear back."

"Tap wood," said Mrs. Herb briefly.

"Aigh?"

"Tap wood."

"What say?"

"I say *tap wood*. W'y, when you brag, if you don't tap wood, it'll happen the other way. Some of your folks 'u'd turn right around an' disgrace you. You'd best tap wood."

"I'm no dumb loon," said Mrs. Purple. "I don't have to tap wood to keep my folks from disgracin' me. I ain't afraid."

"Well," said Mrs. Herb, sighing, "I reckon I'm a dumb loon. I tap wood every time I brag. An' if I held my chin as high as you hold your'n, I don't know but I'd carry a stick o' wood around with me an' beat a regular tattoo on it all the time. As I was sayin', M'liss can't bear to think o' the Children's Home. She just moans to God for some good Christian fambly to take him an' bring him up right."

"Hunh."

"Well, I'll have to be goin'. I've set quite a spell. I've felt to enjoy it."

"I've felt to enjoy havin' you," said Mrs. Purple, rising with cold and formal politeness. "You must run in again."

"I will so."

When Mrs. Herb was gone, Mrs. Purple stood for some time looking out the window with unseeing eyes.

She had laid down her Battenberg lace and stood with one hand resting heavily on a chair; with the other she slowly stroked her chin.

"I don't know what it is to me, anyhow," she said at last, drawing a deep breath. "I can't waste my time on a trollop like her."

All at once she seemed to feel the clasp of a soft baby hand around her fingers. She looked down at her hand in a startled way.

"He was awful sweet," she said reluctantly. "An' he's the only child that ever did come to me, as if he'd took a notion to me." Then her face hardened. "There's no call for me to think about it," she said, going toward the kitchen. "I've got dinners to get for bishops."

...

At nine o'clock that night Mrs. Purple sat in the seldom-used parlor, awaiting her son. Mr. Purple had gone to meeting with the bishop. She sat in state, the lights turned low, her hands folded in her lap. Maybelle had gone down to the gate to meet her brother.

It seemed a long time after the train whistled before Mrs. Purple heard them coming. When she finally heard them in the hall, it seemed strange that they were not talking. Then she heard her son's step coming alone to her door. It was slow and dragging, and before the door opened she knew that something was wrong.

She leaned rigidly forward in her chair, grasping its arms with both stiff hands, but unconsciously holding her head as high as ever.

At sight of his face something seemed to clutch her heart. A grayness flashed over her face, making her look years older. It brought out every wrinkle in the dim light. She tried to get up, but something held her to her chair.

"Herbert!" she gasped out. "Oh, my son, my son! What is it? What's happened?"

She had expected to have him come home so proud and handsome; his head up, with a springing step and the exultant look of success. She had pictured him over and over in her mind.

But here he was staggering across the room to her, his face wild and convulsed with suffering, a cry of horror bursting from him. He flung himself upon his knees—he, her pride, her joy, the light of her hard old heart!—and buried his face in her lap.

"Oh, mother, mother, mother! What shall I do? What *can* I do? To come home to you like this! In such shame, such disgrace, such agony! And I never knew—I never knew!"

"What are you talkin' about, Herbert Purple? Answer up. Who dar's to mention shame and disgrace in the same breath with a Purple? If it's debts, I'll pay 'em, if your father won't. If it's college pranks—"

"Oh, God help me! It's a debt that can never be paid. To think what she must have suffered for nearly two years—and never a word from her! Maybelle knew it all the time; she made Maybelle promise she'd never tell. She wouldn't have told me now if there was any hope. But it's too late, too late!" he burst out wildly. "While I was graduating and having honors heaped on me, she was lying there, dying, disgraced, dishonored."

"Herbert Purple!" cried out his mother, and as long as he lived he never forgot her voice; he felt her rising up from her chair powerfully, as if by no will of her own; a violent trembling had seized her. It seemed as if her words shook against her teeth. "Who are you talkin' about? If you mention Maybelle an' shame in the same breath—"

"Oh, mother! As long as Maybelle lives, as long as you live, we will never any of us get away from shame again—and all through me! Oh, how can I bear it? How can we all bear it? Wretch that I am, to even think of myself while poor M'liss—"

His mother uttered a hoarse cry that was like the cry of an animal in torture.

"The child is mine. Oh, mother, I never knew there was one! Yet I did want to do what I could. I wanted to marry her before I went away—I begged her to marry me—it seemed the only thing that could make me hold up my head again—but she wouldn't; for your sake and Maybelle's she wouldn't. She said she was different, and it would nearly kill you to have me marry her. She said it wasn't my fault any more than hers; that we were so young we'd live it down, and it would be a lesson to us forever—she tried to comfort *me*, mother, and make it easy for me. She said I must go away and study, and put it behind me, and grow to be a good man, so God would forgive us and would forget it. M'liss Dement, the drunkard's daughter, talked that way to me, mother, to your son. And it did help me. I went away and worked hard and prayed to be forgiven, and I did outgrow it, and feel that God was forgiving me and blessing me in my work—and all the time there was a child, and I never knew! She wouldn't tell. She bore the shame for both of us! She was an outcast—disgraced, deserted, trodden upon. While I was going higher she was sinking lower. Maybelle says she tried at last to get into the church—the church to which *my* life is dedicated!—and they wouldn't let her in—while *I*—oh, I shall go mad with thinking of it! A lifetime's service to God will not pay the debt to her; will not atone for what she has suffered through me—alone, motherless, cast off!"

He ceased, conscious, of a sudden, of the convulsive shuddering of his mother's whole body. She was standing; and he, too, got to his feet, releasing her shaking, unresponsive hand, and faced her. He looked once, and once only, into her eyes. The supreme anguish written upon her proud old face was more than he could bear. He bowed his head and stood before her dumb.

Through the early June dawn Mrs. Purple came out of her home and went through the orchard to the house where M'liss lay dying. The air was sweet with all sweet, blowing things, and musical with the song of birds. The pale green foliage floated above and about her. Cherries hung scarlet from the trees, and currants in rich ruby globes from their vines; early apples were yellowing among their leaves, and the indescribable fragrance of strawberries mingled with the breath of old-fashioned flowers. But Mrs. Purple saw none of the beauty, heard none of the melody, smelled none of the sweet. She was an old, broken-down woman. She had lived—somehow—through a night of such suffering as she had never dreamed could be for her. She had never had much sympathy for people who suffer. "Let 'em do what's right an' they won't have to suffer!" had ever been her hard thought. She had kept her head high; she had held herself aloof from wrongdoers, judging them without mercy and crushing them with scorn.

For the first time her own head was low. It was bowed with shame. It seemed to her that the very path she trod was red with shame. Along this same path her son's feet had gone on their way to ruin; her daughter's, on their secret missions of the mercy and charity that had never been in her mother's heart.

The old woman saw everything clearly at last. She had not been spared one torturing thought, one remembrance of her own hardness and pride. Every denunciation of sin and sinners she had ever uttered, every sneer at shame, every bitter judgment, had come back to her in the long hours of the night. God's message had come to her as she deserved—without mercy; had written itself through her consciousness with a kind of exquisite torture. In the pitiless searchlight turned upon her heart she had read all the truth there.

Her head was low and her heart was broken; but she was a better woman than she had ever been before.

The dying girl shrank at sight of her, but only for a moment. Her first look at the face on the pillow, gray and drawn with physical suffering and with such mental torture as she herself was passing through, broke down the last remnant of the old woman's pride. Great tears came slowly to her eyes and filled them full; they stood there for a moment, cold and blinding; then they brimmed over and fell upon M'liss's hand—slowly at first, then faster and faster—until, at last, she burst out into passionate sobbing and fell upon her knees beside the bed.

"Oh, M'liss, M'liss," she uttered chokingly, "if ever a mortal woman was sorry, I'm sorry for the way I've treated you. God had to make me suffer to make me see my sin. I don't ask you to forgive me; but I want you to trust me enough to give me the child. I promise you before God that I'll raise it right—an' by *right* I don't mean proud an' hard, like I've been livin' myself. With that child near me, I'll never be hard again; I'll never judge any livin' soul again. I'm a greater sinner than you, an' I'll work to the last day o' my life to atone-up for the way I've treated you."

Death was so close to poor M'liss that she could scarcely speak.

"I'm—sorry—too," she whispered, in the slow and painful utterance of the dying. "But I wasn't—as bad—as you thought—as I acted… Don't worry—you didn't know… May God forever—bless you—bless you—" There was silence in the room while she tried to finish the sentence; when the words came they were barely audible—"for taking—the—child."

M'liss's hand moved weakly to reach Mrs. Purple's head, but fell back upon the bed in pitiful helplessness. But M'liss's child stretched his hand over his mother's still form and patted the old woman's bowed head.

"M'liss's Child" was awarded a prize of $400 from *Collier's Magazine* which published the story on 4 November 1905. It was reprinted in the collection *Collier's Prize Stories* in 1916.

"M'liss's Child" is a mystery story that is set in a rural town. The main character is unmarried M'liss Dement whose mother has died and whose father is an alcoholic. M'liss has had a child and has defiantly refused to tell anyone who the child's father is. The story centers on her steadfast refusal and the resolute efforts of the other women in town to determine both the child's paternity and how they should act toward this young woman whose behavior has been and continues to be so flagrantly disruptive. In "M'liss's Child," Higginson considers questions of morality, judgment, and privacy.

"The Message of Ann Laura Sweet"
• 1914 •

"WELL, GOOD GRIEF!" exclaimed Ann Laura Sweet, coming in at eight o'clock in the morning to spend the day. "It does a soul good to see you once more. It's been ten year, if it's been a day, since I laid eyes on you. Well—the dimple in your chin ain't any older—even if the rest of you is."

My feathers fell. "Take off your hat, Ann Laura," said I. "You must be tired after getting up so early and riding so far in the rain."

"Oh, not very," responded Ann Laura, cheerfully. She sat down in a large rocking-chair and leaned back as comfortably as though it had been made for her. She was sixty years old, and looked scarcely fifty. She was large, but well girdled; gray-haired, but rosy; roughened by hard work, but unlined by worry. "You see, I'm used to getting up early." She pulled off her silk gloves and rolled them together neatly before laying them on the table at her side. "I've got up early all my life. I don't know anything but getting up early and working hard all day."

A pang of remorse shot through me. It had been hard to rise so early to receive her.

"And as for the rain," she went on, happily, "why, Emmeline, I just love the rain. You know—well, I never had a dollar that I didn't earn, and I haven't now; and the Almighty knows how hard I've worked for every one I have—but still sometimes, when I find myself enjoying clean through the things that other people complain about, why, it seems to me that I'm about the richest woman on earth."

She took off her hat, pushed the long pins into it thoughtfully, and laid it beside her gloves.

"Now, this very morning, Emmeline: as I look back over it, every minute was perfect, but nothing quite so good as the rain. It made every field and every orchard and every flower ten times sweeter than they'd 'a' been without it. No, no." She laughed humorously. "If you've got to pity me, take something besides the rain and getting up early. I never sensed that there was anything to pity me for. I can work as hard at sixty as I could at twenty-six; my back's straight, my shoulders up, and my legs are good; nearly all my teeth's my own; my hair's coming out some, but I only wear one switch and it's made out of my own hair; I can see and hear and smell and, God knows, *talk*"—she laughed again—"and I've been back to Kansas twice in twenty years," she bragged proudly.

"Twice?" asked I feebly, feeling myself shrinking away into nothingness.

"Yes, Emmeline, twice. I tell you, there are lots and lots of people"—her eyes fairly sparkled—"well-to-do people who don't have to work hard for a living, who can't say they've been to Kansas twice on visits—let alone being born there and living there till they're twenty."

"No, indeed," said I.

"No, indeed," said Ann Laura Sweet. "And, Emmeline, if I've ever done anything good in my life—any real good deed—it was on my visits to Kansas."

She sat back in her chair and looked into the fire with earnest, reminiscent eyes.

"I was born in a dugout on the Kansas prairie. When I was about two year old my father died. My mother struggled along trying to make a living for herself, my two older sisters, and me; but with grasshoppers and gophers—it was too much for her. She married steppaw. He had three sons and three daughters, and as we only had two rooms and a lean-to in our dugout, we went to live in his, which had three rooms, a lean-to, and a loft without any windows. Two of the rooms were only big enough to hold a bed, though, and the windows were only a foot square."

"For eleven people!" said I. "Mercy, Ann Laura!"

She looked at me. There was kind disapproval in her eyes.

"That was nothing," said she. "We had company to stay nearly all the time. Steppaw was the best man that ever lived. He was never satisfied unless he was feeding somebody. I swan, Emmeline! There wa'n't a Sunday come that he didn't bring home a wagonload from church to dinner, and maybe stay all night."

"Did you find so many stepbrothers and stepsisters congenial?" I asked, not thinking of anything more original in the silence that followed.

"Tiptop," exclaimed Ann Laura. Her eyes shone. "They were the nicest boys and girls. It wa'n't no time till we loved 'em like our own flesh. My, my!" Her eyes filled of a sudden with tears. "How happy we all used to be in that old dugout! I've never been so happy since—and I've been married three times and am a widow again," she added, in a proud tone.

There seemed to be no possible reply to this; so I looked into the fire and was silent.

"I *could* marry again," she went on cheerfully; "over and over, the land knows. But I don't know as I will. There ain't so all-fired much in marrying, when all's said and done, Emmeline. There was a woman back in Kansas married so often they called her 'Marrying Semia'; but I didn't see as she was so terribly happy. So I don't know."

She ceased speaking and looked at me fixedly.

"Do you save your combings?"

"Do I save—what?"

"Why, your combings? Do you save your combings?"

"No, Ann Laura," I faltered, feeling a little giddy.

"Well, I do wish you'd save them for me. The hair woman could mix in some gray, so's they'd be a real good match for my hair. The time's coming when I'll need a new switch; and even though we're only relations by marriage, I'd rather wear your hair, Emmeline, than an out-and-out stranger's; so you needn't feel a bit backward or squeamish about saving your combings for me... Well, let me see. Where was I at, anyhow? Oh, yes, I remember. I got married and come out West. My first husband died when Lela was a little thing. That was a terrible trouble, Emmeline." Her face wrinkled suddenly and quick tears rolled down her cheeks again. "But after a while I got married, and that was worse. It was like jumping out of the frying pan into the fire. He was just no-account; so I upped and left him. I won't filly-fool around with any man that ain't worth his salt. That's one thing about me. They've got to be worth their salt... The third one wa'n't worth his'n, so I left him and took my first one's name again... Well, one day when Lela was a good-sized girl, she was in the sitting room one day, tatting, and I was in the kitchen—*standing* room, I call it—" she broke off with her cheerful laugh. "I was ironing. It was eighteen year ago, but I remember just as well what I was ironing. It was a blue-and-white stripe gingham, and just as I got half way down the stripe a kind o' vision come to me. It was just as if I saw steppaw sitting all alone in the door of that Kansas dugout. I saw him just as plain; and I stood so still that the iron burned a hole in the gingham. You see, my mother had died about four months before that, and steppaw was seventy-nine years old."

She counted on her fingers.

"Yes, seventy-nine... Well, that vision took such a holt of me that I cried right out: 'Lela! Lela! I'm going back to Kansas to see steppaw.' 'You lost your mind?' Lela calls back. She's great at her jokes. 'No, I ain't lost my mind,' I calls back to her. 'I'm going to start this very week.' 'I smell something burning,' calls Lela, calls she. 'Well, I don't care if you do,' calls I. 'It's only this gingham. You can buy gingham any day, but you can't go to Kansas once in a coon's age.' "

Ann Laura paused for breath, coaxing it along with a sigh.

"Well, I guess nobody ever had such a time getting to go anywheres. Lela and everyone else fought it. We argified, too, and pro and con, but I was just like all possessed. It seemed as if I could see steppaw day and night, sitting in the door of the dugout with one hand over his eyes, looking for me, and calling: 'Ann Laura! Ann Laura!' So one day I just upped and started, taking Lela along with me. I didn't let anybody know, so when we got to the little station on the Kansas prairie we had to hire a buckboard. We stopped at Sister Lib Deal's first and she came out to the gate to see who her comp'ny was. We hadn't seen one another for eighteen year.

'Lib Deal,' says I, solemnly. 'Don't you sense your own flesh and blood?'

She gave a scream like, 'Oh, Ann Laura! Ann Laura! Is that you? What do you think has happened to steppaw?'

She burst right out crying and threw her apron over her head.

'Is steppaw dead, Lib Deal?' says I—and I begun to cry, too, for he was dear as an own father, and I'd come all that way to see him.

'Oh, no, no, no!' cries Lib Deal, sobbing awful. 'Ann Laura, he's gone and *got married!* Seventy-nine-year old and maw gone only four months!... And who do you suppose he's married? *That old Delilah Hand!*' "

"*Delilah!*" ejaculated I, quite unexpectedly even to myself, yet firmly repressing all appearances of mirth.

"Yes, Delilah. I never'd heard of her before; I just stood gazing at Lib Deal; I guess my mouth fell open. 'Are you telling the truth, Lib Deal?' says I at last. 'God knows I am,' says she. 'She's sixty-nine, Ann Laura; and she's got six children; and steppaw's got 'em all huddled up in his dugout. I bet they sleep standing up in the chimbly, for I can't think of any other place for 'em. They're all married but one daughter, and steppaw's going to dig dugouts all around his'n—like gophers' holes, I expect!—for Delilah Hand's children to live in. Live on steppaw! That's what it means. I swan, I'll never set a foot inside his dugout as long as I live! Ain't you coming in, Ann Laura?'

'I guess I'll go on,' says I, 'and see Hat Em, and take her by surprise. I'll come back and visit you in a few days.'

We drove off and left her standing at the gate with the apron over her head, and her skirts blowing out every which way for Sunday. When we got to Hat Em's, well, she sensed who I was right away. Hat Em wa'n't very strong. She was little and frail, and she just seemed to blow around, like a thistledown. She threw her arms around my neck and burst into the most terrible crying.

'Oh, Ann Laura! What do you think steppaw has done? He's gone and got married... And who do you think he's married?' Here the tears just run down Hat Em's cheeks like streams. '*Why, that old Delilah Hand!* Sixty-nine year old, Ann Laura, and she's got six children, all married but one, and all living off of steppaw in that old dugout—and where they sleep I don't know, unless it's in trun-el beds and on top o' the kitchen stove. I'll never go a-near 'em as long as God gives me breathing. Maw only gone four months—and that *old Delilah Hand* a-setting there in maw's chair, and a-cooking on maw's cookstove she was so proud of—it had four holes—and a-eating up maw's praserves and sweet pickles. I almost lose my mind with dwelling on it day and night.'

'Well, don't dwell on it, Hat Em,' says I, drawing a long breath. 'What's the use? Steppaw's been a mighty good father to us, and he was a mighty good husband to maw; and now she's gone—and he's all alone—and old—and—'

'Oh, go on a-taking his part!' cries out Hat Em wildly, sobbing right out loud. 'Him seventy-nine year old! And all them children! I wouldn't feel so awful terrible about it, I reckon, if it wa'n't for all them children.'

'Well, as for the children, Hat Em,' says I, 'steppaw took a lot of us in and hovered us and we all turned out pretty well. I don't see as it's so much agin anybody, having a lot of children. It's Kansas and Mizzoura agin the world for children. And if they're all married—'

'Don't you talk to me,' weeps Hat Em. 'I'll never go a-near 'em. It ain't the dugout; I don't want the dugout when steppaw's earthly lot is spun, as the Bible says. It's maw's things and maw's place. And to think of its being that old Delilah Hand—'

'Hat Em,' says I sternly, 'once and for all what is there agin this old Delilah Hand?'

Hat Em, she just sobbed on and on for some time. 'Ain't?' says I.

'Oh, I don't know what all there is agin her,' sobs

she at last, 'nor what there *ain't*. It's just *her*—and all them children. A-trompin' around!'

Well, Emmeline, I went in and stayed all night and tried to get her mind off of steppaw, but you might as well of tried to put Jonah's whale through the eye of a needle. She wept and wept, till it seemed as if Kansas couldn't ever have another drought; and it was just like that for two weeks, till I couldn't stand it any longer. I upped all of a sudden and went to see steppaw. The girls had cried for sorrow, but poor old steppaw cried for joy.

'You're the first to come to see me, Ann Laura,' says he. 'Even my own flesh and blood won't come. But, Emmeline, I was so lonesome I couldn't stand it; and poor old Delilah, she was lonesome, too; and it didn't seem any harm to get married. I didn't mean any disrespect to your mother, Ann Laura, God knows. I worshiped the ground she trod on, and Delilah knows it, and she never complains when I set here and think of your mother. Nobody but old, old people, Ann Laura, knows how awful it is to live a lifetime with somebody and be left all alone. Children don't understand, but Delilah and me do. We make allowance for one another, and we could have some peaceful days yet before we die, if only my children would come to see me. They are breaking my old heart, Ann Laura, staying away from me; and you look like an angel to me for coming. I can't have a happy minute till they forgive me.'

I never was so surprised in anybody as I was in old Delilah. She wa'n't a bit pushing, and just as kind to me. All her children had got settled in dugouts around steppaw's but one young woman daughter who wa'n't married. It made so many dugouts, Lib Deal, she called it *Hand*ville, and Hat Em, for all she's been called the gentle one of us girls, she called it *Delilah* town. I had to laugh at that, but I bet I did it in my sleeve. I wouldn't 'umor them to let them see me laugh.

Isaphene, the young woman daughter, just about carried me on two chips. My own nieces wa'n't half, nor a hundredth part, so kind to me as she was; and after I'd visit around with my own kin and then come back to steppaw and Delilah and Isaphene, it begin to glimmer in on me that steppaw hadn't been such an awful dunce to choose Delilah and her folks to live with, instead of his own flesh. They didn't find fault and pick him to pieces; they seemed to think he was just perfect, and they let him do just as he pleased. They even seemed to think I was all right—and that was more than any of my own kin ever did. Instead of praising the good in me and helping me to put my best foot forwud, my own kin always held up my faults and rattled 'em at me day and night, like a nigger playing bones. Mebbe you've heard it said that Heaven gives us our kin, but, thank the Almighty, we can choose our friends. And sometimes it seems just so—If you could of seen poor old steppaw—seventy-nine year old—a-setting with tears running down his old cheeks over the way his own fambly treated him; and then these strange women doing for him and making over him and even making excuses for his fambly, you wouldn't of blamed him. I'll admit, when all's said and done, this marrying is terrible guesswork—"

Here Ann Laura Sweet paused and looked at me fixedly.

"Emmeline," said she in a kind of embarrassed way, "it does seem so good to have this visit with you that I'm going to admit that I *have* thought of marrying again. I don't know as I will, though," she added hastily, "for it is terrible guesswork. But I can—Well, let me see; where was I at?... Oh, yes, I remember. Well, I stayed all summer, visiting around, and winter come on, and I'd ought to come home, if oughts count for anything; but whenever I'd mention it, poor old steppaw would set with tears running down his cheeks, and old Delilah'd get up heavy out of her chair and sly away into the lean-to, so's we'd be alone. He'd beg me not to leave him without any kin in his old age. I'd get so wrought up I'd cry, too. And so it was."

"At last Christmas come. One night old Delilah comes to me as white as a sheet. She'd been crying.

'Ann Laura,' wails she, 'don't you think you might get all your family to come to dinner on Christmas Day, if my daughter and me'll get the dinner all by ourselves, and then stay out in the kitchen while you all eat?'

'Oh, Delilah,' says I, and something begun to hurt in my throat; 'I wouldn't let you do that.'

'I know *you* wouldn't,' says she, 'but I'd do anything on this earth to get them to make [up] with your poor old steppaw, and I thought, mebbe, if it seemed like me knucklin' down to them, instead of them to me—why, mebbe they'd come—'

Right here her old voice quivered so she couldn't finish, and all of a sudden it come to me that here all my life long I'd ached to do some great deed; and that there ain't anything greater than to make people happy; and that here was my chance; and that it 'u'd be all the greater deed because it 'u'd be all in my own heart and not shouted out loud from the housetops. You see, Emmeline, it's just like this. I took a long ocean voyage once with a friend that was just aching to do good.

She was under heavy obligations to me, but that just seems to make some kind of people haughty. Well, she went around that ship a-searching for sickness, so's she could air off what she knew and distinguish herself by her noble kindness to complete and utter strangers. If anybody had a headache or a toeache, behold and lo! There she was with her camphire bottle a-bathing his or her head or toe like a bathing machine—while all the time I was lying alone in my berth, as sick as a dog, and the ship a-rolling so's I couldn't eat even when my stomach would let me, because I couldn't hold the tray and get food to my mouth at the same time. Then she'd come in at bedtime and smear her face with cold cream and crawl into her berth so heavy it 'u'd crack and say: 'You wouldn't be so sick if you'd put a mustard plaster on your arm.' A mustard plaster on my *arm!* Now, Emmeline, God knows that the very last place on me I'd put a mustard plaster is my *arm!* I never was seasick in my *arm* in all my born days, and what's more, I don't expect to be taken with seasickness there. But so it is. Lots and lots of people, good people, go around aching so hard to do good that they look so far from them they don't see the good they might do right under their noses. It ain't the real good they want to do; it's the kind that attracts attention. There's people that give right and left where it'll be found out and then let their poor old parents hobble around with rheumatiz and not even give them somebody to do their work. And so, 'Ann Laura Sweet,' says I, 'right here and now is your great deed to be done that you've been a-pining for, so set to and do it.'

Well, I just set to work on first one relation and then another. You'd be surprised, but the first one I got was Lib Deal. She'd always been the hard and stubborn one of the fambly, and I no more expected to see her give in than I'd expect to see blue kernels on a yellow roasting ear or a yellow roasting ear with eardrums— but I do reckon that she just give in so's she could see old Delilah humiliate herself. Anyhow, after Lib Deal give in, the whole fambly give in, one after another, like a flock of sheep jumping over a pastur' bars."

Here Ann Laura leaned back in her chair and laughed silently for some time, with tiny wrinkles running around her kind and humorous eyes.

"Well, Emmeline, after every last one, little and big, haughty and meek, had ba-a-ed and jumped over the fence, I just set down all alone and laughed till I cried till I laughed. It didn't seem possible I'd done it," she added.

"When I told old Delilah to go ahead with her Christmas dinner, poor old steppaw just begun to cry like a child. 'God bless you, Ann Laura,' says he. 'If you never do another good deed, God forever bless you for this one.' Old Delilah never opened her head and never shed a tear; but as long as I live I'll not forget her old chin. I never saw anybody's chin quiver the way hers did. She come close to me and laid her hand on my shoulder, and kep' trying to say something, but her chin kep' on quivering so there wa'n't a sound come from her lips. Her face was just as gray as a stun. I hadn't sensed till that minute how much it all meant to old Delilah.

Well, Emmeline, Christmas come and they all come trooping in and made up with steppaw. He just set before the fireplace and cried for joy. After a while everybody softened up with forgiving feelings, and talked just as if nothing had happened. Then Isaphene brought in the dinner, and there wa'n't a one of our family that could of got up such a dinner.

'For the land's sake!' cries out Lib Deal, a-staring as the dinner come in.

'I want to know!' falters out Hat Em.

'Wall,' says Hat Em's husband Eli, drawling the way he always done, 'I don't want to know; I want to *eat*.' Eli was the worst old stubborn head in the hull fambly. He was so stubborn he set down on a live coal one time, and he was so stubborn he wouldn't humor the coal to get up, but just set there and turned as purple as a starfish on a piling. And hisses out: 'Burn, damn you, burn!'

I'll tell you what we had for dinner: Two big turkeys, brown and juicy, with the best stuffing and gravy; mash potato as light as feathers, with little wells of melted butter running into it—or out of it; little onions boiled, with cream sauce poured over them; corn and tomatoes, and macaroni with cheese browned on top; watermelon pickle so clear you could see yourself in it; currant jelly that set up in the dish and wavered from side to side without toppling over; tomato pickle and strawberry jam; baking-powder biscuit folded over with butter oozing out of the flap, and so light they just faded away agin your palate; salad and salted nuts and cottage cheese; and for dessert she had three kinds of pie—one was a custard two inches thick, flavored with nutmeg and vanilla; it was as smooth as velvet and just the right thickness; it wavered and wavered like the jelly, but didn't break apart—I tell you," Ann Laura laughed out suddenly, "I didn't waver any about eating it. There ain't one cook in a thousand can make good custard pie… And then she had two kinds of layer cake, and floating island.

Steppaw waited on us and beamed all over and seemed so happy till Hat Em goes and sets her foot in it. 'Ann Laura,' says she, 'what's in that glass dish down there by you?' 'It looks like peach praserve,' says I, as innocent as a lamb.

'Looks like *what?*' says steppaw. He laid down his knife and fork and leaned over the table to peer.

'Peach praserve,' says I, passing it to him. He looked at it and burst into tears—and it wa'n't for joy. 'Oh, girls,' says he. 'Them's your mother's peach praserves.' He looks at Hat Em, Lib Deal, and me. "I have been so cruel to poor Delilah; I wouldn't let her or Isaphene tech 'em because your ma worked so hard over 'em. And now she's saved 'em and set 'em out for your ma's children to eat up—and her out in that kitchen a-cooking and a-waiting on you. Oh, children, children! It ain't right to treat Delilah that way, and it ain't anything to be proud of.'

Well, we all set there like stuns. At last Lib Deal says: 'We didn't ask her to ask us.' 'No, you didn't,' cackles old Eli, 'but we all come a-running when she ast us.'

Lib Deal just glared. Pretty soon Hat Em blew up out of her chair and fluttered away into the kitchen. It was a long time before she come back, but when she did, old Delilah was with her; they'd both been crying, but they looked happy then.

'I wish you-all a Merry Christmas,' says old Delilah Hand, 'every one of you, and many a Christmas besides. Hat Em wants I should set down and eat with you-all, but I ask you to excuse me. Some other time, mebbe. Today I want you all to forget there is any old Delilah

Hand, and just have a good time eating and visiting together. If you want to give me a happier Christmas than I reckoned I'd ever have again, that's the way to do it. You don't know how welcome you are.' Then she turned and walked out into the kitchen, but not before I'd seen her chin quivering again. But such dignity!"

"Emmeline"—Ann Laura sat back in her chair and folded her toil-worn hands, they were swollen and the joints were enlarged—"I had to leave for home the next day, and it was fifteen year before I heard another word about that day's work. Last summer Sister Hat Em was dying and she wanted I should come, so I upped and went. Old Delilah had been dead a year and I didn't even know it. There was poor old steppaw, ninety-four-year-old, a-living alone in the same dugout and hobbling over to take his meals at Delilah's granddaughter's.

" 'Nobody ever did a better deed than you did, Ann Laura, when you persuaded us-all to make up with old Delilah,' says Lib Deal to me, alongside Sister Hat Em's dying bed. 'There ain't no better folks than her and her folks. We all thought as much of her as we do of steppaw; and as for him—well, he couldn't let her out of his sight, and if any of us was sick or in trouble, why, there was old Delilah a-standing at the door to help, like an angel from heaven. When she was dying we all stood around her, crying, and all at once she spoke up and whispers: 'God bless you-all; and God bless Ann Laura. If it hadn't been for Ann Laura, mebbe you'd never forgive me for marrying steppaw, and mebbe we'd never of got to understanding and loving each other so.'

Then Hat Em got hold of my hand. 'Yes, God bless you, Ann Laura, sister,' trembles she in her dying voice.

'If it hadn't of been for you—' "

But Ann Laura could say no more for tears. It was some time afterward that she continued in a shaken voice:

"So, you see, Emmeline, everybody can do something if they want to take the trouble. I expect your life now seems so full and you have so many ways of doing good that my story don't amount to much to you. But when a body has been poor and hard-working all his life, little things get to seeming big; and for that matter, mebbe what seems big to you wouldn't seem big to somebody else. I don't believe there's anybody so poor or 'umble that he ain't got a message to pass on to people higher up, if only he knew how. My story of old Delilah Hand always sounded to me like a message to everybody not to go a-seeking high and low for good to do when there's a-plenty chance to do it at home. I used to *ache* to do some big thing that people would hear about and talk about, but I don't any more. It was a poem that cured me."

She took her bag from a table and fumbled in it. "I've carried it with me so long it's most worn out... Now I don't know any more about a poem than I do an elephant's hind foot; but there's something in this'n that took hold of me."

She leaned forward in her chair and read aloud with great earnestness:

"I could content myself to be one drop
   Among the myriad drops that swell the breast
   Of life's full sea, if I might ride the crest
Of some proud wave that none can overtop;

If I might catch the sun's sweet morning light,
    When swift he mounts into the day's cool space,
    And paint his tinted clouds upon my face,
And wear the stars upon my breast at night.

But, oh, to lie a hundred fathoms deep,
    Down in a cold, dim cavern of the sea,
    Where no sun ray can ever come to me,
Where shadows dwell and sightless creatures creep;

To gaze forever up, with straining eyes,
    To where God's day illumines the shining sands,
    To grope, and strive, and reach with pallid hands,
You never see the light, and never rise.

I should go mad, but for a still, small voice,
    A pitying voice, that sometimes says to me;
    'It takes so many drops to fill life's sea,
Ye cannot all have places of your choice.' "

"Now, there," said Ann Laura Sweet, lifting her head and looking at me steadily, "if there ain't a message in that there poem for people like me, why, I don't know a message when I hear it. Sometimes it's seemed as if I'd earned my bread with the sweat of my *heart*, instead of the sweat of my face, as the Bible says, but that poem has helped me to make the best of everything and do the nearest good and not go around a-mooning to be something, or do something, that I can't be or do any more than a rhinoceros can be a lizard or a cow can ketch a mouse... *So there!*" wound up Ann Laura Sweet with a laugh; but there was a sound as of tears, shaken through her laugh; and there was something fine and beautiful shining upon her face.

"The Message of Ann Laura Sweet" won the *Collier's Magazine* best short story prize of $500 in 1914. The panel that judged the contest consisted of former United States President Theodore Roosevelt and well-known investigative journalists Mark Sullivan and Ida Tarbell. The story was reprinted in the collection *Collier's Prize Stories* in 1916.

"The Message of Ann Laura Sweet" was written twenty years after "The Mother of 'Pills,' " Higginson's first award-winning story. "The Message of Ann Laura Sweet" reflects Higginson's skill and artistry in the prime of her literary career. In this story, elderly Ann Laura Sweet arrives at the home of Emmeline, a young female relative, to spend the day visiting. In the course of the visit, Ann Laura tells Emmeline an extended story of family drama and conflict that had occurred back on the Kansas prairie. "The Message of Ann Laura Sweet" is rich in dialogue and in descriptions of pioneer life in Kansas and in the West. In this story, Higginson explores the significance of a person's actions and considers the ways that any one person, no matter what their situation in life, may be able to help others and make a lasting difference.

Higginson was the author of over one hundred short stories which regularly appeared in leading periodicals of the day such as *The Atlantic, Collier's, Harper's, Lippincott's,* and *McClure's Magazine.* Her stories were widely reprinted in magazines and newspapers across the nation. Many of Higginson's poems were set to music during her lifetime by well-known composers such as Leila Brownell, Charles Willeby, Horatio Parker, and Whitney Coombs.

Book Titles & Covers

A Bunch of Western Clover (1894)
The Flower that Grew in the Sand and Other Stores (1896)
A Forest Orchid and Other Stories (1897)
The Snow Pearls (1897)
From the Land of Snow-Pearls: Tales from Puget Sound (1897)
When the Birds Go North Again (1898)
Four-Leaf Clover (1901)
Mariella, of Out-West (1902)
The Voice of April-Land and Other Poems (1903)
The Vanishing Race and Other Poems (1911)
Alaska, the Great Country (1908)

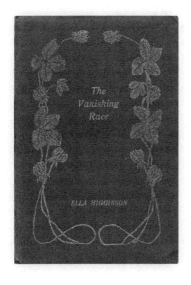
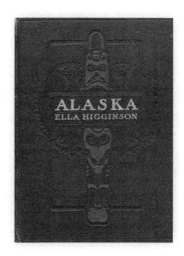

HIGGINSON STRATEGICALLY EMPLOYED the wide popularity of her poem "Four-Leaf Clover" (1890) to increase her regional and national literary reputation. She wore four-leaf clover jewelry and requested that her publisher incorporate the four-leaf clover symbol into the designs of her book covers. Through print ephemera such as sheet music and postcards, her public association with the symbol flourished.

HOME OF ELLA HIGGINSON, BELLINGHAM, WASH.

THIS POSTCARD from the early 1900s depicts the Higginson home at 605 High Street in Bellingham, Washington. Named "Clover Hill" by Higginson, she and her husband had the house built in 1890. She lived there until her death in 1940. The staircase on the right descends westward from High Street and aligns with Pine Street.

HIGGINSON LATER IN LIFE in front of Clover Hill, with her Model T and dog Clover. (Ella Higginson Collection, Whatcom Museum, 1981.76.6.)

LOOKING EAST from below High Street, this early-1900s view of Clover Hill shows Sehome Hill in the background. (Galen Biery Papers and Photographs #802, Center for Pacific Northwest Studies, Western Libraries Heritage Resources, Western Washington University.)

AERIAL PHOTO (1939) shows Clover Hill in relation to Edens Hall of the Bellingham State Normal School, later Western Washington University. The house was demolished in the mid '60s to clear room for a new dormitory, Mathes Hall. (Campus History Collection, Special Collections, Western Libraries Heritage Resources.)

"Here is the home of color and of light," a line from the poem "The College by the Sea" (1904), is inscribed in marble over the front of Edens Hall. Higginson's prominence was such that no authorship accompanied the quotation; it was assumed the source would always be known. Nearly a century later the inscription remains while Higginson's authorship is long forgotten. Built in 1921, Edens Hall remains one of the oldest buildings on campus. (Photograph by David Scherrer, courtesy Western Washington University.)

PORTRAIT OF ELLA HIGGINSON (c.1885) by the Frank G. Abell Studio in Portland, Oregon. (Ella Higginson Papers, courtesy Center for Pacific Northwest Studies, Western Libraries Heritage Resources, Western Washington University.)

BEFORE TRAVELING TO ALASKA to conduct research for her first book of nonfiction, Higginson studied photography in order to take the pictures to be included in *Alaska, the Great Country*. (Ella Higginson Collection, Whatcom Museum, 1981.76.4.)

AN AILING HIGGINSON at home at the end of her life. (Ella Higginson Collection, Whatcom Museum, 1981.76.7.)

SELECTED CHAPTERS FROM
Mariella, of Out-West
· 1902 ·

Chapter XI

MARIELLA WENT TO THE STAIR-DOOR and stumbled up in the dark, sliding her hands along the walls. Her mother came to the foot of the stairs.

"Oh, Mariella," she called, in her most affectionate tone, "you goin' right up?"

"Yes." Mariella stumbled on without stopping.

"What are you goin' to do up there?"

"Nothin'."

"Well, you goin' right to bed?"

"Yes."

"You got a drink with you?"

"Don't want none."

"You might want one 'n the night. Mercy, child! Don't be a snappin' turtle. I'll set a drink here on the stair steps, so's if you want it, it'll be right here. Well, good-night."

"Good-night."

"Oh, Mariella."

"Hunh?"

"Don't 'hunh' me!"

"Ma'am?"

"Your window open?"

"Unh-hunh—yes, ma'am."

"Shut it, will you? The wind might come up 'n the night, an' bang things around. You'd ketch cold too. Hear?"

For answer Mariella went stumbling down to the window. She closed it with a loud noise, and instantly slid it up again as high as it had been before, and slipped the stick that held it up in place. She heard her mother close the stair-door and go away. She sat down on the floor beside the open window.

She was breathless with amazement at her own act. When she had put her hands on the window to lower it, she had not been conscious of any intention to lift it again. It was as if the window had lifted itself and had got the stick under it, somehow. Her mother's peculiar nervousness and solicitude had betrayed her. The child was seized with the certainty that something unusual—something in which she was not to share—was occurring or about to occur. Her mother did not wish her to go down-stairs for a drink of water, and she desired the window closed.

"She must think I'm green," muttered the child, in her mother's language, which she always spoke when off guard, "not to see through her! She never brings me drinks unless I'm sick. Maybe it's a surprise party! She acts just like she did the night the Mallorys got one up on pa, and she knew about it. She went tiptoeing around from window to door, and door to window."

At that moment she heard a faint step on the path beneath her window. The path led through the orchard to the front door. Just at first she was frightened and drew back. Then the front door was opened cautiously; not so cautiously, however, that its customary brief squeak did not accompany its opening. Mariella leaned out suddenly then, but she was too late. Some one had entered from the outer darkness. She caught a glimpse of a large, dark figure. A narrow beam of light was streaming across the porch and the grass, clear to the row of currant bushes. There was another faint squeak; then the beam withdrew, and all was darkness and silence.

Mariella set her lips together. She unlaced and drew off her copper-toed shoes. She stood up and stole with limber, stealthy movements toward the stairway. She moved on her toes. Her shoulders were drawn up. Her arms swung bonelessly at her sides, a little in advance of her body. Her head was

Chapter XI

bent forward. Her steps were long and noiseless. She felt as if she were a mass of boneless flesh, propelled not by her own will or desire, but by some unknown power. Once or twice a board creaked, and she stood still, with red lights shaking before her eyes. She wanted to make her way down-stairs unheard. It was a silly wish to be working so desperately for. But Mariella never did anything by halves. Her reaching the stairs undetected could scarcely have been of more importance had her life depended on it.

She reached them and descended noiselessly. She put her hand on the knob—it turned without sound; she held it firmly, so it could not click, and pushed the door. It did not move. It was locked on the outside.

After a while Mariella returned to the window, and huddled down again on the floor. The brilliant Orion was rising in the east. Sirius was still tangled in the dark firs on the crest of the hill. The child knew nothing of astronomy; but the most beautiful of the planets and constellations were familiar to her, from long and loving watches. She looked nightly for the three brilliant stars in Orion's belt; she knew that down below would be a splendid, changeful star. They were all stars to her.

The "dipper" was the only constellation she knew by name. Her mother had pointed it out to her one cold winter's night. She had gone out to the pump to get water, and had called: "Oh, here's the dipper! Mariella, come an' see the dipper."

"The *what*," said the child, coming out.

"The dipper. W'y, up'n the sky, dumby! Look-ee there!"

She pointed it out, also the North Star.

"What makes you call it the dipper?" Mariella had then asked contemptuously.

"W'y, that's the name. The books an' grammars all call it that."

"How silly! To call anything as beautiful as a star, or a lot of stars, a *dipper!* ugly tin thing!" Mariella had replied, going in without waiting for any more lessons in astronomy.

To-night the stars appealed to her more powerfully than usual.

She had forgotten the mystery below when, about ten o'clock, she was startled by the faint creak of the front door. She leaned out quickly. A man was stepping stealthily across the porch. He was a large man. The narrow strip of light was again streaming across the porch and across the yard to the currant bushes. At the steps the man looked back into the room, and smiled. The light struck full on his face. Mariella never forgot the smile on that face. She drew back; her heart was beating to suffocation. She had recognized him.

When Mariella went down-stairs the following morning, the men had breakfasted and were already out in the orchards with their blue-bedded, creaking wagons, gathering apples. Mr. Palmer had returned, and he and Mrs. Palmer were in the midst of a violent quarrel.

"Well, I know somebody was here," Mr. Palmer was saying as the child entered, "because the orchud bars wa'n't the way I left 'em. There was a man's tracks in the soft ground; he'd had on high-heel boots."

"The preacher wears high-heel boots," said Mrs. Palmer, attempting humor, although there was no appreciation of it in her face. "Sundays," she added, "Oh, here's Mariella! Why don't you ask Mariella? Mariella, your pa thinks there was comp'ny here last night."

Mariella looked at her mother and smiled. It was a smile that brought that lady's heart up into her throat. It took some of the fine color out of her face, too. "You tell him there wa'n't anybody here. He don't see fit to believe me. I do enjoy to see the day your pa don't believe my solemn word! I told him solemn there wa'n't a soul here."

Chapter XI

Mariella looked full at her father, without faltering. "There wasn't anybody here," she said.

"Oh, ho, Miss Steel Trap! How d' you know? Did you stay up till bedtime?"

"Yes, I stayed upstairs."

"Would you of see if anybody had come?"

"Yes."

"Oh, ho. Where was you?"

"Sitting by the window."

"Window open?"

"Yes."

"Mariella," said her mother, piously, "don't tell a lie, not even to make your mother's word good. My word's good."

Mariella tittered.

"Didn't you shut the window when I told you to, for fear you'd ketch cold?"

Mariella looked at her mother, and laughed contemptuously. "Yes, but I opened it again."

"When, child?" Mrs. Palmer's face was a study in purple.

"Right away. Before you locked the door."

"Locked—the—door!" stammered Mrs. Palmer. "I didn't lock the door."

"Didn't you?" said Mariella, indifferently. "Then it just locked itself. It does sometimes, only it was unlocked this morning."

"You must be mistaken about it's bein' locked." Mrs. Palmer was pulling herself together with difficulty. "Well, pa, I guess you'll take Mariella's word about nobody a-bein' here, if you won't take mine. I'd like to know who'd come! The preacher at church!"

She was going out into the kitchen with some dishes as she spoke. She gave her husband an injured look. It was intercepted half-way by Mariella—who returned the look, and smiled.

Chapter XII

When Mariella was gone to school, Mrs. Palmer did some thinking. She was bending over the wash-tub on the back porch. She considered Clary, the hired girl, "mighty fiddlin' stuff" when it came to washing. She either got too much bluing in the clothes or not enough.

Then, all the towels and all the tea-towels and bread cloths, which were made out of raveled flour-sacks, should have been always spread out carefully over the currant and gooseberry bushes to bleach; this Clary could not be driven to do. As Mrs. Palmer was rather under Clary's thumb, hired girls being, as she frequently declared, scarcer than hen's teeth, she decided to do the washing herself.

Mrs. Palmer was a real laundress. She loved the work. Instead of wearing an old torn dress and coming forth on wash-day with untidy hair, as slatterns do, she always put on a neat calico dress and a big apron, checked black and white so finely that the effect was lavender. Her hair was always neatly combed, and her sleeves, rolled above the elbows, revealed plump, well-formed arms. Her waist was simply bound at the neck, without a disfiguring collar, and edged with narrow, crocheted lace of Mariella's making on long winter evenings. Mrs. Palmer's neck was fair. Her movements were alert and vigorous, her face full of animation; in a word, this was Mrs. Palmer at her best—the careful, neat housekeeper, the cheerful mistress, the solicitous mother, neighbor, and wife. Alas! that wash-days only came once a week.

It was a pleasure to see her washing the linen. She did not huddle all over the tub; she held her back straight naturally,

Chapter XII

and bent forward from the waist. With light movements of her powerful arms she spread piece after piece of linen on the bluish, accordion-plaited zinc of the wash-board, and rubbed over it carefully the great bar of yellow soap; then up and down she rubbed the piece itself—three times and then into the soapy water it went with a splash, three times again, and then into the water—over and over until all stains were removed. Then into the big bright boiler on the stove it went for a boiling; afterward it was lifted on, and twisted around a clean bleached broom-stick, and held suspended above the boiler until the soap-suds had dripped from it, when it was lowered into a tub of clear water, wrung, and then put through another tub of clear water; last of all it was plunged quickly into the tub of bluing water.

When there was no danger of being invited to assist, Mariella loved to watch her mother washing. She liked the regular, rhythmic rubbing, and the soft splash into the water; she liked the bluing and the making of the starch; she liked the white folds curling around her mother's arm, and the rainbow-tinted flecks of bubbled foam scattered over her apron; most of all, she liked the long line of neatly hung clothes, and the clean, pleasant smell of their drying in the sun.

On this particular Monday morning Mrs. Palmer was not taking as cheerful pleasure as usual in her laundry work. If her thoughts, as she bent over the big tub, had been put into words, they would have been something like this: "Well, don't that beat you! She slipped down there an' found that door locked, and she knows I locked it! She put that window down when I told her, an' then she put it up again, right off, an' *set* by it. I bet my soul she saw through the drink, an' the window, too. I bet my soul she knows somebody was here! But she wouldn't tell on me! Lord Almighty—if she had!" Mrs. Palmer paled through all the steam that enveloped her like a cloud and freshened her as a bath of dew freshens flowers. "Well, she didn't—but, my soul! The way she laughed when I told her she mustn't lie! It almost made my teeth chatter in my head! If her pa wa'n't too terrible dumb, he'd of see there was something up the way she laughed. It wa'n't a natural laugh. I never see her beat. She sees right through everybody an' everything. It does my soul good, the way she sees through the sky-pilot, as Mr. Hoover calls him. An' pa—she sees right through *him*, as if he was a strip of isinglass. He's almost as thin as isinglass—My-*O!* But I don't propose to have her a-seein' through me, not by a jugful! The worst of it is—I don't believe I'll ever dare to shake her again. I believe she knows she's got the dead-wood on me. I can't do anything with her if I can't shake her. I'll get her a new dress."

Mrs. Palmer stopped washing suddenly and straightened up. She stood a long time, thinking deeply. From time to time she gathered up a handful of foam and let it fall in flecks, like beaten cream, back into the tub. Finally she stripped all the foam off her arms and then wiped them on a towel.

She went around to the front of the house with the porch broom in her hand. Under a pretence of sweeping, but looking over-pale for the exertion, she peered along the edge of the porch with her eyelids wrinkled together, and a strained look in her eyes. When she had finished the porch she began sweeping the narrow path from side to side. She swept slowly and calmly, as if challenging the whole world to look, clear on out through the orchard to the bars.

"You must be pushed," said her husband's voice suddenly, from under a nearby tree.

She started violently. "That you? My-O! You give me a turn. What-a-say?"

"W'y, I say you must be pushed. Sweepin' the *path!* On a wash-day! You must be pushed. What ails you?"

"I don't know as anything ails me. What ails you?"

Chapter XII

"Nothin' ails me. I was a-comin' back to the house, when I see you a-sweepin' the path off. On a wash-day! It looked so funny I thought somethin' must ail you."

Mrs. Palmer faced him now, defiant and at her ease; one hand held the broom; the other was spread out, thumb up, on her generous hip. A slow, tantalizing smile went over her face. "'D you come back for bale-rope?" she asked.

A dull red flamed across Mr. Palmer's brow and eyes, paling off toward the lower part of his face. This was a sure indication that he was at once furious and helpless.

"No, I didn't come back for bale-rope!" he hissed out.

"Oh, I was just goin' to say,"—Mrs. Palmer laughed again,—"there wa'n't any more. It's all gone. You took it all the other mornin' when you come back so all of a sudden—as if *you* was pushed! What ailded you?"

"Maybe you'll find out yet what ailded me!" said Mr. Palmer, fiercely. "Maybe you'll find out. A-jacketty-pinchin' around out here, sweepin' *paths*—on a wash-day! A-sweepin' out *high-heeled tracks*—that's what you're a-doin'! You think I ain't got any eyes 'n my head—"

"Eyes!" interrupted Mrs. Palmer, laughing now without restraint. "Oh, no; I know you've got eyes. But high-heeled tracks! Good grieve! You do act so! I can't see what ails you. For the land's sake! Don't you know *stilt* tracks when you see 'em yet? You're awful dumb."

"*Stilt* tracks?" Mr. Palmer looked dazed.

"Yes, pa, stilt tracks. Mr. Harrison's boy was over here yesterday on his stilts. I reckon some o' his tracks went right into boot-heel tracks—an' you went an' thought it was a high-heel track. You must think the preacher had lots to do, a-comin' here after church was out! If he'd of come, I'd of put him up all night—a preacher that way."

Mr. Palmer removed his hat, and, taking out of it an old

silk handkerchief of an indescribable color, wiped the perspiration from his brow. He had a silly look. "I've see stilt tracks afore," he remarked, "but I never see any that fitted right into heel tracks the way them did."

"You'll see a lot before you die that you never see before," replied Mrs. Palmer, with good-humored contempt. "Which apples the men a-getherin'?"

"The blue pearmains, an' the yallow pippins."

"Hunh? Fallin' off?"

"Terrible."

"I never see their beat for lateness. It's an awful late season. We had the apples all in the fruit-house a month earlier 'n this last year. When you goin' to make the cider?"

"I do' know," he said. He had a shamed, routed look. "Soon 's we get the apples all stored in, an' sort 'em over."

"It's high time. Well, I got the path all swep' off. You comin' on to the house?" she questioned sociably. "Oh, what was it you said you was a-comin' back all of a sudden so for?"

"I didn't say."

"Oh. Well, what was it you was a-comin' for?"

Mr. Palmer turned and gave her a look of helpless rage. His blue eyes blazed at her. His face went red and white in streaks. He stuck his thumbs into his palms and shut his fingers down over them hard.

"Gunny-sacks," he hissed out at her between his teeth. "God A'mighty—*gunny-sacks!*"

"Oh," said Mrs. Palmer, blandly. Her husband flung himself around and went on toward the house, down the newly swept path. He stepped short and high. Mrs. Palmer walked behind him, her face wrinkled up with noiseless laughter. Once a little sound of mirth escaped her lips unexpectedly. "Haigh?" she exclaimed instantly, as if he had spoken; but he walked right on, with his chin up. Mrs. Palmer made short apologetic dabs

Chapter XII

here and there, to the right and to the left, with her broom.

"There, your wash-water's all cold!" hissed Mr. Palmer, passing the porch.

"Plenty more where it come from," replied his wife, cheerfully.

When he came back from the barn with his arms full of the gunny-sacks he did not want, his face was dark with helpless fury. She straightened up, and, leaning the wash-board over on its stomach, slushed a sheet up and down in the water behind it. He gave her one look. She returned it. She was shaking with laughter.

"Heavy?" she asked. This time no words came from his lips in reply; he only hissed, speech being quite beyond him.

When he had passed on and was entirely out of sight, Mrs. Palmer crossed the porch and looked into a square, wavy mirror that hung upon the wall. The humor which had served her so well in allaying suspicion had all gone out of her face; only the pallor of fright remained. She looked long into her own eyes.

"You're a pretty smart woman," she said slowly, and with some admiration. "You ought to of had an education; but you're a pretty smart woman without it. I bet my soul you could learn the multification-table backwards in no time! *Stilt* tracks! My land! There ain't another woman on the face o' the earth would of thought of stilt tracks. All is, them heels'll come off o' them boots!" She rubbed her face with her fingers, grooved white from washing, to bring some color back. Then she said slowly, going back to the tubs: "I bet a picayune I never sweep another path off again on a wash-day! Excuses like stilts don't come to the same body more 'n once in a lifetime."

Clary appeared suddenly in the door. "Mis' Parmer," she said loudly, as if doubtful of that lady's hearing, "Mr. Mall'ry's come."

Mrs. Palmer started violently. "How?" she faltered.

"W'y, I say Mr. Mall'ry's come. He's in the parlor. I took him in. He wanted he should see you just a minute. I wanted he should go out in the orchud an' see Mr. Parmer, but he wanted he should see you just a minute. I put up the window shades, an' took his hat an' set it on the table," she added, in a lower tone, looking at her mistress for a word of praise.

But Mrs. Palmer did not even hear. She was wiping her hands and arms; her hands shook strangely. She pulled down her sleeves and fastened them. "How did he come?" she asked, with a fine carelessness. "Which way?"

"Up from the water. He come in a sail-boat."

Mrs. Palmer breathed again.

"Pin in these ends of my hair, will you? I look like all-fire. I wish people wouldn't come of a wash-day. I expect Mis' Mall'ry's sent him for some Kansas-starter—she always bakes a-Tuesday. I'm all het up, washing. Do I look like all-fire?"

"You don't look so terrible bad," replied Clary, with cold cheer. "But I've see you look lots better."

Mrs. Palmer's feathers drooped.

"I wish I didn't get all het up so, washing." She looked in the mirror, and started reluctantly for the parlor.

"You don't look so terrible bad," repeated Clary, putting a little more warmth into her assurance.

Mrs. Palmer went on slowly. She smoothed down her sleeves and pulled out the bows of her apron strings as she went. She had on her old shoes. They creaked, so she went on her tip-toes.

In ten minutes she returned. Clary looked at her with breathless curiosity. "He gone?"

"Unh-hunh?"

"He went terrible sudden. Did he come after Kansas-starter?"

"No, she'd got some."

Clary meditated. "Maybe he was just going along by?"

Chapter XII

"Maybe he was."

"Did he go out in the orchud to see the men?"

"I do' know. The apple-sauce made?"

"I'm makin' it. It's terrible odd for a man to go a-visitin' on Monday forenoons, ain't it?"

The humor of this appealed to Mrs. Palmer. She laughed suddenly.

"I expect it is." Whenever the humor of a difficult situation presented itself to Mrs. Palmer with sufficient force to make her laugh, she was saved.

"Maybe he come to borrow the harrow," suggested Clary, her mind flying wildly from one need of a man to another.

"Clary," said Mrs. Palmer, confidentially, "you mustn't tell a soul Mr. Mall'ry's been here. You mustn't tell Mariella nor her pa, nor a *soul*. I'm—I'm—thinkin' of gettin' my life insured," she looked impressively at the girl, "an' I'd want it to be a terrible surprise to 'em both."

"Oh, my!" said Clary, letting out deep breathings of awe. "How much?"

Mrs. Palmer turned her head to one side and looked modest, as if deploring admiration. "A thousand dollars," she said, with solemnity. "You must never tell a soul."

"I never will," breathed Clary. "It'll come in awful handy when—"

She stopped, and coughed politely. "Sho-o-o!" she cried, shaking her apron at a hen, to cover her confusion.

"My mercy! Don't scare No-tail so's she hurts herself, or Mariella'll have a duck-fit."

Clary faced around; her eyes were big. "W'y, is Mr. Mall'ry an agent? I didn't know he was an agent."

Mrs. Palmer hesitated a moment, and then, at her wit's end, went into a violent spell of coughing. She coughed long and hard. She coughed Clary's question down three times.

When she finally came out of the paroxysm, she said hastily: "Now, don't let's talk any more. I'll never get that washin' out. You put some cinnamon in your apple-sauce, an' set it away to cool. Then you take an' make the starch for me. Don't fool any more time. We'll just pick up some scriddlin's for dinner."

She was bending over the tub again, and chuckling to herself over having disposed of Clary's curiosity, when that young person appeared in the doorway. She held the pan of apple-sauce in her hand. In the other was a long-handled tin spoon, with which she was stirring the cinnamon into the sauce.

"Say! Mis' Parmer! Well, say! Did you ever see such high-heel boots as he had on? What makes him wear such high heels? And on a Monday forenoon! He must be pushed. Maybe he was a-goin' somewheres, though."

Mrs. Palmer's face had turned to the crimson-purple of a starfish.

"Look a-here!" she exclaimed sternly. "Don't let me ever hear you a-criticisin' anybody's clo's! Never again. An' don't you ever let me hear the word high-heel boots out of your mouth again. Never! If you ever tell a livin' soul Mr. Mall'ry had on high-heel boots, I'll send you a-pikin' home, with your duds."

"I didn't think it was any crime." Clary was beginning to cry. "I just thought it was terrible strange—on a Monday morning."

"Well, don't think." Then she changed her tone. "Clary, if you'll be a good girl, an' not cry, an' never speak Mr. Mall'ry's name before a soul, I'll—I'll give you that buff calico to make yourself a dress. But Mr. Mall'ry 'll be comin' here so much about that insurance I expect I'll get sick of hearin' his very name. Don't ever let me hear his name out of you. That's a good girl. I'll give you that buff calico."

"You're awful clever," said Clary, with feeling. "I declare,

Chapter XII

you're awful clever to me, Mis' Parmer. I'll have it made with a V neck and flowin' sleeves," she added proudly.

"That'll be nice. Go on now an' don't fool any more time."

Clary turned away, beating the sauce hard. She took three steps; then she paused. "Maybe he was on his way to town," she said. "It was terrible odd."

Chapter XIII

It was evening at the Mallorys'. The family was gathered together in the sitting-room. It was a big room, and would have been a cheerful one but for its painful neatness and precision. Everything that was capable of shining shone. The chairs were ranged evenly around the sides of the room. There was a bright fire on the hearth, which was well swept. A crane swung across the fireplace. The andirons were polished, as were the shovel and tongs, standing each in its corner. A table in the centre of the room held books and papers and a coal-oil lamp, whose chimney had not a blur.

Mr. Mallory was leaning back in a big chair, reading the weekly paper. He looked handsome and very comfortable. Mrs. Mallory sat opposite, upright, thin, unattractive. Her hair was drawn plainly away from her face, accentuating the sharpness of her features. She was sewing on white muslin. Isaphene sat between them, reading. The smaller children were playing "doll" in a quiet corner.

Mrs. Mallory looked at Isaphene over her sewing. "You learnin' that piece to speak?"

"Yes, ma'am."

"Let's hear how much you've learned."

Isaphene handed over the book with a sigh. She began at once:—

"From the Cascades' frozen gorges—"

"Stand up," commanded her mother, sternly. Isaphene stood up, meekly, and bowed—a short, bobby bow.

Chapter XIII

"Leaping like a child at play—"

"Here, stand straight. There. Now put your heels together an' your toes this way." Mrs. Mallory arose, held her dress high in front, and illustrated. Isaphene imitated faithfully.

"Winding, widening thro' the valley,
Bright Willamette glides away.
Onward ever—"

"There, there! Hold your shoulders back! More yet!"

"Onward ever, lovely river,
Softly calling to the sea!
Time that scars us,
Maims and mars us,
Leaves no track or trench on thee."

"That ain't bad. Don't run your words all together so. Don't hold your hands so stiff. When you say 'onward ever, lovely river,' make a gesture." Mrs. Mallory made a solemn, soaring movement with her thin arm. Isaphene imitated, following the soaring of her own arm with bewildered eyes.

"There, that's it," said her mother, with admiration. "You did that real graceful. I'm glad you ain't all arms an' legs, like Mariella Palmer! I don't know, though, but what I'd as live be all arms an' legs as to be all flesh, like her mother." She raised her voice, that her husband might hear. The paper rustled a little in his hands.

"I declare, of the two, I'd rather be a *leetle* too thin than to have so much flesh to carry around. She's always a-complainin' of gettin' het up so. No wonder! All that flesh to carry around! She's no more shape! She thinks she is, though."

"She makes good floatin'-island," said Isaphene, with reminiscent eyes.

"She does so," said her mother, cordially. "An' a pretty sum it costs to make it that way. Eggs! My mercy! She puts a dozen in, I expect; an' them forty cents a dozen now. I'd like to see your father if I'd cook so extravagant. I'd like to see him. He wouldn't think floatin'-island was so good then. It's easy to be a good cook, if you just cut an' slash into butter, an' eggs, an' cream. She's no housekeeper when it comes to savin'. She fries in butter half the time… Well, go on. What you waitin' for?"

> "Spring's green witchery is weaving
> Braid and border for thy side,
> Onward ever—"

"There, that don't come in there."

> "Spring's green witchery is—"

"Oh, don't go clear back to the beginnin'! You'll be sayin' the title over next."

> "Hither poetry would dream—"

"Oh, goodness me!" Mrs. Mallory flung the reader down on the table contemptuously. "You don't half know it. You'll study it twenty minutes before you go to bed. Do you know the 'Prize Banner Quickstep' yet?"

"Yes'm."

"Well, go an' play it. Be careful when you open the organ; you're so careless. Pull that flute stop out slow. Now, hold on! Screw your stool up higher; always have it high enough so's your elbows are even with the keys. I'd enjoy to see a daugh-

Chapter XIII

ter of mine set hunched over the way Jemima Watson does, a-playin' in church. I'd enjoy to see that! Now."

Isaphene played with rigid fingers the "Prize Banner Quickstep." She sat erect and stiff, her shoulders even, her elbows held in close to her waist, her chin level. Her eyes were set painfully upon the music. She did not make a mistake, but hammered every note out sharp and hard, without expression.

Mrs. Mallory sat with equal stiffness in her chair, regarding her daughter. Her face was wrinkled up around her eyes. Her thin lips were closed tightly and drawn down at the corners, tracing a narrow line across her face in the shape of a new moon. Not until the last note was sounded and Isaphene folded her hands in her lap, after an apologetic cough, awaiting praise or blame, did the muscles of Mrs. Mallory's face relax. Then she breathed her delight out and in with deep breathings.

"You know *that*," she said, with a crow of triumph in her throat. "I enjoy to hear a daughter of mine play like that. That's a terrible difficult piece to learn in such a short time. I'd enjoy to watch Mis' Parmer's face the first time she hears you play that piece—I'd enjoy to watch her. They're always a-talkin' about that Mariella a-bein' so smart. Look at her. All skin an' bone! She holds her elbows every which way for Sunday. She'd look pretty at an organ, I must say… Can you play 'General Percifor F. Smith's Grand March' yet?" she added, with tremblings of doubtful awe in her tone.

"I'll see."

She played the piece through without a mistake. Her mother glowed at her, and even her father lowered his paper and looked over it at this brilliant performance, caressing his full cheek with one hand.

"Well, I never see the way she improves," announced Mrs. Mallory, looking at her husband. "She ain't been no time a-learnin' that piece; an' she don't know a one that's similar to it—not a one. All the runs an' trills are different, an' had to be learned a-special. Can you sing 'Gypsy's Warning'?"

Isaphene took a sheet of music from a neatly arranged pile on the organ, played the prelude, and began the song in a weak treble:—

> "Do not trust him, gentle lady,
>   Tho' his voice be low and sweet,
> Heed not him who kneels before thee,
>   Gently pleading at thy feet."

"That's too low," interrupted Mrs. Mallory, sternly; "pitch it higher."

Isaphene pitched it higher.

> "Now thy life is in its morning,
>   Cloud not thou thy happy lot;
> Listen to the gypsy's warning,
>   Gentle lady, trust him not;
> Listen to the gypsy's warning,
>   Gentle lady, trust him not."

"That's terrible sad," said Mrs. Mallory, when the song was concluded. "Sing that last verse over; you listen," she added, to her husband.

Isaphene sang:—

> "Lady, once there lived a maiden,
>   Young and sweet, and like thee fair,
> But he wooed and wooed and won her,
>   Filled her gentle heart with care;
> Then he heeded not her weeping,
>   Nor cared he her life to save;

Chapter XIII

Soon she perished—now she's sleeping
  In the cold and silent grave;
Soon she perished—now she's sleeping
  In the cold and silent grave."

"Don't that beat you? Where'd she get her voice from, I'd like to know."

"I sung some when I was younger," said Mr. Mallory, modestly.

"You didn't set the well afire. I sung some too; but we didn't either of us carry a toon that way. Where'd she get her voice from? She'd ought to be encouraged."

"Well, encourage her."

"When she learns a piece like 'General Percifor F.' in such a short time, an' plays it without a mistake, we'd ought to buy her something."

Mr. Mallory resumed his reading at once.

"I say we'd ought to buy her something. She wants some ear-bobs the worst way. A pair of ear-bobs would encourage her to do her—her utmost endeavor."

Mr. Mallory held the paper high and read on.

"She'd like a pair we saw the other day. They're round, kind of crusted gold, with a pearl in the centre and a black stripe around the pearl; and there's a little gold drop danglin' down underneath. They're real gold"—Mrs. Mallory was warming to the occasion, encouraged by the silence behind the newspaper—"anybody can see that with half an eye. Isaphene 'u'd like 'em. They'd encourage her up, I know."

She stopped to draw breath. She expected a reply; but none came.

"Eben, you hear? Why don't you answer me up? You want I should select 'em out next time I go to town?"

Still there was no reply. A certain kind of woman can live

with one man fifty years without learning to recognize a sign when she looks it squarely in the face. Mrs. Mallory was that kind of woman. Not receiving a reply, she added, with a petulant inflection, "Eben! Hear?"

The newspaper quivered and came down. Mr. Mallory glared at his wife. His face was white with anger. He was not handsome now. "I hear." His voice shook.

"No, I don't want you should 'select 'em out' "—he mimicked her tone—"the next time you go to town, nor the last time. Buy, buy, buy! It's all a woman can find fit to talk about! You'd drive a man insane with your encouragin's here an' your encouragin's there! I don't want to hear any more about it. It's a pity if you can't encourage a twelve-year-old without forever a-buyin' her somethin'."

"My land!" stammered out Mrs. Mallory. "You needn't get worked up so. What's a pair of ear-bobs? They only cost five dollars."

"Only cost five dollars, aigh? What's a pair of ear-bobs? A pair of ear-bobs is a pair of ear-bobs! My Lord! Why don't you say *five hells?* That's what you'd drive a man to, with your buyin' here an' your buyin' there; an' your only costin' this and your only costin' that!"

"Oh, if you're goin' to swear," said Mrs. Mallory, weeping, "all about a little thing like a pair of ear-bobs! A body'd think I'd asked you to give her a *farm* to encourage her!"

"It 'u'd amount to a farm. It's a pair of ear-bobs here, an' a pair o' shoes there, an' a petticoat som'ers else—"

A sudden ray of humor glimmered across Mrs. Mallory's face, like a rainbow across a storm. "Well, we can't wear everything in the same place," she said.

"I don't want to hear any more of your encouragin's an' your buyin's! You understand? It's come to a pretty pass! A man can't set foot 'n the house without your hollerin' at him for money!

Chapter XIII

If it ain't somethin' to eat, it's somethin' to wear; an' if it ain't somethin' to wear, it's somethin' to act the fool over in your ears. It's come to a pretty pass! I don't want to ever hear ear-bobs out o' you again. You'll drive me to the poor-house yet!"

"Oh, I guess not," said Mrs. Mallory, contemptuously. "Not as long as you can buy seed-drills, an' harrows, an' rakes, an' ploughs—all with spring-seats on 'em! I guess you won't go to the poor-house as long as you can make yourself so comfortable. I never see a man yet that thought his own buyin's 'u'd send him to the poor-house; it's always his wife's! Isaphene, you get an' study that 'Beautiful Willamette' piece over again; I'll make a lady out of you, ear-bobs or no ear-bobs. I'd be ashamed to not encourage a child that nobody else can hold a candle to—an' then set up lazy on a spring-seat! I'd be condemned! I'd—"

Mr. Mallory arose heavily, and crushed the paper down on the table.

"I'd rather be condemned any day than to get your tongue started," he said, in a desperate tone, going off to bed.

Chapter XIV

"Why, for pity's sake," said Mrs. Mallory, "you don't rub your cake of cleaning soap right on the woodwork, do you?"

She was sitting erect on a straight chair in Mrs. Palmer's kitchen. She had come early one January afternoon. "Mr. Mallory was goin' right by to town," she explained cordially, "so I thought I'd come an' visit."

"Well, do," said Mrs. Palmer, without warmth. "I'm rill glad; but my work ain't all done up yet, so I'll have to invite you into the kitchen till I get through. Clary's home. She has to go every so often, rain or shine."

So they had gone into the warm and pleasant kitchen. Mrs. Palmer turned around now and looked at her guest.

"What's it for?" she asked briefly.

"Why, I wouldn't say it was for rubbin' right on to woodwork."

"Why not?"

"It seems to me it must be terrible wasteful."

There was a silence, then Mrs. Palmer said slowly, "What do you use it for?"

"Oh, just a little on the dish-cloth to polish my nicest things up. I don't use a cake in six months."

"Hunh." There was another silence. "What do you clean your woodwork with?"

"Oh, I powder up some Bath brick. It's better an' quicker, an' it costs ten times less. I clean all my pans an' kettles with it, too."

Mrs. Palmer went on rubbing the white cake of cleaning soap on her table. "I thought it was to use, myself," she said. "I'd

Chapter XIV

call a cake in six months no more use 'n a hen's teeth to clean with."

"Oh, it's nice if you can afford it," said Mrs. Mallory, in a thin tone that went far; her lips seemed to get thinner as she spoke, and her nose sharper because of the wrinkles that suddenly ran away from it. "I can't afford much wastefulness myself. If I wasn't equinomical I couldn't have more 'n three new dresses a year."

Mrs. Palmer felt her face grow red. It had been two years since she had had a new dress of any material better than calico. She rubbed the table hard. She would have liked to rub the whole cake of cleaning soap away, right before Mrs. Mallory's eyes. Three new dresses a year!

"If I wasn't equinomical," repeated Mrs. Mallory, with her short, exasperating laugh, "I expect I'd have to go to the neighbors' attired in calico."

"Well, I'm savin'," announced Mrs. Palmer, in a deep bass, "but I ain't so savin' that I don't use enough cleanin' soap to keep things clean."

Mrs. Mallory smoothed out the folds of her dress skirt. "This is my third best black alpaco. My new one is as pretty! It fairly glimmers. It makes me think of moonlight."

Mrs. Palmer looked around at her now and smiled scornfully. "*Black* moonlight?" she asked briefly.

A little pink splashed delicately across Mrs. Mallory's face. Even her blushes were ladylike. "*Fine* black goods," she said coldly, "always have a kind of a gleamy look. It's just like moonlight. Common wool stuffs don't have it. I never buy an alpaco that don't look gleamy." She coughed thinly. "I wouldn't feel to afford 'em gleamy if I wasn't equinomical."

"Well," said Mrs. Palmer, slowly, "I'm savin'; but, I swan, I won't squeeze a nickel if I never get anything gleamy. There's some things we don't do here out West. If a thing costs twenty cents an' I throw down a two-bit piece, I don't wait for no nickel change. I notice that. Everybody comes out here from New England sooner or later, but we come sooner, an' we got some o' the picayunishness took out o' us. I drether," she spoke out fiercely, walking around the big kitchen with short, high steps, and rattling pans and things for emphasis, "I drether go with one dress for six year than to be picayunish. Scrimp, scrimp, scrimp! I know people that wouldn't put twelve eggs in floatin' isle to save the minister's soul. No wonder he's so bent on comin' here to dinner. I expect gleamy dresses ain't so terrible good to eat! About as good as bread puddin' with one egg in it, I expect!"

Mrs. Mallory looked a little frightened. "You are a beautiful cook," she declared, in a conciliatory tone. "That's universally preceded. Everybody precedes that. Your rules are always in demand. I hear only the other day your Kansas-starter was unsurpassed."

"Hunh," said Mrs. Palmer.

"Yes, I did. Your puddin's, too."

"Well, I ain't afraid to put cream an' butter an' eggs into my cookin' if I do say it myself," bragged Mrs. Palmer.

Mrs. Mallory was making tatting. She held her work high, and made short, jabbing movements into her left hand, with the shuttle held stiffly in her right.

"No, indeed," she said, with cordial warmth, "your cookin' is unsurpassed. Mr. Mallory fairly declares by your floatin' isle."

A little pleased red came to Mrs. Palmer's face. Her movements became less vigorous. "I hope he won't get caught in a storm comin' from town," she said. She drew a chair near her guest and sat down more sociably. "That's a rill pretty pattern," she said, narrowing her eyes at the tatting.

"Yes, it is so; it's a five-leaf clover."

"Mariella does all our tattin'."

Chapter XIV

"Isaphene don't have time; she spends so much time on her practisin'," said Mrs. Mallory, overcoming her fright and beginning to brag again. "She can play 'General Percifor F. Smith's Grand March.'"

"Mariella can learn anything an' have plenty of time left for tattin'," said Mrs. Palmer, who was always on the watch for the waving of a red rag. "She don't spend much time a-practisin' anything she wants to learn."

"I didn't know she was so quick with her sums."

"Well, they're one thing she ain't so terrible quick with," confessed Mrs. Palmer, with bitter reluctance. "Tom-fool things! I can't see any sense in 'em myself."

There were danger signals in her face again. Mrs. Mallory recognized them, and shied away from them.

"What have you got to say about Mr. Leaming's doin's?" she inquired; her tone invited gossip.

Mrs. Palmer set her lips together.

"It's a sin an' a shame!" she declared, "for him to up an' leave right 'n the middle of a term this way just because that old Englishman he calls his—his—"

"Factotum?" suggested Mrs. Mallory, undaunted.

"Well, then, factotum—just because he teached him an' was good to him when he was a boy! Now he's wrote he's a-dyin', an' he wants Leaming to hike right over there all the way to England, an' he ups an' offs, as if he was pushed! I never see the beat!"

"His factotum's rich, ain't he?"

"Yes, he's rich; but his son 'll get it all. I don't believe in skuropin' all over the earth unless there's somethin' to be got out of it."

"He got a teacher to take his place?"

"Yes, he telegrafted right down to Seattle an' Tacoma, an' he got one. It's a wonder he did, too; pneumony o' the lungs is terrible brief up there this weather, they say."

"It's brief enough here. Like as not a new teacher 'll have a hard row to hoe with Mahlon Proudfoot. He's so stubborn."

Mrs. Palmer laughed. "I expect. I know he's stubborn. He gets it honest, though. His father's the stubbornest man on the sound. He's one o' the oldest settlers round here. The old pioneers tell on him that he's so stubborn that he set down on a live coal o' fire once, an' was so stubborn he just set still an' let it burn. Mule-head!"

"I expect Mariella 'll miss the teacher," hazarded Mrs. Mallory.

"She's pickin' now," reflected Mrs. Palmer, shrewdly. "Well, let her pick. I'd just as 'lieve she'd know."

"She will so," she admitted candidly. "I don't know what to do with her; she's most cried her eyes out a'ready. He come around last night an' took her out for a walk, an' told her. We were all eatin' supper when she come home—all except her pa—an' I told her to set down an' eat, but she wouldn't; she'd been cryin'. The hands teased her. Gus said her eyes was like boiled gooseberries, an' Hoover, he said her sweetheart was a-goin' to England. She was terrible sassy to 'em." Mrs. Palmer paused, as if remembering. "She was sassy to me too," she said more slowly.

Mrs. Mallory sent the shuttle to and fro with little short emphatic jabs. "That's one thing about Isaphene. She never is sassy. She's always polite."

"I don't mind a girl bein' sassy," said Mrs. Palmer, holding her head high. "I brought Mariella up that way. It shows a girl has got some spunk in her. Anything but skim-milk!"

"Isaphene never is," insisted Mrs. Mallory. "I want her to be a lady. I mean to send her to a seminary. Well, I declare! If he hasn't returned a'ready!" She waved her thin hand across the window; her husband had just driven up to the gate.

Chapter XIV

"He's just like a child about me. He's perfectly devoted to me."

"He is?" said Mrs. Palmer; her face was eloquent with exclamations.

"My, yes. He hardly lets me out o' his sight. He humors me high an' low. Once a lover, always a lover."

"Pfew! but it is warm in here!" Mrs. Palmer's face was crimson. "Come again soon. I'm sorry he come for you so sudden."

She went out on the porch with her guest, making conversation in a difficult way, until her humor came to her aid. Then she laughed out suddenly.

"You tell Mr. Mall'ry I think he's as smart as a steel trap," said she, still laughing. "I always did think he was smart; but I didn't know as he was so *terrible* smart."

"What's he so smart about?" Mrs. Mallory's face took on a thin, suspicious look.

But Mrs. Palmer had already said good-by and was going back into the house. The wind blew her skirts about her stout ankles.

"I'd like to know what she thinks he's so smart about," reflected Mrs. Mallory, going to the gate. She had a feeling that there was a joke somewhere.

Mrs. Palmer had not faithfully reported the scene of the evening before with Mariella. When the child returned from her walk with Leaming she sped through the dining-room like a wraith. The family was at supper.

"Here, you Mariella!" cried her mother. "Where you been? Come here an' eat your supper."

"I don't want any."

"Come an' eat some, anyhow. Look round here. Why, good grieve! What's got into you? You look like you'd been drawed through a knot-hole! What ails you?"

"Nothing."

"Nothin', aigh? With eyes like boiled gooseberries! What ails you?"

Mariella was silent. She stood looking steadily at her mother. There were devils in her eyes.

"Come an' eat your supper now. Hear?"

"I don't want any."

"Ho, ho!" cried out Gus, chuckling coarsely. "The teacher's a-goin' to England to-morrow. It's a-makin' his little sweetheart sick."

The child flashed around on him, as he spoke. "Shut up!" she cried instantly. "You old ignorant fool!"

The other men roared. Her mother flushed scarlet. "I'll punish you for that. Come an' eat your supper."

"I don't want any."

"Come an' eat, anyhow."

Mariella did not move.

"Where you been? You've got to tell."

Mariella did not speak.

Mrs. Palmer arose in a threatening manner. "You little heifer! You answer me when I ask you questions. Where you been?"

Mariella laughed in her mother's face.

"I've been looking for *high-heel tracks!*" she said, and went on upstairs, banging the door behind her.

She threw herself on the bed in the dark, without undressing, and lay there, face downward, all night.

MARIELLA, OF OUT-WEST is Higginson's only completed novel. Published in 1902, *Mariella* was reprinted a second time in 1902, and then in 1903, 1905, and 1924.

Chapter XIV

At age 41, for the first and only time in her extended literary career, Higginson completed the writing of a novel. The resulting work, *Mariella, of Out-West* ranks as one of the earliest published novels written by a woman born west of the Mississippi. Reviewers compared *Mariella* to novels by celebrated authors such as Jane Austen, Charles Dickens, William Makepeace Thackeray, Leo Tolstoy, and Émile Zola, among others. When later asked in an interview to name her best writing, "Without hesitation Mrs. Higginson answered, '*Mariella*. I like it better than anything I have ever written' " (Coyney).

Mariella centers on the life of fourteen-year old Mariella Palmer, who grows to early adulthood in the novel. Mariella is an only child who lives with her parents on a remote ranch in Puget Sound. In this breathtakingly beautiful region, Mariella's parents have lived together unhappily for years, laboring for economic stability as they contend with the hardships of early twentieth-century farming in the Pacific Northwest. In the chapters excerpted here, Mariella accidentally discovers a shocking secret, tension flares between her parents and their neighbors, and Mariella must begin to come to terms with the private knowledge that she has stumbled upon. In these chapters, as in the novel as a whole, Higginson considers issues of family bonds, secrecy, and the struggles between choosing a truth that will disrupt her family or a falsehood that will maintain appearances.

SELECTED CHAPTERS FROM
Alaska, the Great Country
· 1908 ·

Chapter I

EVERY YEAR, from June to September, thousands of people "go to Alaska." This means that they take passage at Seattle on the most luxurious steamers that run up the famed "inside passage" to Juneau, Sitka, Wrangell, and Skaguay. Formerly this voyage included a visit to Muir Glacier; but because of the ruin wrought by a recent earthquake, this once beautiful and marvellous thing is no longer included in the tourist trip.

This ten-day voyage is unquestionably a delightful one; every imaginable comfort is provided, and the excursion rate is reasonable. However, the person who contents himself with this will know as little about Alaska as a foreigner who landed in New York, went straight to Niagara Falls and returned at once to his own country, would know about America.

Enchanting though this brief cruise may be when the weather is favorable, the real splendor, the marvellous beauty, the poetic and haunting charm of Alaska, lie west of Sitka. "To Westward" is called this dream-voyage past a thousand miles of snow-mountains rising straight from the purple sea and wrapped in coloring that makes it seem as though all the roses, lilies, and violets of heaven had been pounded to a fine dust and sifted over them; past green islands and safe harbors; past the Malaspina and the Columbia glaciers; past Yakutat, Kyak, Cordova, Valdez, Seward, and Cook Inlet; and then, still on "to Westward"—past Kodiak Island, where the Russians made their first permanent settlement in America in 1784 and whose sylvan and idyllic charm won the heart of the great naturalist, John Burroughs; past the Aliaska Peninsula, with its smoking Mount Pavloff; past Unimak Island, one of whose active volcanoes, Shishaldin, is the most perfect and symmetrical cone on the Pacific Coast, not even excepting Hood—and on and in among the divinely pale green Aleutian Islands to Unalaska, where enchantment broods in a mist of rose and lavender and where one may scarcely step without crushing violets and bluebells.

The spell of Alaska falls upon every lover of beauty who has voyaged along those far northern snow-pearled shores with the violet waves of the North Pacific Ocean breaking splendidly upon them; or who has drifted down the mighty rivers of the interior which flow, bell-toned and lonely, to the sea.

I know not how the spell is wrought; nor have I ever met one who could put the miracle of its working into words. No writer has ever described Alaska; no one writer ever will; but each must do his share, according to the spell that the country casts upon him.

Some parts of Alaska lull the senses drowsily by their languorous charm; under their influence one sinks to a passive delight and drifts unresistingly on through a maze of tender loveliness. Nothing irritates. All is soft, velvety, soothing. Wordless lullabies are played by different shades of blue, rose, amber, and green; by the curl of the satin waves and the musical kiss of their cool and faltering lips; by the mists, light as thistle-down and delicately tinted as wild-rose petals, into which the steamer pushes leisurely; by the dreamy poise of seabirds on white or lavender wings high in the golden atmosphere; by the undulating flight of purple Shadow, tiptoe, through the dim fiords; by the lap of waves on shingle, the song of birds along the wooded shore, the pressure of soft winds on the temples and hair, the sparkle of the sea weighing the eyelids down. The magic of it all gets into the blood.

The steamer slides through green and echoing reaches; past groups of totems standing like ghosts of the past among the

Chapter I

dark spruce or cedar trees; through stonewalled canyons where the waters move dark and still; into open, sunlit seas.

But it is not until one sails on "to Westward" that the spell of Alaska falls upon one; sails out into the wild and splendid North Pacific Ocean. Here are the majesty, the sublimity, that enthrall; here are the noble spaces, the Titanic forces, the untrodden heights, that thrill and inspire.

The marvels here are not the marvels of men. They are wrought of fire and stone and snow by the tireless hand that has worked through centuries unnumbered and unknown.

He that would fall under the spell of Alaska, will sail on "to Westward," on to Unalaska; or he will go Northward and drift down the Yukon—that splendid, lonely river that has its birth within a few miles of the sea, yet flows twenty-three hundred miles to find it.

Alaskan steamers usually sail between eight o'clock in the evening and midnight, and throngs of people congregate upon the piers of Seattle to watch their departure. The rosy purples and violets of sunset mix with the mists and settle upon the city, climbing white over its hills; as hours go by, its lights sparkle brilliantly through them, yet still the crowds sway upon the piers and wait for the first still motion of the ship as it slides into the night and heads for the far, enchanted land—the land whose sweet, insistent calling never ceases for the one who has once heard it.

Passengers who stay on deck late will be rewarded by the witchery of night on Puget Sound—the soft fragrance of the air, the scarlet, blue, and green lights wavering across the water, the glistening wake of the ship, the city glimmering faintly as it is left behind, the dim shores of islands, and the dark shadows of bays.

One by one the lighthouses at West Point on the starboard side, and at Point-No-Point, Marrowstone, and Point

Wilson, on the port, flash their golden messages through the dusk. One by one rise, linger, and fade the dark outlines of Magnolia Bluff, Skagit Head, Double Bluff, and Liplip Point. If the sailing be early in the evening, midnight is saluted by the lights of Port Townsend, than which no city on the Pacific Coast has a bolder or more beautiful situation.

The splendid water avenue—the burning "Opal-Way"—that leads the ocean into these inland seas was named in 1788 by John Meares, a retired lieutenant of the British navy, for Juan de Fuca (whose real name was Apostolos Valerianos), a Greek pilot who, in 1592, was sent out in a small "caravela" by the Viceroy of Mexico in search of the fabled "Strait of Anian," or "Northwest Passage"—supposed to lead from the Pacific to the Atlantic north of forty degrees of latitude.

As early as the year 1500 this strait was supposed to have been discovered by a Portuguese navigator named Cortereal, and to have been named by him for one of his brothers who accompanied him.

The names of certain other early navigators are mentioned in connection with the "Strait of Anian." Cabot is reported vaguely as having located it "neere the 318 meridian, between 61 and 64 degrees in the eleuation, continuing the same bredth about 10 degrees West, where it openeth Southerly more and more, until it come under the tropicke of Cancer, and so runneth into Mar del Zur, at least 18 degrees more in bredth there than where it began"; Frobisher; Urdaneta, "a Fryer of Mexico, who came out of Mar del Zur this way into Germanie"; and several others whose stories of having sailed the dream-strait that was then supposed to lead from ocean to ocean are not now considered seriously until we come to Juan de Fuca, who claimed that in his "caravela" he followed the coast "vntill hee came to the latitude of fortie seuen degrees, and that there finding that the land trended North and North-east, with a broad Inlet

Chapter I

of Sea between 47 and 48 degrees of Latitude, hee entered thereinto, sayling therein more than twenty days, and found that land trending still sometime Northwest and North-east and North, and also East and Southeastward, and very much broader sea then was at said entrance, and that hee passed by diuers Ilands in that sayling. And that at the entrance of this said Strait, there is on the North-west coast thereof, a great Hedland or Iland, with an exceeding high pinacle or spired Rocke, like a pillar, thereupon."

He landed and saw people clothed in the skins of beasts; and he reported the land fruitful, and rich in gold, silver, and pearl.

Bancroft and some other historians consider the story of Juan de Fuca's entrance to Puget Sound the purest fiction, claiming that his descriptions are inaccurate and that no pinnacled or spired rock is to be found in the vicinity mentioned.

Meares, however, and many people of intelligence gave it credence; and when we consider the differences in the descriptions of other places by early navigators, it is not difficult to believe that Juan de Fuca really sailed into the strait that now bears his name. Schwatka speaks of him as, "An explorer—if such he may be called—who never entered this beautiful sheet of water, and who owes his immortality to an audacious guess, which came so near the truth as to deceive the scientific world for many a century."

The Strait of Juan de Fuca is more than eighty miles long and from ten to twelve wide, with a depth of about six hundred feet. At the eastern end it widens into an open sea or sound where beauty blooms like a rose and from which forest-bordered water-ways wind slenderly in every direction.

From this vicinity, on clear days, may be seen the Olympic Mountains floating in the west; Mount Rainier, in the south; the lower peaks of the Crown Mountains in the north; and

Mount Baker—or Kulshan, as the Indians named it—in the east.

The Island of San Juan, lying east of the southern end of Vancouver Island, is perhaps the most famous, and certainly the most historic, on the Pacific Coast. It is the island that barely escaped causing a declaration of war between Great Britain and the United States, over the international boundary, in the late fifties. For so small an island,—it is not more than fifteen miles long, by from six to eight wide,—it has figured importantly in large affairs.

The earliest trouble over the boundary between Vancouver Island and Washington arose in 1854. Both countries claimed ownership of San Juan and other islands near by, the Oregon Treaty of 1846 having failed to make it clear whether the boundary was through the Canal de Haro or the Strait of Rosario.

I.N. Ebey, American Collector of Customs, learning that several thousand head of sheep, cattle, and hogs had been shipped to San Juan without compliance with customs regulations, visited the island and was promptly insulted by a British justice of the peace. The *Otter* made her appearance in the harbor, bearing James Douglas, governor of Vancouver Island and vice-admiral of the British navy; but nothing daunted, Mr. Ebey stationed Inspector Webber upon the island, declaring that he would continue to discharge his official duties. The final trouble arose, however, in 1859, when an American resident shot a British pig; and serious trouble was precipitated as swiftly as when a United States warship was blown up in Havana Harbor. General Harney hastily established military quarters on one end of the island, known as the American Camp, Captain Pickett transferring his company from Fort Bellingham for this purpose. English Camp was established on the northern end. Warships kept guard in the harbors.

Chapter I

Joint occupation was agreed upon, and until 1871 the two camps were maintained, the friendliest social relations existing between them. In that year the Emperor of Germany was chosen as arbitrator, and decided in favor of the United States, the British withdrawing the following year.

Until 1895 the British captain's house still stood upon its beautiful bluff, a thousand feet above the winding blue bay, the shore descending in steep, splendid terraces to the water, stairwayed in stone, and grown with old and noble trees. Macadam roads led several miles across the island; the old block-house of pioneer days remained at the water's edge; and clustered around the old parade ground—now, alas! a meadow of hay—were the quarters of the officers, overgrown with English ivy. The captain's house, which has now been destroyed by fire, was a low, eight-roomed house with an immense fireplace in each room; the old claret- and ivory-striped wall-paper—which had been brought "around the Horn" at immense cost—was still on the walls. Gay were the scenes and royal the hospitalities of this house in the good days of the sixties. Its site, commanding the straits, is one of the most effective on the Pacific Coast; and at the present writing it is extremely probable that a captain's house may again rise among the old trees on the terraced bluff—but not for the occupancy of a British captain.

Every land may occasionally have a beautiful sunset, and many lands have gorgeous and brilliant ones; but nowhere have they such softly burning, milky-rose, opaline effects as on this inland sea.

Their enchanting beauty is doubtless due to the many wooded islands which lift dark green forestated hills around open sweeps of water, whereon settle delicate mists. When the fires of sunrise or of sunset sink through these mists, the splendor of coloring is marvellous and not equalled anywhere. It is as though the whole Sound were one great opal, which had broken apart and flung its escaping fires of rose, amethyst, amber, and green up through the maze of trembling pearl above it. The unusual beauty of its sunsets long ago gave Puget Sound the poetic name of Opal-Sea or Sea of Opal.

Chapter XXIV

Port Valdez—or the Puerto de Valdés, as it was named by Vancouver after Whidbey's exploration—is a fiord twelve miles long and of a beauty that is simply enchanting.

On a clear day it winds like a pale blue ribbon between colossal mountains of snow, with glaciers streaming down to the water at every turn. The peaks rise, one after another, sheer from the water, pearl-white from summit to base.

It has been my happiness and my good fortune always to sail this fiord on a clear day. The water has been as smooth as satin, with a faint silvery tinge, as of frost, shimmering over its blue.

At the end, Port Valdez widens into a bay, and upon the bay, in the shadow of her mountains, and shaded by her trees, is Valdez.

Valdez! The mere mention of the name is sufficient to send visions of loveliness glimmering through the memory. Through a soft blur of rose-lavender mist shine houses, glacier, log-cabins, and the tossing green of trees; the wild, white glacial torrents pouring down around the town; and the pearly peaks linked upon the sky.

Valdez was founded in 1898. During the early rush to the Klondike, one of the routes taken was directly over the glacier. In 1898 about three thousand people landed at the upper end of Port Valdez, followed the glacier, crossed over the summit of the Chugach Mountains, and thence down a fork of the Copper River. The route was dangerous, and attended by many hardships and real suffering.

At first hundreds of tents whitened the level plain at the

foot of the glacier; then, one by one, cabins were built, stocks were brought in for trading purposes, saloons and dance halls sprang up in a night,—and Valdez was.

In this year Captain Abercrombie, of the United States Army, crossed the glacier with his entire party of men and horses and reached the Tanana. In the following year, surveys were made under his direction for a military wagon trail over the Chugach Mountains from Valdez to the Tanana, and during the following three years this trail was constructed.

It has proved to be of the greatest possible benefit, not only to the vast country tributary to Valdez, but to the various Yukon districts, and to Nome. After many experiments, it has been chosen by the government as the winter route for the distribution of mail to the interior of Alaska and to Nome. Steamers make connection with a regular line of stages and sleighs. There are frequent and comfortable road houses, and the danger of accident is not nearly so great as it is in travelling by railway in the eastern states.

The Valdez military trail follows Lowe River and Keystone Canyon. Through the canyon the trail is only wide enough for pack trains, and travel is by the frozen river.

The Signal Corps of the Army has constructed many hundreds of miles of telegraph lines since the beginning of the present decade. Nome, the Yukon, Tanana, and Copper River valleys are all connected with Valdez and with Dawson by telegraph. Nome has outside connection by wireless, and all the coast towns are in communication with Seattle by cable.

The climate of Valdez is delightful in summer. In winter it is ten degrees colder than at Sitka, with good sleighing. The annual precipitation is fifty per cent less than along the southeastern coast. Snow falls from November to April.

The long winter nights are not disagreeable. The moon and the stars are larger and more brilliant in Alaska than can be

Chapter XXIV

imagined by one who has not seen them, and, with the changeful colors of the Aurora playing upon the snow, turn the northern world into Fairyland.

Valdez has a population of about twenty-five hundred people. It is four hundred and fifty miles north of Sitka, and eighteen hundred miles from Seattle. It is said to be the most northern port in the world that is open to navigation the entire year.

There are two good piers to deep water, besides one at the new town site, an electric light plant and telephone system, two newspapers, a hospital, creditable churches of five or six denominations, a graded school, private club-rooms, a library, a brewery, several hotels and restaurants, public halls, a court-house, several merchandise stores carrying stocks of from fifty to one hundred thousand dollars, a tin and sheet metal factory, saw-mills,—and almost every business, industry, and profession is well represented. There are saloons without end, and dance halls; a saloon in Alaska that excludes women is not known, but good order prevails and disturbances are rare.

The homes are, for the most part, small,—building being excessively high,—but pretty, comfortable, and frequently artistic. There are flower-gardens everywhere. There is no log-cabin so humble that its bit of garden-spot is not a blaze of vivid color. Every window has its box of bloom. La France roses were in bloom in July in the garden of ex-Governor Leedy, of Kansas, whose home is now in Valdez.

The civilization of the town is of the highest. The whole world might go to Alaska and learn a lesson in genuine, simple, refined hospitality—for its key-note is kindness of heart.

The visitor soon learns that he must be chary of his admiration of one of the curios on his host's wall, lest he be begged to accept it.

The Tillicum Club is known in all parts of Alaska. It has a

very comfortable club-house, where all visitors of note to the town are entertained. The club occasionally has what its own self calls a "dry night," when ladies are entertained with cards and music. (The adjective does not apply to the entertainment.)

The dogs of Valdez are interesting. They are large, and of every color known to dogdom, the malamutes predominating. They are all "heroes of the trail," and are respected and treated as "good fellows." They lie by twos and threes clear across the narrow board sidewalks; and unless one understands the language of the trail, it is easier to walk around them or to jump over them than it is to persuade them to move. A string of oaths, followed by "*Mush!*" all delivered like the crack of a whip, brings quick results. The dogs hasten to the pier, on a long, wolflike lope, when the whistle of a steamer is heard, and offer the hospitality of the town to the stranger, with waving tails and saluting tongues.

It is a heavy expense to feed these dogs in Alaska, yet few men are known to be so mean as to grudge this expense to dogs who have faithfully served them, frequently saving their lives, on the trail.

The situation of Valdez is absolutely unique. The dauntlessness of a city that would boldly found itself upon a glacier has proved too much for even the glacier, and it is rapidly withdrawing, as if to make room for its intrepid rival in interest. Yet it still is so close that, from the water, it appears as though one might reach out and touch it. The wide blue bay sparkles in front, and snow peaks surround it.

Beautiful, oh, most beautiful, are those peaks at dawn, at sunset, at midnight, at noon. The summer nights in Valdez are never dark; and I have often stood at midnight and watched the amethyst lights on the mountains darken to violet, purple, black,—while the peaks themselves stood white and still, softly outlined against the sky.

Chapter XXIV

But in winter, when mountains, glacier, city, trees, lie white and sparkling beneath the large and brilliant stars, and the sea alone is dark—to stand then and see the great golden moon rising slowly, vibrating, pushing, oh, so silently, so beautifully, above the clear line of snow into the dark blue sky—that is worth ten years of living.

"Why do you not go out to 'the states,' as so many other ladies do in winter?" I asked a grave-eyed young wife on my first visit, not knowing that she belonged to the great Alaskan order of "Stout Hearts and Strong Hearts"—the only order in Alaska that is for women and men.

She looked at me and smiled. Her eyes went to the mountains, and they grew almost as wistful and sweet as the eyes of a young mother watching her sleeping child. Then they came back to me, grave and kind.

"Oh," said she, "how can I tell you why? You have never seen the moon come over those mountains in winter, nor the winter stars shining above the sea."

That was all. She could not put it into words more clearly than that; but he that runs may read.

The site of Valdez is as level as a parade ground to the bases of the near mountains, which rise in sheer, bold sweeps. A line of alders, willows, cottonwoods, and balms follows the glacial stream that flows down to the sea on each side of the town.

The glacier behind the town—now called a "dead" glacier—once discharged bergs directly into the sea. The soil upon which the town is built is all glacial deposit. Flowers spring up and bloom in a day. Vegetables thrive and are crisp and delicious—particularly lettuce.

Society is gay in Valdez, as in most Alaskan towns. Fort Liscum is situated across the bay, so near that the distance between is travelled in fifteen minutes by launch. Dances, receptions, card-parties, and dinners, at Valdez and at the fort, occur several times each week, and the social line is drawn as rigidly here as in larger communities.

There is always a dance in Valdez on "steamer night." The officers and their wives come over from the fort; the officers of the ship are invited, as are any passengers who may bear letters of introduction or who may be introduced by the captain of the ship. A large and brightly lighted ballroom, beautiful women, handsomely and fashionably gowned, good music, and a genuine spirit of hospitality make these functions brilliant.

The women of Alaska dress more expensively than in "the states." Paris gowns, the most costly furs, and dazzling jewels are everywhere seen in the larger towns.

All travellers in Alaska unite in enthusiastic praise of its unique and generous hospitality. From the time of Baranoff's lavish, and frequently embarrassing, banquets to the refined entertainments of to-day, northern hospitality has been a proverb.

"Petnatchit copla" is still the open sesame.

Chapter XXV

THE TRIP OVER "the trail" from Valdez to the Tanana country is one of the most fascinating in Alaska.

At seven o'clock of a July morning five horses stood at our hotel door. Two gentlemen of Valdez had volunteered to act as escort to the three ladies in our party for a trip over the trail.

I examined with suspicion the red-bay horse that had been assigned to me.

"Is he gentle?" I asked of one of the gentlemen.

"Oh, I don't know. You can't take any one's word about a horse in Alaska. They call regular buckers 'gentle' up here. The only way to find out is to try them."

This was encouraging.

"Do you mean to tell me," said one of the other ladies, "that you don't know whether these horses have ever been ridden by women?"

"No, I do not know."

She sat down on the steps.

"Then there's no trail for me. I don't know how to ride nor to manage a horse."

After many moments of persuasion, we got her upon a mild-eyed horse, saddled with a cross-saddle. The other lady and myself had chosen side-saddles, despite the assurance of almost every man in Valdez that we could not get over the trail sitting a horse sidewise, without accident.

"Your skirt'll catch in the brush and pull you off," said one, cheerfully.

"Your feet'll hit against the rocks in the canyon," said another.

"You can't balance as even on a horse's back, sideways, and if you don't balance even along the precipice in the canyon, your horse'll go over," said a third.

"Your horse is sure to roll over once or twice in the glacier streams, and you can save yourself if you're riding astride," said a fourth.

"You're certain to get into quicksand somewhere on the trip, and if all your weight is on one side of your horse, you'll pull him down and he'll fall on top of you," said a fifth.

In the face of all these cheerful horrors, our escort said:—

"Ride any way you please. If a woman can keep her head, she will pull through everything in Alaska. Besides, we are not going along for nothing!"

So we chose side-saddles, that having been our manner of riding since childhood.

We had waited three weeks for the glacial flood at the eastern side of the town to subside, and could wait no longer. It was roaring within ten steps of the back door of our hotel; and in two minutes after mounting, before our feet were fairly settled in the stirrups, we had ridden down the sloping bank into the boiling, white waters.

One of the gentlemen rode ahead as guide. I watched his big horse go down in the flood—down, down; the water rose to its knees, to its rider's feet, to *his* knees—

He turned his head and called cheerfully, "Come on!" and we went on—one at a time, as still as the dead, save for the splashing and snorting of our horses. I felt the water, icy cold, rising high, higher; it almost washed my foot from the red-slippered stirrup; then I felt it mounting higher, my skirts floated out on the flood, and then fell, limp, about me. My glance kept flying from my horse's head to our guide, and back again. He was tall, and his horse was tall.

"When it reaches *his* waist," was my agonized thought, "it

Chapter XXV

will be over *my* head!"

The other gentleman rode to my side.

"Keep a firm hold of your bridle," said he, gravely, "and watch your horse. If he falls—"

"Falls! *In here!*"

"They do sometimes; one must be prepared. If he falls—of course you can swim?"

"I never swam a stroke in my life; I never even tried!"

"Is it possible?" said he, in astonishment. "Why, we would not have advised you to come at this time if we had known that. We took it for granted that you wouldn't think of going unless you could swim."

"Oh," said I, sarcastically, "do all the women in Valdez swim?"

"No," he answered, gravely, "but then, they don't go over the trail. Well, we can only hope that he will not fall. When he breaks into a swim—"

"*Swim!* Will he do that?"

"Oh, yes, he is liable to swim any minute now."

"What will I do then?" I asked, quite humbly; I could hear tears in my own voice. He must have heard them, too, his voice was so kind as he answered.

"Sit as quietly and as evenly as possible, and lean slightly forward in the saddle; then trust to heaven and give him his head."

"Does he give you any warning?"

"Not the faintest—ah-h!"

Well might he say "ah-h!" for my horse was swimming. Well might we all say "ah-h!" for one wild glance ahead revealed to my glimmering vision that all our horses were swimming.

I never knew before that horses swam so *low down* in the water. I wished when I could see nothing but my horse's ears that I had not been so stubborn about the saddle.

The water itself was different from any water I had ever seen. It did not flow like a river; it boiled, seethed, rushed, whirled; it pushed up into an angry bulk that came down over us like a deluge. I had let go of my reins and, leaning forward in the saddle, was clinging to my horse's mane. The rapidly flowing water gave me the impression that we were being swept down the stream.

The roaring grew louder in my ears; I was so dizzy that I could no longer distinguish any object; there was just a blur of brown and white water, rising, falling, about me; the sole thought that remained was that I was being swept out to sea with my struggling horse.

Suddenly there was a shock which, to my tortured nerves, seemed like a ship striking on a rock. It was some time before I realized that it had been caused by my horse striking bottom. He was walking—staggering, rather, and plunging; his whole neck appeared, then his shoulders; I released his mane mechanically, as I had acted in all things since mounting, and gathered up the reins.

"That was a nasty one, wasn't it?" said my escort, joining me. "I stayed behind to be of service if you required it. We're getting out now, but there are, at least, ten or fifteen as bad on the trail—if not worse."

As if anything *could* be worse!

I chanced to lift my eyes then, and I got a clear view of the ladies ahead of me. Their appearance was of such a nature that I at once looked myself over—and saw myself as others saw me! It was the first and only time that I have ever wished myself at home when I have been travelling in Alaska.

"Cheer up!" called our guide, over his broad shoulder. "The worst is yet to come."

He spoke more truthfully than even he knew. There was one stream after another—and each seemed really worse than

Chapter XXV

the one that went before. From Valdez Glacier the ice, melted by the hot July sun, was pouring out in a dozen streams that spread over the immense flats between the town and the mouth of Lowe River. There were miles and miles of it. Scarcely would we struggle out of one place that had been washed out deep—and how deep, we never knew until we were into it—when we would be compelled to plunge into another.

At last, wet and chilled, after several narrow escapes from whirlpools and quicksand, we reached a level road leading through a cool wood for several miles. From this, of a sudden, we began to climb. So steep was the ascent and so narrow the path—no wider than the horse's feet—that my horse seemed to have a series of movable humps on him, like a camel; and riding sidewise, I could only lie forward and cling desperately to his mane, to avoid a shameful descent over his tail.

Actually, there were steps cut in the hard soil for the horses to climb upon! They pulled themselves up with powerful plunges. On both sides of this narrow path the grass or "feed," as it is called, grew so tall that we could not see one another's heads above it, as we rode; yet it had been growing only six weeks.

Mingling with young alders, fireweed, devil's-club and elder-berry—the latter sprayed out in scarlet—it formed a network across our path, through which we could only force our way with closed eyes, blind as Love.

Bad as the ascent was, the sudden descent was worse. The horse's humps all turned the other way, and we turned with them. It was only by constant watchfulness that we kept ourselves from sliding over their heads.

After another ascent, we emerged into the open upon the brow of a cliff. Below us stretched the valley of the Lowe River. Thousands of feet below wound and looped the blue reaches of the river, set here and there with islands of glistening sand or rosy fireweed; while over all trailed the silver mists of morning. One elderberry island was so set with scarlet sprays of berries that from our height no foliage could be seen.

After this came a scented, primeval forest, through which we rode in silence. Its charm was too elusive for speech. Our horses' feet sank into the moss without sound. There was no underbrush; only dim aisles and arcades fashioned from the gray trunks of trees. The pale green foliage floating above us completely shut out the sun. Soft gray, mottled moss dripped from the limbs and branches of the spruce trees in delicate, lacy festoons.

Soon after emerging from this dreamlike wood we reached Camp Comfort, where we paused for lunch.

This is one of the most comfortable road houses in Alaska. It is situated in a low, green valley; the river winds in front, and snow mountains float around it. The air is very sweet.

It is only ten miles from Valdez; but those ten miles are equal to fifty in taxing the endurance.

We found an excellent vegetable garden at Camp Comfort. Pansies and other flowers were as large and fragrant as I have ever seen, the coloring of the pansies being unusually rich. They told us that only two other women had passed over the trail during the summer.

While our lunch was being prepared, we stood about the immense stove in the immense living room and tried to dry our clothing.

This room was at least thirty feet square. It had a high ceiling and a rough board floor. In one corner was a piano, in another a phonograph. The ceiling was hung with all kinds of trail apparel used by men, including long boots and heavy stockings, guns and other weapons, and other articles that added a picturesque, and even startling, touch to the big room.

In one end was a bench, buckets of water, tin cups hanging

Chapter XXV

on nails, washbowls, and a little wavy mirror swaying on the wall. The gentlemen of our party played the phonograph while we removed the dust and mud which we had gathered on our journey; afterward, *we* played the phonograph.

Then we all stood happily about the stove to "dry out," and listened to our host's stories of the miners who came out from the Tanana country, laden with gold. As many as seventy men, each bearing a fortune, have slept at Camp Comfort on a single night. We slept there ourselves, on our return journey, but our riches were in other things than gold, and there was no need to guard them. Any man or woman may go to Alaska and enrich himself or herself forever, as we did, if he or she have the desire. Not only is there no need to guard our riches, but, on the contrary, we are glad to give freely to whomsoever would have.

Each man, we were told, had his own way of caring for his gold. One leaned a gunnysack full of it outside the house, where it stood all night unguarded, supposed to be a sack of old clothing, from the carelessness with which it was left there. The owner slept calmly in the attic, surrounded by men whose gold made their hard pillows.

They told us, too, of the men who came back, dull-eyed and empty-handed, discouraged and footsore. They slept long and heavily; there was nothing for them to guard.

Every road house has its "talking-machine," with many of the most expensive records. No one can appreciate one of these machines until he goes to Alaska. Its influence is not to be estimated in those far, lonely places, where other music is not.

In a big store "to Westward" we witnessed a scene that would touch any heart. The room was filled with people. There were passengers and officers from the ship, miners, Russian half-breeds, and full-blooded Aleuts. After several records had filled the room with melody, Calvé, herself, sang "The Old

Folks At Home." As that voice of golden velvet rose and fell, the unconscious workings of the faces about me spelled out their life tragedies. At last, one big fellow in a blue flannel shirt started for the door. As he reached it, another man caught his sleeve and whispered huskily:—

"Where you goin', Bill?"

"Oh, anywheres," he made answer, roughly, to cover his emotion; "anywheres, so's I can't hear that damn piece,"—and it was not one of the least of Calvé's compliments.

Music in Alaska brings the thought of home; and it is the thought of home that plays upon the heart-strings of the North. The hunger is always there,—hidden, repressed, but waiting,—and at the first touch of music it leaps forth and casts its shadow upon the face. Who knows but that it is this very heart-hunger that puts the universal human look into Alaskan eyes?

After a good lunch at Camp Comfort, we resumed our journey. There was another bit of enchanting forest; then, of a sudden, we were in the famed Keystone Canyon.

Here, the scenery is enthralling. Solid walls of shaded gray stone rise straight from the river to a height of from twelve to fifteen hundred feet. Along one cliff winds the trail, in many places no wider than the horses' feet. One feels that he must only breathe with the land side of him, lest the mere weight of his breath on the other side should topple him over the sheer, dizzy precipice.

It was amusing to see every woman lean toward the rock cliff. Not for all the gold of the Klondike would I have willingly given one look down into the gulf, sinking away, almost under my horse's feet. Somewhere in those purple depths I knew that the river was roaring, white and swollen, between its narrow stone walls.

Now and then, as we turned a sharp, narrow corner, I could

not help catching a glimpse of it; for a moment, horse and rider, as we turned, would seem to hang suspended above it with no strip of earth between. There were times, when we were approaching a curve, that there seemed to be nothing ahead of us but a chasm that went sinking dizzily away; no solid place whereon the horse might set his feet. It was like a nightmare in which one hangs half over a precipice, struggling so hard to recover himself that his heart almost bursts with the effort.

Then, while I held my breath and blindly trusted to heaven, the curve would be turned and the path would glimmer once more before my eyes.

But one false step of the horse, one tiniest rock-slide striking his feet, one unexpected sound to startle him—the mere thought of these possibilities made my heart stop beating.

We finally reached a place where the descent was almost perpendicular and the trail painfully narrow. The horses sank to their haunches and slid down, taking gravel and stones down with them. I had been imploring to be permitted to walk; but now, being far in advance of all but one, I did not ask permission. I simply slipped off my horse and left him for the others to bring with them. The gentleman with me was forced to do the same.

We paused for a time to rest and to enjoy the most beautiful waterfall I saw in Alaska—Bridal Veil. It is on the opposite side of the canyon, and has a slow, musical fall of six hundred feet.

When we went on, the other members of our party had not yet come up with us, nor had our horses appeared. In the narrowest of all narrow places I was walking ahead, when, turning a sharp corner, we met a government pack train, face to face.

The bell-horse stood still and looked at me with big eyes, evidently as scared at the sight of a woman as an old prospector who has not seen one for years.

I looked at him with eyes as big as his own. There was only one thing to do. Behind us was a narrow, V-shaped cave in the stone wall, not more than four feet high and three deep. Into this we backed, Grecian-bend wise, and waited.

We waited a very long time. The horse stood still, blowing his breath loudly from steaming nostrils, and contemplated us. I never knew before that a horse could express his opinion of a person so plainly. Around the curve we could hear whips cracking and men swearing; but the horse stood there and kept his suspicious eyes on me.

"I'll stay here till dark," his eyes said, "but you don't get me past a thing like *that!*"

I didn't mind his looking, but his snorting seemed like an insult.

At last a man pushed past the horse. When he saw us backed gracefully up into the V-shaped cave, he stood as still as the horse. Finding that neither he nor my escort could think of anything to say to relieve the mental and physical strain, I called out graciously:—

"How do you do, sir ? Would you like to get by?"

"I'd like it damn well, lady," he replied, with what I felt to be his very politest manner.

"Perhaps," I suggested sweetly, "if I came out and let the horse get a good look at me—"

"Don't you do it, lady. That 'u'd scare him plumb to death!"

I have always been convinced that he did not mean it exactly as it sounded, but I caught the flicker of a smile on my escort's face. It was gone in an instant.

Suddenly the other horses came crowding upon the bell-horse. There was nothing for him to do but to go past me or to go over the precipice. He chose me as the least of the two evils.

"Nice pony, nice boy," I wheedled, as he went sliding and

Chapter XXV

snorting past.

Then we waited for the next horse to come by; but he did not come. Turning my head, I found him fixed in the same place and the same attitude as the first had been; his eyes were as big and they were set as steadily on me.

Well—there were fifty horses in that government pack train. Every one of the fifty balked at sight of a woman. There were horses of every color—gray, white, black, bay, chestnut, sorrel, and pinto. The sorrel were the stubbornest of all. To this day, I detest the sight of a sorrel horse.

We stood there in that position for a time that seemed like hours; we coaxed each horse as he balked; and at the last were reduced to such misery that we gave thanks to God that there were only fifty of them and that they couldn't kick sidewise as they passed.

I forgot about the men. There were seven men; and as each man turned the bend in the trail, he stood as still as the stillest horse, and for quite as long a time; and naturally I hesitated to say, "Nice boy, nice fellow," to help him by.

There were more glacier streams to cross. These were floored with huge boulders instead of sand and quicksand. The horses stumbled and plunged powerfully. One misstep here would have meant death; the rapids immediately below the crossing would have beaten us to pieces upon the rocks.

Then came more perpendicular climbing; but at last, at five o'clock, with our bodies aching with fatigue, and our senses finally dulled, through sheer surfeit, to the beauty of the journey, we reached "Wortman's" road house.

This is twenty miles from Valdez; and when we were lifted from our horses we could not stand alone, to say nothing of attempting to walk.

But "Wortman's" is the paradise of road houses. In it, and floating over it, is an atmosphere of warmth, comfort and good cheer that is a rest for body and heart. The beds are comfortable and the meals excellent.

But it was the welcome that cheered, the spirit of genuine kind-heartedness.

The road house stands in a large clearing, with barns and other buildings surrounding it. I never saw so many dogs as greeted us, except in Valdez or on the Yukon. They crowded about us, barking and shrieking a welcome. They were all big malamutes.

After a good dinner we went to bed at eight o'clock. The sun was shining brightly, but we darkened our rooms as much as possible, and instantly fell into the sleep of utter exhaustion.

At one o'clock in the morning we were eating breakfast, and half an hour later we were in our saddles and off for the summit of Thompson Pass to see the sun rise. This brought out the humps in the horses' backs again. We went up into the air almost as straight as a telegraph pole. Over heather, ice, flowers, and snow our horses plunged, unspurred.

It was seven miles to the summit. There were no trees nor shrubs,—only grass and moss that gave a velvety look to peaks and slopes that seemed to be floating around us through the silvery mists that were wound over them like turbans. Here and there a hollow was banked with frozen snow.

When we dismounted on the very summit we could hardly step without crushing bluebells and geraniums.

We set the flag of our country on the highest point beside the trail, that every loyal-hearted traveller might salute it and take hope again, if he chanced to be discouraged. Then we sat under its folds and watched the mists change from silver to pearl-gray; from pearl-gray to pink, amethyst, violet, purple,—and back to rose, gold, and flame color.

One peak after another shone out for a moment, only to withdraw. Suddenly, as if with one leap, the sun came over the

Chapter XXV

mountain line; vibrated brilliantly, dazzlingly, flashing long rays like signals to every quickened peak. Then, while we gazed, entranced, other peaks whose presence we had not suspected were brought to life by those searching rays; valleys appeared, filled with purple, brooding shadows; whole slopes blue with bluebells; and, white and hard, the narrow trail that led on to the pitiless land of gold.

We were above the mountain peaks, above the clouds, level with the sun.

Absolute stillness was about us; there was not one faintest sound of nature; no plash of water, nor sough of wind, nor call of a bird. It was so still that it seemed like the beginning of a new world, with the birth of mountains taking place before our reverent eyes, as one after another dawned suddenly and goldenly upon our vision.

Every time we had stopped on the trail we had heard harrowing stories of saddle-horses or pack-horses having missed their footing and gone over the precipice. The horses are so carefully packed, and the packs so securely fastened on—the last cinch being thrown into the "diamond hitch"—that the poor beasts can roll over and over to the bottom of a canyon without disarranging a pack weighing two hundred pounds—a feat which they very frequently perform.

The military trail is, of necessity, poor enough; but it is infinitely superior to all other trails in Alaska, and is a boon to the prospector. It is a well-defined and well-travelled highway. The trees and bushes are cut in places for a width of thirty feet, original bridges span the creeks when it is possible to bridge them at all, and some corduroy has been laid; but in many places the trail is a mere path, not more than two feet wide, shovelled or blasted from the hillside.

In Alaska there were practically no roads at all until the appointment in 1905 of a road commission consisting of Major

W.P. Richardson, Captain G.B. Pillsbury, and Lieutenant L.C. Orchard. Since that year eight hundred miles of trails, wagon and sled roads, numerous ferries, and hundreds of bridges have been constructed. The wagon road-beds are all sixteen feet wide, with free side strips of a hundred feet; the sled roads are twelve feet wide; the trails, eight; and the bridges, fourteen. In the interior, laborers on the roads are paid five dollars a day, with board and lodging; they are given better food than any laborers in Alaska, with the possible exception of those employed at the Treadwell mines and on the Cordova Railroad. The average cost of road work in Alaska is about two thousand dollars a mile; two hundred and fifty for sled road, and one hundred for trails. These roads have reduced freight rates one-half and have helped to develop rich regions that had been inaccessible. Their importance in the development of the country is second to that of railroads only.

The scenery from Ptarmigan Drop down the Tsina River to Beaver Dam is magnificent. Huge mountains, saw-toothed and covered with snow, jut diagonally out across the valley, one after another; streams fall, riffling, down the sides of the mountains; and the cloud-effects are especially beautiful.

Tsina River is a narrow, foaming torrent, confined, for the most part, between sheer hills,—although, in places, it spreads out over low, gravelly flats. Beaver Dam huddles into a gloomy gulch at the foot of a vast, overhanging mountain. Its situation is what Whidbey would have called "gloomily magnificent." In 1905 Beaver Dam was a road house which many chose to avoid, if possible.

The Tiekel road house on the Kanata River is pleasantly situated, and is a comfortable place at which to eat and rest.

For its entire length, the military trail climbs and falls and winds through scenery of inspiring beauty. The trail leading off to the east at Tonsina, through the Copper River, Nizina, and

Chapter XXV

Chitina valleys, is even more beautiful.

Vast plains and hillsides of bloom are passed. Some mountainsides are blue with lupine, others rosy with fireweed; acres upon acres are covered with violets, bluebells, wild geranium, anemones, spotted moccasin and other orchids, buttercups, and dozens of others—all large and vivid of color. It has often been said that the flowers of Alaska are not fragrant, but this is not true.

The mountains of the vicinity are glorious. Mount Drum is twelve thousand feet high. Sweeping up splendidly from a level plain, it is more imposing than Mount Wrangell, which is fourteen thousand feet high, and Mount Blackburn, which is sixteen thousand feet.

The view from the summit of Sour-Dough Hill is unsurpassed in the interior of Alaska. Glacial creeks and roaring rivers; wild and fantastic canyons; moving glaciers; gorges of royal purple gloom; green valleys and flowery slopes; the domed and towered Castle Mountains; the lone and majestic peaks pushing up above all others, above the clouds, cascades spraying down sheer precipices; and far to the south the linked peaks of the Coast Range piled magnificently upon the sky, dim and faintly blue in the great distance,—all blend into one grand panorama of unrivalled inland grandeur.

Crossing the Copper River, when it is high and swift, is dangerous,—especially for a "chechaco" of either sex. (A chechaco is one who has not been in Alaska a year.) Packers are often compelled to unpack their horses, putting all their effects into large whipsawed boats. The halters are taken off the horses and the latter are driven into the roaring torrent, followed by the packers in the boats.

The horses apparently make no effort to reach the opposite shore, but use their strength desperately to hold their own in the swift current, fighting against it, with their heads turned pitifully up-stream. Their bodies being turned at a slight angle, the current, pushing violently against them, forces them slowly, but surely, from sand bar to sand bar, and, finally, to the shore.

It frequently requires two hours to get men, horses, and outfit from shore to shore, where they usually arrive dripping wet. Women who make this trip, it is needless to say, suffer still more from the hardship of the crossing than do men.

In riding horses across such streams, they should be started diagonally up-stream toward the first sand bar above. They lean far forward, bracing themselves at every step against the current and choosing their footing carefully. The horses of the trail know all the dangers, and scent them afar—holes, boulders, irresistible currents, and quicksand; they detect them before the most experienced "trailer" even suspects them.

I will not venture even to guess what the other two women in my party did when they crossed dangerous streams; but for myself, I wasted no strength in trying to turn my horse's head up-stream, or down-stream, or in any other direction. When we went down into the foaming water, I gave him his head, clung to his mane, leaned forward in the saddle,—and prayed like anything. I do not believe in childishly asking the Lord to help one so long as one can help one's self; but when one is on the back of a half-swimming, half-floundering horse in the middle of a swollen, treacherous flood, with holes and quicksand on all sides, one is as helpless as he was the day he was born; and it is a good time to pray.

According to the report of Major Abercrombie, who probably knows this part of Alaska more thoroughly than any one else, there are hundreds of thousands of acres in the Copper River Valley alone where almost all kinds of vegetables, as well as barley and rye, will grow in abundance and mature. Considering the travel to the many and fabulously rich mines already discovered in this valley and adjacent ones, and the cost

Chapter XXV

of bringing in grain and supplies, it may be easily seen what splendid opportunities await the small farmer who will select his homestead judiciously, with a view to the accommodation of man and beast, and the cultivation of food for both. The opportunities awaiting such a man are so much more enticing than the inducements of the bleak Dakota prairies or the wind-swept valleys of the Yellowstone as to be beyond comparison.

Major Abercrombie believes that the valleys of the sub-drainage of the Copper River Valley will in future years supply the demands for cereals and vegetables, if not for meats, of the thousands of miners that will be required to extract the vast deposits of metals from the Tonsina, Chitina, Kotsina, Nizina, Chesna, Tanana, and other famous districts.

The vast importance to the whole territory of Alaska and to the United States, as well, of the building of the Guggenheim railroad from Cordova into this splendid inland empire may be realized after reading Major Abercrombie's report.

We have been accustomed to mineralized zones of from ten to twelve miles in length; in the Wrangell group alone we have a circle eighty miles in diameter, the mineralization of which is simply marvellous; yet, valuable though these concentrates are, they are as valueless commercially as so much sandstone, without the aid of a railroad and reduction works.

If the group of mines at Butte could deflect a great transcontinental trunk-line like the Great Northern, what will this mighty zone, which contains a dozen properties already discovered,—to say nothing of the unfound, undreamed-of ones,—of far greater value as copper propositions than the richest of Montana, do to advance the commercial interests of the Pacific Coast?

The first discovery of gold in the Nizina district was made by Darnel Kain and Clarence Warner. These two prospectors were urged by a crippled Indian to accompany him to inspect a vein of copper on the head waters of a creek that is now known as Dan Creek.

Not being impressed by the copper outlook, the two prospectors returned. They noticed, however, that the gravel of Dan Creek had a look of placer gold.

They were out of provisions, and were in haste to reach their supplies, fifty miles away; but Kain was reluctant to leave the creek unexamined. He went to a small lake and caught sufficient fish for a few days' subsistence; then, with a shovel for his only tool, he took out five ounces of coarse gold in two days.

In this wise was the rich Nizina district discovered. The Nizina River is only one hundred and sixty miles from Valdez. In Rex Gulch as much as eight ounces of gold have been taken out by one man in a single day. The gold is of the finest quality, assaying over eighteen dollars an ounce.

There is an abundance of timber suitable for building houses and for firewood on all the creeks. There is water at all seasons for sluicing, and, if desired, for hydraulic work.

Chapter XXXII

We found only one white woman at Karluk, the wife of the manager of the cannery, a refined and accomplished lady.

Her home was in San Francisco, but she spent the summer months with her husband at Karluk.

We were taken ashore in a boat and were most hospitably received in her comfortable home.

About two o'clock in the afternoon we boarded a barge and were towed by a very small, but exceedingly noisy, launch up the Karluk River to the hatcheries, which are maintained by the Alaska Packers Association.

It was one of those soft, cloudy afternoons when the coloring is all in pearl and violet tones, and the air was sweet with rain that did not fall. The little make-believe river is very narrow, and so shallow that we were constantly in danger of running aground. We tacked from one side of the stream to the other, as the great steamers do on the Yukon.

On this little pearly voyage, a man who accompanied us told a story which clings to the memory.

"Talk about your big world," said he. "You think it 'u'd be easy to hide yourself up in this God-forgotten place, don't you? Just let me tell you a story."

"A man come up here a few years ago and went to work. He never did much talkin'. If you ast him a question about his-self or where he come from, he shut up like a steel trap with a rat in it. He was a nice-lookin' man, too, an' he had an education an' kind of nice clean ways with him. He built a little cabin, an' he didn't go 'out' in winter, like the rest of us. He stayed here at Karluk an' looked after things.

Well, after one-two year a good-lookin' young woman come up here—an' jiminy-cricket! He fell in love with her like greased lightnin' an' married her in no time. I God, but that man was happy. He acted like a plumb fool over that woman. After while they had a baby—an' then he acted like two plumb fools in one. I ain't got any wife an' babies myself an' I God! it ust to make me feel queer in my throat.

Well, one summer the superintendent's wife brought up a woman to keep house for her. She was a white, sad-faced-lookin' woman, an' when she had a little time to rest she ust to climb up on the hill an' set there alone, watchin' the sea-gulls. I've seen her set there two hours of a Sunday without movin'. Maybe she'd be settin' there now if I hadn't gone and put' my foot clean in it, as usual.

I got kind of sorry for her, an' you may shoot me dead for a fool, but one day I ast her why she didn't walk around the bay an' set a spell with the other woman.

'I don't care much for women,' she says, never changin' countenance, but just starin' out across the bay.

'She's got a reel nice, kind husband,' says I, tryin' to work on her feelin's.

'I don't like husbands,' says she, as short as lard piecrust.

'She's got an awful nice little baby,' says I, for if you keep on long enough, you can always get a woman.

She turns then an' looks at me.

'It's a girl,' says I, 'an' Lord, the way it nestles up' into your neck an' loves you!'

Her lips opened an' shut, but she didn't say a word;

Chapter XXXII

but if you'd look 'way down into a well an' see a fire burnin in the water, it 'u'd look like her eyes did then.

'Its father acts like a plumb fool over it an' its mother,' says I. 'The sun raises over there, an' sets over here but *he* thinks it raises an' sets in that woman an' baby.'

'The woman must be pretty,' says she, suddenly, an' I never heard a woman speak so bitter.

'She is,' says I; 'she's got—'

'Don't tell me what she's got,' snaps she, gettin' up off the ground, kind o' stiff-like. 'I've made up my mind to go see her, an' maybe I'd back out if you told me what she's like. Maybe you'd tell me she had red wavy hair an' blue eyes an' a baby mouth an' smiled like an angel—an' then devils couldn't drag me to look at her.'

Say, I nearly fell dead, then, for that just described the woman; but I'm no loon, so I just kept still.

'What's their name?' says she, as we walked along.

'Davis,' says I; an' mercy to heaven! I didn't know I was tellin' a lie.

All of a sudden she laughed out loud—the awfullest laugh. It sounded as harrable mo'rnful as a sea-gull just before a storm.

'*Husband!*' she flings out, jeerin'; '*I* had a husband once. I worshipped the ground he trod on. *I* thought the sun raised an' set in *him*. He carried me on two chips for a while, but I didn't have any children, an' I took to worryin' over it, an' lost my looks an' my disposition. It goes deep with some women, an' it went deep with me. Men don't seem to understand some things. Instid of sympathizin' with me, he took to complainin' an' findin' fault an' finally stayin' away from home.'

'There's no use talkin' about what I suffered for a

year; I never told anybody this much before—an' it wa'n't anything to what I've suffered ever since. But one day I stumbled on a letter he had wrote to a woman he called Ruth. He talked about her red wavy hair an' blue eyes an' baby mouth an' the way she smiled like an angel. They were goin' to run away together. He told her he'd heard of a place at the end of the earth where a man could make a lot of money, an' he'd go there an' get settled an' then send for her, if she was willin' to live away from everybody, just for him. He said they'd never see a human soul that knew them.'

She stopped talkin' all at once, an' we walked along. I was scared plumb to death. I didn't know the woman's name, for he always called her 'dearie,' but the baby's name was Ruth.

'You've got to feelin' bad now,' says I, 'an' maybe we'd best not go on.'

'I'm goin' on,' says she.

After a while she says, in a different voice, kind of hard, 'I put that letter back an' never said a word. I wouldn't turn my hand over to keep a man. I never saw the woman; but I know how she looks. I've gone over it every night of my life since. I know the shape of every feature. I never let on, to him or anybody else. It's the only thing I've thanked God for, since I read that letter—helpin' me to keep up an' never let on. It's the only thing I've prayed for since that day. It wa'n't very long—about a month. He just up an' disappeared. People talked about me awful because I didn't cry, an' take on, an' hunt him.'

'I took what little money he left me an' went away. I got the notion that he'd gone to South America, so I set out to get as far in the other direction as possible. I

Chapter XXXII

got to San Francisco, an' then the chance fell to me to come up here. It sounded like the North Pole to me, so I come. I'm awful glad I come. Them sea-gulls is the only pleasure I've had—since; an' it's been four year. That's all.'

Well, sir, when we got up close to the cabin, I got to shiverin' so's I couldn't brace up an' go in with her. It didn't seem possible it *could* be the same man, but then, such darn queer things do happen in Alaska! Anyhow, I'd got cold feet. I remembered that the cannery the man worked in was shut down, so's he'd likely be at home.

'I'll go back now,' I mumbles, 'an' leave you women folks to get acquainted.'

I fooled along slow, an' when I'd got nearly to the settlement I heard her comin'. I turned an' waited—an' I God! she won't be any ash-whiter when she's in her coffin. She was steppin' in all directions, like a blind woman; her arms hung down stiff at her sides; her fingers were locked around her thumbs as if they'd never loose; an' some nights, even now, I can't sleep for thinkin' how her eyes looked. I guess if you'd gag a dog, so's he couldn't cry, an' then cut him up *slow*, inch by inch, his eyes 'u'd look like her'n did then. At sight of me her face worked, an' I thought she was goin' to cry; but all at once she burst out into the awfullest laughin' you ever heard outside of a lunatic asylum.

'Lord God Almighty!' she cries out—'where's his mercy at, the Bible talks about? You'd think he might have a little mercy on an ugly woman who never had any children, wouldn't you—especially when there's women in the world with wavy red hair an' blue eyes—women that smile like angels an' have little baby girls!

Oh, Lord, what a joke on me!'

Well, she went on laughin' till my blood turned cold, but she never told me one word of what happened to her. She went back to California on the first boat that went, but it was two weeks. I saw her several times; an' at sight of me she'd burst out into that same laughin' an' cry out, 'My Lord, what a joke! Did you ever see its beat for a joke?' but she wouldn't answer a thing I ast her. The last time I ever see her, she was leanin' over the ship's side. She looked like a dead woman, but when she see me she waved her hand and burst out laughin'.

'Do you hear them sea-gulls?' she cries out. 'All they can scream is *Kar*-luk! *Kar*-luk! *Kar*-luk! You can hear'm say it just as plain. *Kar*-luk! I'll hear 'em when I lay in my grave! Oh, my Lord, what a joke!'"

ALASKA, THE GREAT COUNTRY, Higginson's only book of nonfiction, was first published in 1908. It was reprinted at least eight times in Higginson's lifetime. Higginson significantly revised and updated the book for the 1919 edition. Higginson's publisher, Macmillan, later republished *Alaska* as part of their Macmillan Travel Series. The excerpt reprinted here is taken from the 1908 first edition.

Higginson's *Alaska, the Great Country* is a mix of history, travel narrative, and guidebook. In order to conduct research for this book, Higginson traveled to Alaska for four consecutive summers to collect material. She later recounted that once she began writing the book, "I was at my desk at eight o'clock in the morning and worked till five o'clock in the afternoon; then from eight at night till one or two in the morning, for a full year" (Powers 433). The book was very popular and widely praised.

Chapter XXXII

Readers who are accustomed to Higginson's fiction and poetry will immediately recognize in *Alaska* her characteristic use of lyrical language, extensive descriptions of nature, and strong narrative story line. In the chapters excerpted here, Higginson provides detailed descriptions of locations such as Washington's San Juan Islands and Alaska's Port Valdez. She also recounts a comic incident of riding horseback over a very rough trail in Alaska, a scene all the more entertaining for those who knew that Higginson was herself a very accomplished equestrian. Additionally, this excerpt includes the tale of a forsaken white woman who had fled to Alaska to escape the distressing memories of her earlier life.

Explanatory Notes

"The Snow Pearls"
1. *sardonyx*: a mineral with colored bands of red.
2. *Mount Baker*: an active volcano located in Whatcom County, Washington, USA. Mount Baker is part of the North Cascade Mountain range.

"Yet am I Not for Pity"
1. *Sappho*: famed Greek female lyric poet, born on the isle of Lesbos.

"The Lamp in the West"
1. *Venus*: second planet from the sun, named after the Roman goddess of love and beauty. Aside from Earth's Moon, Venus is the brightest natural object in the night sky.

"Sunrise on the Willamette"
1. *Willamette*: the Willamette River, major river in northwestern Oregon State.
2. *tulés*: a rush-like plant that grows on the shores of marshes and lakes. Common in the Pacific Northwest and the Western United States
3. *Mount Hood*: active volcano and highest mountain located in Northern Oregon State. Mount Hood is part of the Cascade Volcanic Arc.

"Midnight on Brooklyn Bridge"
1. *Sehome Hill*: second-growth forest composed of 180-

acres of Douglas fir and other trees located in the city of Bellingham Washington, adjacent to Western Washington University.
2. *Puget Sea*: typically used to refer to the Puget Sound or waters leading to the Puget Sound.

"The College by the Sea"
1. *Sehome Hill*: second-growth forest composed of 180-acres of Douglas fir and other trees located in the city of Bellingham Washington, adjacent to Western Washington University.

"The Mother of 'Pills'"
1. *graduated glasses*: a glass container such as a beaker marked on the side with lines indicating volume of milliliters contained.
2. *corde-ruche*: pleated fabric decorative trim.
3. *hop-pickin'*: Before the invention of the mechanical hops picker in the late nineteenth century, hops were picked by hand. The labor-intensive annual hops harvest drew large groups of people to areas such as the Yakima Valley (Washington) and the Willamette Valley (Oregon).
4. *Nooksacks, Lummis, Alaskas*: The Nooksack and the Lummi tribes are Salish Native groups of Puget Sound. Alaskas is a more general term that refers to indigenous peoples of Alaska such as the Aleut, Haida, Tlingit, and other native groups.
5. *cochineal*: an insect that produces carminic acid, often used for cosmetic purposes, including, in this case, the coloring of pills and ointments.
6. *tincture cantharides*: substance derived from dried beetles and used topically to soothe irritation. Also

known as Spanish fly.
7. *aconite*: a highly toxic herb traditionally used for a variety of medicinal purposes such as an anesthetic and to reduce fever. Also known as wolf's bane.
8. *Jamaica ginger*: An extract from prized ginger grown in Jamaica with high concentration of ethanol. Used to treat pain and nausea.
9. *canton-flannel portieres*: door curtains made of a heavy cotton material.
10. *"Annie Laurie"*: a popular old Scottish ballad.

"Patience Appleby's Confessing-Up"
1. *canton flannel*: a heavy cotton material.
2. *Century liniment*: a brand of oil sold as "Twentieth Century Liniment" and advertised as relieving symptoms of rheumatism.
3. *arnicky*: arnica. A perennial flower long-used for pain relief.
4. *pulse-warmers*: knitted garments to cover the wrists in cold weather.
5. *gaiter-tops*: a cloth or leather garment to cover the tops of boots and keep out cold and snow.
6. *phthisicy*: to have difficulty breathing.
7. *liniment bottles*: bottles of various products marketed to relieve pain stemming from rheumatism.

"The Takin' In of Old Mis' Lane"
1. *pleg*: plague.
2. *poor-farm*: A working farm run by the county and supported by the public where the poor and elderly who had no resources were sent to live and, if they were physically able, to work.
3. *phaeton*: a lightweight carriage.

4. *"Lilly Dale," "Hazel Dell," "General Persifor F. Smith's Grand March"*: popular songs from the mid-nineteenth-century United States; Persifor Frazer Smith (1798-1858), celebrated US military commander during the Mexican-American War (1846-48).

"Mrs. Risley's Christmas Dinner"
1. *stun crock*: stone crock.

"The Arnspiker Chickens"
1. *Corbett and Fitzsimmons*: James Corbett (1866-1933) and Robert Fitzsimmons (1863-1917), both boxing champions, fought for the heavyweight title on March 17, 1897 in Carson City, Nevada. The celebrated match was titled "The Fight of the Century." Fitzsimmons won the match in the 14th round.
2. *a felon:* a skin irritation.
3. *catarrh*: literally a mucus discharge. Here Mrs. Worstel is mispronouncing "guitar."

"A Point of Knuckling-Down"
1. *ball bluin'*: small blue balls composed of blue iron powder used in laundering to make yellowed white fabric appear temporarily whiter.
2. *han'kachers*: handkerchiefs.
3. *pennyrile*: penny royal. An herb traditionally used for a variety of medicinal purposes.
4. *floating island*: a rich dessert of meringue, custard, and caramel.
5. *calico washed in alum water*: economical fabric made from unbleached cotton; inexpensive chemical used to brighten and soften fabric.
6. *sacque*: a loosely fitting hip-length jacket.

7. *stunned*: stoned, with the pits removed.
8. *quinsy sore throat*: throat pain from abscessed tonsils.
9. *Carry me on two chips*: to pamper or treat very well.
10. *Saint Vitus dance*: a colloquial name for Sydenham's chorea, an illness causing rapid movements of the face, hands, and feet thought most often to affect children.

"The Blow-Out at Jenkins's Grocery"
1. *At home cards*: in this case, commercial announcements that resembled invitations.
2. *"Home, Sweet Home"*: popular song of the US mid-nineteenth-century often played at saloon closing hours.

"The Stubbornness of Uriah Slater"
1. *Braymin*: Brahma hen. A breed of hen probably originating in India. The Brahma hen became well-known and expensive in the nineteenth century after two were presented to Britain's Queen Victoria.
2. *quivass*: crevice. A narrow crack.

"M'liss's Child"
1. *stun*: stone.
2. *lylocks*: lilacs.
3. *Battenburg lace*: strips of fabric embellished by hand-stitched needlework. Popular in the nineteenth century.
4. *Sparrow-grass*: colloquial name for asparagus.
5. *tews*: to vex or complain.

"The Message of Ann Laura Sweet"
1. *feathers fell*: to feel embarrassed or diminished.
2. *switch*: hairpiece made of human hair used to give hair volume or conceal baldness.
3. *dugout*: a shelter dug into the ground or into a hillside.

4. *tatting*: handcrafting decorative lace edging.
5. *buckboard*: basic four-wheeled wagon drawn by a horse, popular in newly settled regions of the nineteenth-century United States.
6. *camphire*: camphor.
7. *carried me on two chips*: to pamper or treat very well.
8. *nigger playing bones*: "The bones" are a musical instrument devised from animal bones or pieces of wood and are played between the fingers. They are used in a variety of musical traditions, including the blues, traditional Irish music, zydeco, and some French-Canadian music. This reference is probably to the use of the bones in US nineteenth-century minstrel shows. Ann Laura Sweet's fluent use of the word "nigger" is testament to the pervasive casual racism that is the backdrop to both the time and place of the story and Higginson's own early twentieth-century Pacific Northwest milieu.
9. *stun*: stone.
10. This poem, titled "My Discontent," was written by Higginson's sister, Carrie Blake Morgan. It was published in *Lippincott's Magazine* in 1895 and widely reprinted. The poem also appears in Carrie Blake Morgan's sole book of poetry *The Path of Gold* (1900).

FROM *MARIELLA, OF OUT-WEST*
1. *copper-toed shoes*: girls' and boys' shoes made with copper encasing the toe area to prevent the shoe leather from easily wearing out. Typically worn in more rural areas of the country.
2. *bluing*: a liquid containing blue dye that made faded or yellowed white garments appear temporarily whiter.
3. "*From the Cascades' frozen gorges*": stanzas from "Beautiful Willamette" (1868), a poem by nineteenth-

century Oregon writer Samuel L. Simpson (1845-1900) that celebrates Oregon's Willamette River.
4. *Kansas-starter*: a sourdough bread starter using Kansas wheat, often brought to the West by female settlers.
5. *floatin' island*: a rich dessert of meringue, custard, and caramel.
6. *"Prize Banner Quickstep"*: popular instrumental piece from the mid-nineteenth-century United States.
7. *"General Persifor F. Smith's Grand March"*: popular song from the mid-nineteenth-century United States; Persifor Frazer Smith (1798-1858), celebrated United States military commander during the Mexican-American War (1846-48).
8. *"Gypsy's Warning"*: popular song from the mid-nineteenth-century United States.
9. *Bath brick*: a brick made of clay that was used for cleaning. Powder could be scraped from the brick to scour surfaces.
10. *alpaco*: alpaca. A warm, natural fiber with a silky appearance made from alpaca fleece.
11. *factotum*: servant, main assistant.

FROM *ALASKA, THE GREAT COUNTRY*
1. *Muir Glacier*: located in Alaska's Glacier Bay and named after famed naturalist John Muir (1838-1914) who popularized it in his writings.
2. *John Burroughs*: American naturalist, 1837-1921.
3. *petnatchit copla*: literally, "fifteen drops" in Russian. In Russian culture in Alaska, this phrase was used to offer the hospitality of a glass of liquor.
4. *Calvé*: Emma Calvé (1858-1942), famous French opera singer. She sang poems of Higginson's that had been set to music.

Whatcom County Historical Society
• BOOKS IN PRINT •

The Journal

AS AN OPEN FORUM for the publication and presentation of local history, *The Journal of the Whatcom County Historical Society* showcases articles, photographs, maps, and artistic depictions of Whatcom County history submitted by members of the Society and the community. *The Journal* is published annually and copies are provided as a benefit to specified levels of annual membership in the Society. For information about becoming a member or about submitting material for an upcoming *Journal,* or to purchase copies of the publications listed here, please visit www.whatcomhistory.net or write to The Whatcom County Historical Society at 1308 E Street, Bellingham, WA 98225. In addition to current and back issues, the following special editions of *The Journal* are available:

The Bellingham City Centennial
In Cooperation with the Center for Pacific Northwest Studies, Western Washington University.
April 2004

Model School: A History of the Campus School at Western Washington University, 1899-1967
Celebrates the Campus School as part of a series of commemorations, including a museum exhibit, a class reunion and a documentary film.
August 2007

Also Published by the WCHS

Heart on My Sleeve
By Sue C. Boynton, 1980
Edited by Hope B. Freeman; illustrated by Janet Hardin.

The Sue Boynton Story
By Dorothy Koert, 1982
Whatcom County History Series

The Saxon Story: Early Pioneers on South Fork
By Marie Hamel Royer, 1982

The Harris Journal: Memoir of William H. Harris, Whatcom County Probate Judge, 1883-1889
Galen Biery Memorial Edition, 1994

Mount Baker Theatre: The Early Years
Compiled and edited by Carole Teshima Morris, 2002

The Brothels of Bellingham: A Short History of Prostitution in Bellingham, Washington
By Curtis Smith, DDS, 2004

The Less Subdued Excitement: A Century of Jazz in Bellingham and Whatcom County, Washington
By Milton Krieger, 2012

Selected Writings of Ella Higginson
Edited and with an introduction by Laura Laffrado, 2015